FAMILY DEVOTIONS

WITH HELPFUL HINTS FOR PARENTS

BY

NEIL M. PHELAN, JR.

authorHOUSE™

1663 LIBERTY DRIVE, SUITE 200
BLOOMINGTON, INDIANA 47403
(800) 839-8640
WWW.AUTHORHOUSE.COM

First published by AuthorHouse 06/06/05

ISBN: 1-4208-5737-1 (sc)

Library of Congress Control Number: 2005904479

Printed in the United States of America
Bloomington, Indiana

This book is printed on acid-free paper.

DEDICATION

This book is affectionately dedicated to my loving wife, Marilyn. She has been a "helpmeet" indeed. In every struggle and trial of the ministry she has been my best friend as well as a constant source of encouragement. The pastor's wife is certainly underestimated. Her husband spends many hours in his study, writing, preparing, meditating and counseling with his flock. She must give him up to the Lord for this service. I appreciate her faithfulness, her cheerfulness and the smile I have enjoyed day in and day out. Well has Solomon written, "*Whoso* findeth a wife findeth a good *thing*, and obtaineth favour of the LORD." –Proverbs 18:22. If I were to doubt my Lord's love and favor, I only have to consider His kind hand in providing me with her.

ACKNOWLEDGEMENTS

I appreciate the encouragement and advice of Elder Edward Cagle. He has been a faithful father in Israel to me. I hold him in the highest esteem among the elders of Israel.

I also would like to thank Elder Harold Stumbaugh for his encouragement. He has been a constant friend in all seasons.

Most of all, I appreciate the labor and encouragement of Elder Dickie Halbgewachs. His doctrinal balance and insight were invaluable. I also appreciate his help in the construction of many phrases that might have otherwise been obscure to the casual reader.

Among the many blessings that may be enjoyed in the ministry, the blessing of meeting and knowing men who have dedicated their souls to the service of Jesus Christ is among the greatest. I realize that I do not deserve such friends; I count it another measure of God's grace. How wisely has Solomon written, "A man's gift maketh room for him, and bringeth him before great men."- Proverbs 18:16. I thank God for these great men who have helped me, as well as many others that I have had the opportunity to fellowship.

TABLE OF CONTENTS

PREFACE

Devotional material has always been of *immeasurable* value to God's people. Spurgeon's "Morning and Evening" has encouraged many a pilgrim as they prepared for their day and sought comfort on their pillow at night. We do not aspire to this caliber of thought or experience, yet we feel a burden for the same work. One reason is because there is always a need for *contemporary* authors, people who live and breathe in this present world, who may be identified as a living "brother, and companion in tribulation".

Another reason is more *personal*. It involves our own perusal of the devotional material of our present day. From our personal study, we have found many of the great old themes and doctrines of the Church to be lacking, even vacant. Surely, these truths were given by the Chief Shepherd for the comfort of His sheep and need to be published.

A final reason has given *equal* force to vent our hearts in written form. There was once a day when families gathered together to discuss religious topics. It was by those discussions, however brief and unstructured they may have been, that children became aware of their parents' faith and ultimately, their God. Today, we live in a busy world. With computers, television, VCR's, CD's and a world of entertainment at our fingertips, this opportunity of teaching has become all but extinct. Gadgets, noise and electronics stifle familial communication. Granted, children may know that their parents believe in God because they go to church, yet, the dynamics of personal interactions between parent and child is all but lost. Thus, we come to this final reason for this collection of articles. To give the parent some short *meditations* to enjoy personally and ultimately share with their family and children.

Our homilies are, for the most part, a condensed version of messages delivered to our congregation. Surely, if they were given us by the Chief Shepherd for the feeding of the gathered flock, they will be beneficial to other sheep which are not of our immediate fold. Many lessons may be taught from each short homily which, we hope, will open a door of utterance between parent and child concerning the most important subject that they will ever discuss with their family: God and His wonderful word!

For your benefit, we have included some helpful hints for parents at the conclusion of each devotion. Hopefully, these will serve to exercise the mind and open up avenues of teaching. As a personal note, let us encourage the parent to keep their devotions short, from 10 to 20 minutes. We will never cut off the giant's head if our sword is too long and many a child has gone to sleep while the sword was being pulled from the scabbard. Of course, if questions arise, and Godly discussion ensues, don't cut off the water of life. Let it flow freely!

HOW TO USE THIS BOOK

There are several methods in which this book may be used. Of course, it can be used for the sole purpose of personal devotions and meditations. Yet, we hope it will be used as subject material for family Bible studies. One may read each homily aloud to their particular gathering and discuss the subjects listed in the "HELPFUL HINTS" which are given to stimulate conversation and highlight the most prominent points of the devotion. Another method of study would be for the teacher to read the devotion beforehand and plan a lesson of their own.

Hopefully, this book will serve as an encouragement to those who have recognized the need for family devotions but have been intimidated as to the what, how and how much. It is our prayer that this work will lead someone, somewhere, closer to Jesus Christ, the fount of every blessing!

"THAT GOOD PART"

*".....Mary hath chosen that good part, which
shall not be taken away from her"*
-Luke 10:42

For just a few moments, let us consider a visit our Lord made to the home of some of His friends. It was the home of Mary and Martha. These were the two sisters of Lazarus, that same Lazarus that Jesus called forth from the tomb. It was Mary that washed His feet with her tears, wiped them with the hairs of her head and anointed His body with ointment. From His short visit, we may learn a lot about Jesus, as well as ourselves, and discover what Mary found to be "that good part."

Today, we will find Jesus in many of the same places that we found Him during His earthly ministry. One of those is in the hearts and homes of people that *love* Him. Though He was and is Lord of heaven and earth, he owned no property. He lived with His friends and so He still does. He did not beg, nor do we find Him burdensome to others. But to those who cherished His companionship He made His abode!!

From this we may learn that our religion should be *more* than a Sunday morning or Wednesday night event. It is an abiding presence. Fellowship with Jesus may be enjoyed every day. I am not suggesting that we "forsake the assembling of ourselves together" only to seek Him in our homes. The assembling of the Saints was ordained of God. The light of our *public* testimony should shine ever so bright and we must be present for it to do so. But we are not to put our religion in a compartment only to be taken out once or twice a week. "That good part" transcends *beyond* the public worship. We have all enjoyed many rich and blessed experiences with Jesus in the confines of my home. In prayer, in study, in meditations, we have found His presence. Perhaps you are physically unable to be in God's house on the Sabbath day; perhaps you are in a jail cell as Paul and Silas were; perhaps the winds of persecution have driven you and your family into a den or a cave. Be encouraged, "that good part" may be enjoyed any day, any time and at any place.

In her zeal to sit at the feet of Jesus, Mary's sister was a source of discouragement. Instead of saying, "My sister is seated where I should be", Martha rebukes her sister for her devotional time with Christ. Zeal will always meet Mr. and Mrs. Discouragement. Satan sends them immediately. Why is this? Because zeal has stirred up the nest of the idle, exposed their complacency and set an example that they should have already followed. Is that not why God sent Zeal to His house? "That good part" is reserved for those we find in such a posture.

It is not the big things that hinder our fellowship with Jesus. It is the simple, every day *whirl* of life. Was it not so with Martha? While we should not criticize Martha unjustly for her labors, we must agree with our Lord that Mary had chosen the *good* part. It is a matter of priority! Martha was busy banging pans and preparing meats while Mary enjoyed "that good part". Yes, meals must be served, household affairs must be run, jobs are to be held down and all the necessary burdens of life must be diligently observed. Jesus is not teaching us to be *slothful*. Yet, in the common rush of life, we *must* find the time to sit at the feet of Jesus. It seems to me that Satan has designed more gadgets, more hobbies, more books, more methods of entertainment than a person could explore in a lifetime. People are busier keeping up with the latest diet book than the Book of Books. They wake up with the Good Morning America, spend their day with the soap opera and go to bed with the late night host. No wonder their nights are full of fears and their day is full of doubt. "That good part" is lost in a whirlwind of activity. No wonder there is so much depression. "That good part" doeth good like a medicine. It produces a merry heart(Prov. 17:22).

Surely, that good part must be Mary's posture! She is in a posture of *submission* to Jesus...at His feet, not questioning what He is doing. She has come apart from the world to give Him her *complete* and *undivided* attention. She has given Him her ears, her eyes, her feet and her heart. She is anxious to learn any thing that He has to say. And according to Jesus, "it shall not be taken away from her." Though riches may take wings and fly away, Dagon may fall, the stock market may crash, the economy and towers collapse, this treasure does not belong to this world. It is out of Satan's reach! These experiences leave indelible memories in our heart and soul. While we will forget the headlines of last week, these experiences will be carried all the way to glory. May we learn from Mary and look for every opportunity to sit at Jesus feet. I wonder what He said that day?!!!

Helpful Hints:

1. This is a great lesson to encourage daily devotions for young and old alike. What time do you take each day to talk to Jesus in these ways: in prayer, in meditations, in reading God's word?

2. Show the importance of having Christ as the center of our homes and how He lives in the families of those that love Him.

3. Use this lesson to illustrate how we get so busy with the affairs of work, school and even hobbies that we forget our time with the Lord.

4. Use this lesson to illustrate how others, even those of our own family, can throw cold water upon our fire to serve the Lord.

5. Use this lesson to show that Jesus sees and knows the times we take with Him.

6. Talk about what you think Jesus may have said that day in His conversation with Mary.

"ALL THINGS"

"And we know that all things work together for good to them that love God, to them who are the called according to his purpose. For whom he did foreknow, he also did predestinate to be conformed to the image of his Son, that he might be the firstborn among many brethren. Moreover whom he did predestinate, them he also called: and whom he called, them he also justified: and whom he justified, them he also glorified. What shall we say to theses things? If God be for us, who can be against us?"
-Romans 8:28-31

I love the things that work together for our good. The sinner may draw great comfort from them because they are unlike the shifting things of this world, things that are prone to change and decay. The things that Paul here enumerates are *security* and *serenity* to the sinner. They strengthen our faith and our hope. They nail down our future. These things are Holy things, unchangeable things, things that God has ordained for our "good".

We must not take our "things" out of context. The phrase "all things" must be considered in the context in which it is given. Paul tells us precisely what these "things" are and to whom these blessings belong. His eyes soar much higher than the mundane affairs of this life. Let us soar with the apostle for just a moment!

The things that we shall consider are reserved for a special people: "them that love God". Do you love God? Then you have sufficient evidence that these things belong to you. You have been "called according to his purpose", called from death to life, from Adam's fallen seed to the seed of Christ. His purpose is to bring you home. These people do not love God to get called. They love Him because *they are called*. And since these special people are the only recipients of these special graces and favors we must know that "all things" does not include the persons or actions of the wicked. Only those who love God will be able to respond appropriately to the apostle's interrogation of the heart, "What shall we then say to these things?"

The first "thing" on the apostle's list concerns people: "for whom". *Whom* always refers to people, not places and events. And these particular people are foreknown. God knew them before they were born; before they did any good or evil(Romans 9:11); before Adam's transgression; before time itself. What do you say to this?

The second thing that Paul tells us that works for our good is that God has predetermined that these people shall be conformed to Christ's spotless image. What a wonderful image He has: "holy, harmless, undefiled, separate from sinners and made higher than the heaven"-Heb.7:26. His blood has cleansed them. He did not predestinate Adam to sin. Adam needed no help in that matter, nor do we. Let us not blame God for our failures. Nor did He predestinate people to hell. The Bible does not teach *double* predestination. But out of all of Adam's race He did rescue the objects of His love. Surely, none that God loves nor any that love God will inhabit that awful place. If you love God, take a look at your future and rejoice in your deliverance. You shall not be alone, He is the firstborn among "many brethren".

But this is not the end of Paul's list of "things". We have further security. Those who are predestinated have also been "justified"(v30) or made innocent. They did not make themselves innocent. Christ made them innocent by His blood. And they have also been "glorified"v30. This means that they have been highly *honored*. Not because of any thing that was found in them. He found them in Adam. But because they are found in Christ as He represented them upon Calvary's cross. Could one be predestinated and not called; justified and not glorified; glorified and not predestinated; loved and not justified? Surely, surely, all of these things work "together". They work together for "our good". Today, we must ask the same question to those who love God that Paul asked the church at Rome. "What shall we say to these things?"-v31. What would the apostle say today if he were here with us? His response is found in verses 32-39. Is your response the same? Lord, until we arise in thy spotless image we confess that we are sinners. But we rejoice in our security! Amen.

Helpful Hints:
1. Use this lesson to illustrate the security of those who love God.
2. Break this lesson down into many devotionals and use it to teach the great themes of God's foreknowledge, predestination, calling, depravity, election, specific atonement, irresistible grace and the preservation of the Saints.
3. Use this lesson to teach the sovereignty of God who rules over all things.
4. Use this lesson to show that even suffering and affliction works together for our good and brings us closer to the Lord.

"LOOKING UNTO JESUS"

*"Wherefore seeing we also are compassed about with so great
a cloud of witnesses, let us lay aside every weight, and the sin
which doth so easily beset us, and let us run with patience the
race that is set before us, Looking unto Jesus the author and
finisher of our faith; who for the joy that was set before him
endured the cross, despising the shame, and is set down at the
right hand of the throne of God"*
-Hebrews 12:1,2

Here we find the apostle seeking to encourage his
Hebrew brethren with a nostalgic review of their faithful
ancestors. This "great cloud of witnesses" hovered around
their cots as a constant reminder of faith's triumphs by
men and women just like themselves. Paul was saying,
"If God was with them, surely He will be with us." Today,
we may say by faith, "If God was with them, surely He
will be with us!"

Paul compares the life of faith to the footrace of the
Olympic games of his day, "the race that is set before us."
If you are a Christian, the race is on. You must run it. But
how shall we run?

First we must lay aside "every weight". The word "weight" describes the runner's hindrances. Runners will not pick up weights before they run. Nor should the faithful in their endeavors to live by faith. What is your hindrance today? What is it that keeps you from God's house; from prayer's paths; from the Bible's pages; from God's will in your life? Whatever, or, whoever it is, we must consider it as a heavy hindrance. It may be great, but is it greater than God? Call upon Him and He shall help you to lay it aside by prayer, repentance and faith. We must find the steps that Christian discovered in his first steps of faith when he passed through the slough of Despond!

Secondly, we must lay aside the "sin". How long must we be reminded that sin besets the runners pace? Sin is man's problem. That will never change. It causes the runner to stumble and even fall. But do not let this discourage the runner. I have never known a runner that did not stumble from time to time. Even the best of runners have fallen. David stumbled, Moses stumbled, Abraham stumbled, even Peter had his trip ups. Some falls are private and some are before all. But the faithful runner must get up and finish the race. If he stumbles and falls he is not alone, "The Lord upholdeth all that fall, and raiseth up all those that be bowed down"-Psalm 145:14. Is there a particular sin, past or present, strapped to your back? Let it no longer hinder you. Take it to the cross. There you will find it crucified and your pace will be light once again.

We are next told how to run: "with patience." The life of faith is not a 100 yard dash. It is a long distance run, moment by moment, day by day, week by week, year by year. It must be approached with a prayerful attitude. Therefore, patience must be a Godly virtue. And how does one come by this thing called patience? According to Paul, "tribulation worketh patience". The trials and tribulations of life teach us how to run. Let us learn from them. It is never too late to learn. The hoary head has much to teach us in this arena. Consider our great cloud of witnesses.

Finally, the runner's eyes must be fixed. Looking back is a deadly distraction of Satan. The Grand Canyon may be before you! You can run into a brick wall looking back over your shoulder at past failures. We must be "Looking unto Jesus the author and finisher of our faith." Look to the throne of grace and find forgiveness; look to Calvary and find deliverance; look to Jesus who said, "Father, forgive them".

The look at our cloud of witnesses was indeed encouraging, but here we find the perfect example. One who never stumbled or fell. He is the author. He wrote the book on the life of faith. If we are to learn, let us learn from the Master! Let us notice how He ran. Have we faced the trials; the mockery; the hatred; the blasphemy; the lies; or even the physical torment the He endured? We must keep on running! He, too, ran with His eyes open. He looked straight ahead at the "Joy set before Him." The runner can endure a lot of pain when the trophy is in sight. Jesus endured the cross, despising the shame because He had victory before His eyes: The redemption of His people.

He must have obtained His prize because He is "set down at the right hand of the throne of God." This is the winners circle! He rejoices today. Let us rejoice with Him for His work.

While our days may become lonesome and dark, when our feet grow weary in our run, we must keep our eyes upon Him. With this heavenly view we can gain a glimpse of where we will be seated one day. This joy is set before the eyes of every believer. Lord, help us to be a witness for our posterity!

Helpful Hints:

1. Use this lesson to talk about repentance.

2. Use this lesson to show how Satan weights us down with sin and bad habits and how we rise above these by faith.

3. Use this lesson to talk about someone you all know who lived a life of faith in your own family.

4. Use this lesson to show how Jesus suffered for our sakes, yet remained faithful.

5. Use this lesson to remind your children that they will suffer in this world if they live the Christian life, but that the blessings are worth it.

6. Use this lesson to illustrate the power of a witnessing life.

"THE MATHEMATICS OF GRACE"

"Then came Peter to him, and said, Lord, how oft shall my brother sin against me, and I forgive him? till seven times? Jesus saith unto him, I say not unto thee, Until seven times: but, Until seventy times seven" –
Matthew 18:21-22

These words of Jesus reflect something that seems to be drifting from our vocabulary, a kind of math that is not new, but ancient as the Godhead, treasured up in the person of Christ: it is the mathematics of grace.

Grace reveals God's way of keeping score which goes against the grain of our natural reasoning. Grace disengages a catch 22 situation that occurs between people who love one another. It is a math that Satan hates because it reconciles irreconcilable differences; accepts the prodigal home; frees the woman taken in adultery; calls a murderer to become an apostle; places Rahab in the royal family; and forgives a repentant fornicator in the Corinthian church. Jesus is saying, "Peter, you forgive, I'll keep the books."

If you will notice, Jesus did not give Peter an "out". He didn't say, "Peter, when they ask for your forgiveness you may then extend it." He just said, "Forgive". That's God's mathematics. To forgive whether we are asked to or not.

Paul had been taught this *higher* math as well. He offered grace to sinners because it was the best thing he had ever experienced. To the Ephesians he wrote, "And be ye kind one to another, tenderhearted, forgiving one another, even as God for Christ's sake hath forgiven you"-Eph 4:32. How did Christ forgive us? Did we ask Him to descend from glory? Did we ask Him to take on the form of flesh? Did we ask Him to bleed and die for our sins against Him? Did Christ go to the grave with hard and angry feelings toward those that injured Him? He forgave, He suffered, He bled and died without any one asking Him to do so. That, my dear reader, is agape love. Perhaps our love is not what it should be. Jesus was "full of grace and truth" as He said, "Father, forgive them for they know not what they do". His last words were in the form of a petition for forgiveness for those who did not ask for it nor deserve it.

Grace is a wonderful word. As one writer has recently noticed, it is the "last best word". It carries with it a sound of dignity as well as holiness. He wrote, "Many people 'say grace' before meals, acknowledging daily bread as a gift from God. We are grateful for someone's kindness, gratified by good news, congratulated when successful, gracious in hosting friends. When a person's service pleases us, we leave a gratuity. In each of these uses I hear a pang of childlike delight in the undeserved." That is what makes grace so "amazing". It is a blessing for the "undeserving".

Our problem with "grace" is that it seems unfair. This much grace might serve to encourage one to sin. While Jesus never condoned sin, He offered His grace freely and called upon sinners to repent. Listen to His words to the woman taken in adultery, "Woman, where are those thine accusers? hath no man condemned thee? She said, No man, Lord. And Jesus said unto her, Neither do I condemn thee: go, and sin no more"-John 8:10-11. Grace opens the cage to the one who has been caught and says, "Fly away, you are free, visit this place no more."

Grace is more than theology, it involves be-ology, what we are to be.

C.S. Lewis wrote, "To be a Christian means to forgive the inexcusable, because God has forgiven the inexcusable in you." Some say that being a Christian is believing a particular doctrine. But being a Christian is emulating Christ. The best testament that explains grace to others is not the New or the Old. It is the living testament. As Knute Rockne said, "One man practicing sportsmanship is far better than 50 preaching it." Are you keeping score today? Jesus says, "quit multiplying and start forgiving".

Grace does not offer an advantage to those who have offended us. Grace diffuses; disarms; disengages; restores. That was the subject of the conversation between Peter and Jesus in Matthew 18: restoration. Grace, and grace alone, offers that blessing. Grace calls upon nations, races, families and leaders to forget yesterday and focus on tomorrow. Grace releases the tension between opposing factors as it cries: "All that counting is giving you a headache and keeping you awake at night. Quit keeping score".

Grace is expensive. Though it did not cost me anything, it cost God the Father His Son. Someone must pay for sin. I could not. I did not have the assets to cover the cost. But God did. He gave it freely in the person of Christ and I receive free pardon. That makes the mathematics of grace add up and 70x7 becomes a very small number.

Helpful Hints:

1. Use this lesson to talk about forgiveness.

2. Show that the biblical basis for forgiveness is not a request, but on the basis that we have been forgiven for Christ's sake.

3. Use this lesson to show that we do not write people off, that there is always hope for relationships to be restored.

4. Use this lesson to show that Satan wants us to burn bridges with people we love, even people of our own family and church.

5. Use this lesson to talk about grace, how we are saved by God's grace and how we extend this same grace to others.

"WHEN JESUS RETURNS"

"For the Lord himself shall descend from heaven with a shout, with the voice of the archangel, and with the trump of God: and the dead in Christ shall rise first: Then we which are alive and remain shall be caught up together with them in the clouds, to meet the Lord in the air: and so shall we ever be with the Lord. Wherefore comfort one another with these words"
-1 Thessalonians 4:16-18

When Paul wrote to the church at Thessalonica concerning the second advent of Christ, we find his words to be words of comfort, "Comfort one another with these words." He did not write of a remorseful event, an event that God's people should anticipate with dread and fear. The melody of his heart has the tune of a *homecoming*, a gathering together of loved ones that have gone on before us, the beginning of the eternal worship service of the Lamb slain.

When Jesus returns, He is not coming alone. Paul said, "them also which sleep in Jesus will God bring with him"-v14. Those Saints that have died, that now dwell with Christ on high, are coming with Jesus at His second advent. Moses, Abraham, Paul, Peter, and even those of our own family that we long to see again will return at that day. Surely, this must be a comfort to those who have lost loved ones in Christ, to know that they are presently with Jesus, and when He returns, they shall be with Him. And they are coming back for a purpose. They are coming for their bodies. They shall hover above the circle of the earth as Jesus speaks with the voice that wakes the dead and calls forth their glorified bodies from the dust!

Those that sleep in Christ will rise first, "and the dead in Christ shall rise first." Those bodies that sleep in Christ shall rise first from the grave as they are called, glorified, changed and reunited with those hovering souls and spirits that once occupied the tabernacle of clay. Those who are alive when Jesus returns will not go up before those which sleep in Jesus. They will be eyewitnesses of the dead coming forth from the graves! According to Paul, this will be an event that all will behold. Those who have hated Jesus and opposed God's creation will stand in dumbstruck awe and fear of this terrible event. When the Titanic went down, there were few life rafts and those left on board knew they were going down. Christ is our life raft. We shall rise in Him!

The Saints that live at the time of Jesus' second advent, will then follow. That is the order of events, "We which are alive and remain shall be caught up together with them in the clouds, to meet the Lord in the air". They will not disappear as some have suggested. As Jesus rose from the earth in the presence of the apostles into the clouds, so shall the Saints rise to be with Jesus in the air. All will behold the scene.

According to Paul, that is the end, "so shall we ever be with the Lord." When Jesus returns, He will not set His foot upon this earth again. He has no reason to do so. When He came the first time He was victorious, He justified His people, He paid for their sins, He saved them from the wrath to come, He redeemed them from all iniquity, He established His kingdom, He ascended into the portals of glory a conquering King. His work was "finished". What else could He do? The purpose of His second advent is to collect what He paid for on the first trip, what rightfully belongs to Him, His redeemed family and pronounce His eternal sentence on all unbelievers, "Depart from me, ye cursed, into everlasting fire, prepared for the devil and his angels". And from here, Paul is silent. Should we not be as well?

The scene Paul has before us is a simple one. It is not clouded with types and shadows, with symbolism that we must try to unscramble. Whatever we may believe concerning His second advent, it MUST agree with this simple account of Jesus' return. Lord, come quickly!

Helpful Hints:
1. This lesson allows us the opportunity to talk to our family about the greatest theme of all Christianity: Heaven.
2. Use it to talk about death and what happens to our loved ones at death: the soul and spirit goes back to God and the body, the tabernacle which houses the soul and spirit, is placed in the ground.
3. Use it to comfort the loss of a loved one with our family, to know that for a Christian to be absent from the body is to be present with the Lord.
4. Use it to oppose false doctrines of Christ's return, about the fictitious ideas of people disappearing.
5. Use it to reinforce the idea that the kingdom of God is with us today and today is the time to be active in it.
6. Use it to show that heaven is more than spiritual wisps floating around in eternity knowing nothing or no one. That we shall know one another there as

brothers and sisters in Christ and that Jesus shall be the center of it all.

7. Use it to dismiss fears about millennial reigns and monsters coming up out of the ground. That our battle is today and when Jesus returns our battles will be over.

"A SON IS GIVEN"

"For unto us a child is born, unto us a son is given: and the government shall be upon his shoulder: and his name shall be called Wonderful, Counsellor, The mighty God, The everlasting Father, The Prince of Peace"
-Isaiah 9:6

It is the time of the year that many hearts have been opened to confer a gift or two upon the objects of their love. But let us pause for a moment to consider the greatest gift that has ever graced the halls of time. This gift was given to, and for, the objects of God's love. It was the most expensive gift that has ever been given. It had a purpose that has never been equaled. To those who possess this gift, its value grows more and more each passing day. The gift was God's Son, Jesus Christ.

The same that is the mighty God is a little child born. The ancient of days becomes an infant of a span long. As Mary held the babe in her arms she looked directly into the face of God, her redeemer, the great I Am, the one that would open the eyes of the blind, the ears of the deaf, cause the lame to leap, the leper to be cleansed and speak the dead to life. Though He had just made His advent into this world, He came from another: He had walked where angels tread.

Unto "US" this gift was given. The "US" are God's redeemed family: the elect. Do you have an interest in this gift? Is He your hearts desire, the key to your greatest expectations? Then He must have been given for you! Let us consider His value.

The "Government shall be upon his shoulder". I love the "shalls" of the Bible. When we read them as such, our theology will never waver. This government speaks of His divine authority in the *redemption* and *preservation* of His people. In redemption, He kept all the laws of His Father's judicial government to secure His people. The law was upon "His" shoulders and not the shoulders of the elect. He died for them and redeemed them from all iniquity. He did not leave the legality of salvation for preachers and clergy to figure out. Could man ever agree upon any one plan of redemption if left to himself? Let us just rejoice in the gift. It is complete in every way. Though Peter, Paul and the other apostles declared the gift, they added nothing to payment rendered for our debt. Though Mary brought Him into this world, she too, was of the sons of Adam and will claim no part in the redemption of God's people: He trod the winepress alone. The Government was upon His shoulders, His alone.

Because of His divine authority in the legal phase of His government we "shall" speak many wonderful things of Him. Here, Isaiah provides another "shall" that has proven to be true for almost two-thousand years as His beloved reflect upon Him as "Wonderful". He was wonderful in His birth, in His life, in His miracles, in His patience with sinners, in His death, and certainly in His resurrection. A constant series of wonders attend Him.

He *shall* also be called "Counsellor". Have you sought Him out in your difficulties? There has always been much counsel from the minds of men. But the instruction from this Counsellor is the litmus test for all advice. The wisdom and philosophy of man is sand, let us build upon the Rock. The Psalmist has declared "Thy testimonies also are my delight and my counsellors." His office is always open and it will cost you nothing but to obey.

He is the "Mighty God". Though a babe, El-Shaddai is revealed to Israel. Dagon must fall before Him. He opens and no man can shut. He shuts and no man can open. He is the "Lord of Hosts", the commander of angelic host. All things are upheld by His omnipotent power. At His word, all of creation would dissolve in a fervent heat. All power is given Him by the Father. All of which pale into view before the great and Mighty work of redemption at the cross.

He is the "Everlasting Father". Though a Son, He is yet the Father of a noble seed. His people are, "born again, not of corruptible seed, but of incorruptible, by the word of God, which liveth and abideth for ever" 1 Peter 1:23. All of the elect are His offspring; born of His spirit; the seed that shall serve Him; His seed is in them; His spiritual descendants, not Abraham's. Since, this relationship has no end, He is the "Everlasting Father".

He is the "Prince of Peace". Where genuine peace is found, He is the author of it. Though peace between nations shall falter, peace between men shall be fickle, this peace is permanent: it brought peace between fallen man and God. Though the gulf was great, He spanned it with His blood. "For he is our peace"-Ephesians 2:14. Thanks be to God for His unspeakable gift!

Helpful Hints:

1. Talk about the deity and humanity of Christ.

2. Talk about prophecy being fulfilled which was given thousands of years before and the inspiration and surety of scripture.

3. Talk about salvation being all of God.

4. Talk about worldly counsel, worldly wisdom Vs. God's.

5. Talk about the power of our Mighty God and His miracles.

6. Talk about peace found in our relationship with Christ.

7. Talk about the many attributes of Christ and how He is wonderful to us today.

8. Talk about "everlasting".

"WISE INQUIRERS"

"Where is he that is born King of the Jews? For we have seen his star in the east, and are come to worship him"
-Matthew 2:2

One might have thought that God, making His personal appearance in the form of flesh, would have made a grand entrance, but there was nothing at His birth to attract the attention of the Scribes and Pharisees. Nor would the Caesars find an interest in His lowly birth. As Isaiah had prophesied, "he hath no form nor comeliness; and when we shall see him, there is no beauty that we should desire him"-Isaiah 53:2. The birth of the Christ Child was revealed to lowly shepherds of Bethlehem and a few wise men of the east. From these wise inquirers, we may learn some very practical lessons.

It is always encouraging to find *inquiring* minds concerning the things of God. It is an evidence of grace, an attribute of one who is spiritually alive and hungers for spiritual nourishment. These will learn all that they can about their Lord, from the cradle to the cross, they will leave no stone unturned.

Here we learn that the wise inquirer has a teachable spirit even if he has to go by the way of Herod to learn about the Christ child. Though a rich man, the Ethiopian Eunuch was willing to learn from the humble evangelist, Philip, concerning Christ. When Philip drew near the chariot and asked the Eunuch if he understood the text, his reply was that of an anxious inquirer, "How can I except some man should guide me?" As Spurgeon said, "When a man listens with deep attention to the word of God, searches God's book, and engages in thoughtful meditation with the view of understanding the gospel, we have much hope of him."

In the case of the wise men, we also see ignorance admitted. Wise men are never above asking questions, that is how they became wise. Some persons who have taken the name and degree of wise men sometimes think it beneath them to confess any degree of ignorance. Those who are really wise do not think so. They are too well instructed to be ignorant of their own ignorance. As one man said, "The knowledge of our ignorance is the doorstep of the temple of knowledge." Some know they know all, and therefore never know. The Pharisee claimed to see all spiritual things. What could a poor carpenter teach them? But Jesus must say to them, "If ye were blind, ye should have no sin: but now ye say, We see; therefore your sin remaineth"-John 9:41.

Their search for the Christ child was attended with many encouragements and ultimately....success! God will not leave *wise inquirers* in the dark concerning His Son. Though we do not expect His star to appear again, there are many lesser lights that can guide us to His cot today. We live in a land that we may preach the gospel freely; have a Bible in our homes; and worship unhindered and unharmed. Are not these equally stars of encouragement to lead us closer to Emmanuel? How few are following.

There will be many unchurched this Sabbath day. Surely, they will miss a blessing!

His star was a matter of great *favor*. Not all attended the gathering at the manger. Few knew of the star's significance. These men were, therefore, highly privileged. Has the day star risen in your heart? Is Christ in you, the hope of glory? Follow that light. It must lead us only closer to Him.

Their motive was declared: "...we are come to worship him". A wise one indeed! Surely, He is worthy. Let all of creation adore Him. And how did they do so? They presented to Him their gifts. Gold, frankincense and myrrh were laid at the Redeemer's feet, precious cargo from the east. When the heart is genuinely touched, the hand is generously opened for this is a spontaneous act worship. Mary with her alabaster box of precious ointment; the widow's mite; the gifts of the wise men; the hearts of the shepherds; the chorus of the angels; all became His at His appearance. True worship is found in the spirit of giving.

Dear reader, has the day star arisen in your heart to outshine all lesser lights? Have you come to worship Him? Let us be wise inquirers and never cease to seek for Him, where He dwells, and those who attend Him. We may be sure He will always be found among humble surroundings and other wise inquirers. Let our chorus join the angel's.

Helpful Hints:
1. **Talk about the birth of Jesus, the wise men and their gifts.**
2. **Talk about Herod's attempt to destroy the Christ child.**
3. **Talk about enquiring into the things of God and their profit.**

4. Talk about giving our time, our lips, our mind, our heart and our money to the Lord.

"REJOICE EVERMORE"

"Rejoice evermore. Pray without ceasing. In every thing give thanks: for this is the will of God in Christ Jesus concerning you. Quench not the Spirit. Despise not prophesyings. Prove all things; hold fast that which is good. Abstain from all appearance of evil"
-I Thessalonians 5:16-22

Paul closes out his letter to the brethren at Thessalonica with several Christian encouragements that we might continue in or improve upon in our own personal experience. Perhaps there are those who will join me in an honest attempt to live up to Paul's divine instruction.

To "rejoice" means to be *cheerful* or *calmly happy* and "evermore" means at *all times*. For those who read the words, is it an encouragement to try to retain this posture *from now on*.

Consider the gravity of the statement to a church that was being persecuted by its enemies and had recently buried family and church members from the onslaught. It must be a *noble* goal or the apostle would never have encouraged such an attitude for the believers at Thessalonica.

Rejoicing must be an *attitude* or state of mind that rises above the circumstances of this world. How else could Paul have encouraged such an attitude in the heat of sorrow and battle. When trials and tribulations come, the worldling looks for pleasure, the Christian looks for the lily in the valley. Concerning pleasure and joy, C.S. Lewis wrote, "....I doubt whether anyone who has tasted it(joy)would ever, if both were in his power, exchange it for all the pleasures in the world. But then Joy is never in our power and Pleasure often is." Joy is a fruit of the spirit, pleasure is the gratifying of the flesh. Joy feeds the soul while pleasure feeds the flesh. Thus, rejoicing is not being silly or funny which draws attention to self: is it an experience of the heart that may be invisible to others. Rejoicing and joy are twin cousins: joy is the fruit and rejoicing is the consuming of it. Christians are to be noted by the joy manifested in their life, even in times of struggle. When one *rejoices* evermore, the day does not order the attitude, the attitude orders the day and joy ensues.

I can think of no other people that have more occasion to *rejoice* than those who confess Christ. They have many reasons to rejoice. Jesus died for them; their sins are paid for; He presently intercedes for them; He knows them by name; He is a friend that sticks closer than a brother; He is coming back one day to receive them to Himself; and they shall spend eternity with Him in glory. Paul would rejoice with Silas at midnight in prison. When Peter and the disciple were whipped for their public testimony they rejoiced in that they were allowed to suffer for Jesus' sake. Unless we have failed our Lord in some way, there must be something wrong with our spirit when we do not put on the garments of rejoicing. May we all improve.

"Oh may we all improve,
The grace already given;
And wear the crown of perfect love,
And show we're heirs of heaven!"

Helpful Hints:
1. Talk about the difference between pleasure and joy.
2. Talk about forbidden fruit.
3. Talk about the fruit of the spirit.
4. Count your blessings
5. Enumerate the reasons Christians have to rejoice!

"PRAY WITHOUT CEASING"

"Rejoice evermore. Pray without ceasing. In every thing give thanks: for this is the will of God in Christ Jesus concerning you. Quench not the Spirit. Despise not prophesyings. Prove all things; hold fast that which is good. Abstain from all appearance of evil"
-I Thessalonians 5:16-22

Some have suggested that the remainder of Paul's list contains the *recipe* to help us in our attempt to "rejoice evermore". The first on his list involves our prayer life. Do you have one?

In our busy life, our "Sweet Hour of Prayer" is many times a hectic moment of requests. Though we could not pray every second, the apostle encourages us here to be in the constant *attitude* of prayer. Fellowship with our father is upon our minds and hearts every moment. This means, that during our daily prayer, we do not have to say amen at the conclusion of each visit, we can keep the phone off the hook, the lines open, and take up where we left off. Each time our thoughts take us to our Father is the time to speak whether it is a thank you, a petition for another, a personal request or just a hello, I love you.

To be constantly aware that the Lord is ever present and converse with Him during our daily routine is not only possible, but profitable.

The cold and impenitent heart frequently comes from a lack of *conversation* with our Father. Perhaps we have forgotten Him or we refuse to talk to Him about our present occupations. It is then that we have ceased to attain the attitude of prayer. Paul's encouragement will keep the spiritual lines open and prevent our feet from stumbling.

Prayer should always begin with praise: "Hallowed be thy name!" For a sinner to be able to approach our thrice Holy Lord should send praises in the highest strain. Many times, the praise will do more for us than the request for we are reminded of His perfection, His Holiness, His foreknowledge and His Majesty. How could we be treated wrong in our petitions?

Many times, the psalmist, in his prayers, went from praise, to request, to rejoicing. As he soared on eagles wings to Mt. Rejoicing, his cares were left far below in the valley of Achor. His language lept from the funeral dirge to the chorus of an angelic host. As we read his prayers we can feel the load lifted and the troubled waters calmed at the foot of the mercy seat. Let us not worship prayer in and of itself. It is the Person we talk to that answers the petition and lifts us up. The world tries to make prayer the remedy when it is the Lord that answers and heals the wounded spirit. Before you left your room this morning, did you forget to pray?

Helpful Hints:
1. Talk about your prayer life.
2. Talk about prayers answered in your life.
3. Share your burdens with one another and pray over them.

4. Talk about praying without ceasing.
5. Read some of the psalmist's prayers and other prayers of the Bible.

"IN EVERY THING GIVE THANKS"

"Rejoice evermore. Pray without ceasing. In every thing give thanks: for this is the will of God in Christ Jesus concerning you. Quench not the Spirit. Despise not prophesyings. Prove all things; hold fast that which is good. Abstain from all appearance of evil"-I Thessalonians 5:16-22

While the wordling counts his money, his titles, his honor and his crowns, the Christian counts his blessings. My, what a contrast! This list we must ponder as we give *thanks* to the Father for every good and perfect gift. It is the best cure for P.L.O.M. disease(Poor Little Old Me). If we are to give thanks in "every thing", it must mean more than a generic "thank you for my blessings." We must be specific and name each blessing "one by one". A constant perusal of His grace will keep the pilgrim from the valley of despair. An unthankful child is impossible to please. Giving thanks will keep us in the posture of prayer and on the mountain of rejoicing.

Surely, our thanks must begin with Christ, the channel through which every blessing must flow. Have you thanked your Father for the gift of His Son? This was the greatest gift that has ever graced the halls of time and eternity. It was by this gift that our sins were atoned. An eternal benefit has been received. Let our *eternal* thanks begin here as we look forward to their continuance in glory.

Blessings, both natural and spiritual, are too numerous for us to comprehend if our eyes have been opened. A thankful heart is a constant reminder of our Father's love and kindness. Though there will always be thorns in the flesh, let us be careful to thank Him for the grace that is sufficient for every trial. I stand in constant amazement that our Lord continues to shower His blessing upon us, even when past blessings are enjoyed without a word of thanks. Our Father is so faithful even when we are not.

Some have asked what their Father's will would be for them or "what does the Lord want ME to do?" Here is at least one plain and simple answer to this question: give thanks. If we have not realized what He has done for us thus far, will He use us for greater battles? Will He give more light to those who have not walked in their present light? If we do not see His hand when it is opened perhaps we will seek it when it is closed. His will is for every child to search out and recognize every blessing and give thanks in particular for each one. Oh, how our eyes will be opened!

Helpful Hints:
1. Count your blessings, name them one by one.
2. Take time to thank the Father for His Son.
3. Consider blessings often forgotten like health, breath and life.
4. Consider Jesus giving thanks to His Father.
5. Notice the thanks in the Bible.

"QUENCH NOT THE SPIRIT"

"Rejoice evermore. Pray without ceasing. In every thing give thanks: for this is the will of God in Christ Jesus concerning you. Quench not the Spirit. Despise not prophesyings. Prove all things; hold fast that which is good. Abstain from all appearance of evil"-I Thessalonians 5:16-22

With his "Quench not the Spirit", the apostle here warns us of a fault that must be common among God's people. To quench the influence of the Holy Spirit is something that we are all prone to do, in our personal lives and well as collectively in the church. The thought is very suggestive. It presents the thought of one throwing water upon a fire that is providing light and warmth. The result is spiritual darkness and coldness.

Many times it is *fear* that drowns the flame within. Sometimes it is *pride* or some other inward struggle. The heart must be searched as we consider the source of our greatest hindrance. The Thessalonians were persecuted from without and fear had gripped the hearts of many, hindering their fervent devotions. This fear momentarily quenched Peter's flame as he warmed his hands by the enemy's fire and denied his Lord. Satan's roar can paralyze just long enough for him to advance and devour.

It was *pride* that smoldered the inward flame of the rulers of the synagogues. They preferred their positions and favors in the big synagogues above warmth, light and fellowship with Christ and His humble followers(John 12:42). The inward struggles such as being ashamed of Christ, peer pressure and a desire to be like the world are the common problems for us today and present a quenching of the same magnitude. Heart disease abounds, both naturally and spiritually.

The Holy Spirit is a teacher and a Comforter, the match that sets our hearts ablaze. When we refuse His direction, His comforts and His light, we throw water upon the fire we so desperately need: we have quenched the Spirit. This we do when we are given light upon His word and reject His truths, when we refuse to use a gift that has been freely given, when we could have offered a word of encouragement and didn't, when we could have shed a tear in God's house and held it back, when we could forgive a wrong and did not, when we could have defended a truth and were ashamed, when our heart burned to confess Jesus by water baptism and did not, when we know where His house is and avoid it, in all of this and more, we have extinguished the fire.

This quenching affects our testimony, our security, our joy and we become birds who can no longer sing. Our rejoicing evermore ceases until we the flame is fanned once again by the Holy Spirit. Lord, give us your Spirit!

Helpful Hints:
1. Talk about how we can quench the spirit.
2. Give some specific examples.
3. Talk about ways to revive it.

"DESPISE NOT PROPHESYINGS"

"Rejoice evermore. Pray without ceasing. In every thing give thanks: for this is the will of God in Christ Jesus concerning you. Quench not the Spirit. Despise not prophesyings. Prove all things; hold fast that which is good. Abstain from all appearance of evil"-I Thessalonians 5:16-22

Here, in the apostle's encouragement to the baptized members of Thessalonica, the word "prophesyings" speaks of *forthtelling* and not foretelling. It does not depict the *foretelling* of future events, but rather the expounding of the word. In short, this is *preaching*. Perhaps, there were those at Thessalonica who felt that their baptism was the pinnacle of their experience and there was little need to frequent the house of God. Once saved, always saved, has a two edged sword. The truly saved hunger and thirst for God's word and love to hear God's word expounded. The never saved go back to the world.

There have been days, in this country, when people approached God's house for an all day event that focused upon preaching. Some literature will deride the Puritans, who would expound the word of God for hours at a time, yet they say nothing about those that linger at the honky-tonk. They present those old congregations as a sleepy and bored people. But in spite of how history may present those days, we observe the impact that such an interest in God's word had upon society then and today. I find a deeper knowledge of God and His word in their writings; in their stories; in their prayers and in their poetry. There are many distractions all around us. Let them not cause us to despise prophesyings.

I am not suggesting that we can not worship unless we have an all day event. Charles H. Spurgeon fed thousands and most of his discourses were about forty-five minutes. But I would suggest that many have placed entertainment above preaching on the inside and outside of the church. Many will come to church for a show, but few to know. When the building in back of a church is larger than the sanctuary where the word is expounded we know that the focus of that people is not the word of God. Paul told Timothy to "Preach the word", not play the harp. Much of religion today is centered around the palate and not the soul. No wonder when we talk about Jehudi's pocketknife many have not met the man.

If we are to "deny not prophesyings" we must listen to sermons that not only comfort, but also those that rebuke and reprove our sin. That is part of preaching, to "reprove, rebuke and exhort with all longsuffering and doctrine." That is the threefold cord of preaching: to tell the sinner his faults, to reprove him of his sin and to comfort them with Christ. One must be willing to approach God's house with a willingness to learn from the expounding of God's word and a desire for it to change my life for the better. To the world, preaching is foolishness. Yet, "it pleased God by the foolishness of preaching to save them that believe" -1 Cor. 1:21. Preaching is the power of God unto salvation. Let us not despise the biblical instruction that will save us from Satan and his snares. This spiritual instruction will become a blessing to our families. It will make us better husbands, wives, parents, and citizens. Let us be always willing to lend an ear to those that God has called to expound His word. We either like it or despise it. There is no middle ground. Lord, cause us to hunger for thy word!

Helpful Hints:
1. Talk about preaching and some special sermons that you have enjoyed.
2. Talk about the benefits of preaching.
3. Read some of the sermons in the Bible: Peter's discourse at Pentecost and our Lord's sermon on the Mount.
4. Consider the different preaching gifts you have heard.
5. Consider the perishing of the foolish.

"PROVE ALL THINGS"

"Rejoice evermore. Pray without ceasing. In every thing give thanks: for this is the will of God in Christ Jesus concerning you. Quench not the Spirit. Despise not prophesyings. Prove all things; hold fast that which is good. Abstain from all appearance of evil"-I Thessalonians 5:16-22

The Apostle further calls upon us to "Prove all things". This means to *try* or *examine* what has been preached. Is it truth or "cunningly devised fables"? Is it from God or man? Is the wisdom of God or the wisdom of man? Did it come from scripture or from the mind of sinners? God's true ministers will always encourage their hearers to compare what they say with God's world. They would encourage every believer to own a Bible and search it out. Paul's "prove all things" means, "Don't be taken in" by false apostles or false doctrine. Prove it!

Apparently, there were those at Thessalonica who were prone to believe any thing that they heard. Luke compares them with the believers at Berea who, "were more noble than those in Thessalonica, in that they received the word with all readiness of mind, and searched the scriptures daily, whether those things were so"-Acts 17:11. The believers at Berea had a ready mind as well as a ready Bible to "prove" what had been taught in their church. Even what the apostle Paul taught! This was Luke's mark of nobility.

Proving all things keeps us from every wind of doctrine. It sets a mark on the forehead of the false prophet and leads us through the strait gate.

Helpful Hints:
1. Talk about false doctrines and cults of our day.
2. Talk about worldly wisdom Vs. God's.
3. Demonstrate the importance of truth in our lives.
4. Talk about the dangers of false doctrine.

"HOLD FAST THAT WHICH IS GOOD"

"Rejoice evermore. Pray without ceasing. In every thing give thanks: for this is the will of God in Christ Jesus concerning you. Quench not the Spirit. Despise not prophesyings. Prove all things; hold fast that which is good. Abstain from all appearance of evil"-I Thessalonians 5:16-22

Once the Thessalonians had "proved" what they had been taught, once they had found the truth, Paul encouraged them to hold it fast. "Hold fast" means to hang on with all your might. Concerning truth, it means to retain or possess it in your memory; keep the good, throw away the bad; remember the truth, forget the fable. As some put it, "keep the chicken and throw away the bones."

Surely, the thinking, the use of the mind is a part of Christianity. The Church is to be of "one mind"; a willing mind is accepted of God; Paul served the law of God with his mind; and God has given His people a sound mind. Christians are the deepest thinkers in the world, they see the natural as well as the spiritual realm. When truth is held in the mind it must, it will permeate the whole body and will become a well of water springing up into eternal life.

What good is our hearing if we forget what we have heard? We must remember the law so we will not break it; remember our duties that we may perform them; and consider the promises that we may continually rejoice in them. Hold fast to that which is good.

Why would Paul give such a seemingly simple lesson? Because we are prone to do just the opposite, to remember the things we need to forget and forget the things we need to remember. Surely, this will bring depression and misery. Christians are called upon to keep their minds upon profitable things. Whether it is doctrine, duty, God's promises or our feelings about our fellow man, we are to "hold fast" to that which is good and profitable for our souls. We have heard some say that a mind is a terrible thing to waste. Yet, what is waste? Is it not caring and thinking more upon the world than upon God and His word? Our grip, our holding fast, is not with the fingers, but with the mind. If we are slipping or if things are slipping from us, it is because we are weak minded. We need to exercise our thinking. We need to get out the fitness machine of prayer, scripture reading and meditations of God's law. Then we will be like a tree planted by the rivers of water, bringing forth fruit unto God. Lord, help us to be so!

Helpful Hints:
1. What are some truths we need to remember that will help us each day?
2. What should happen in our mind when truth and error collide?
3. How do we hold fast the truth?
4. Talk about Mr. Pliable in Pilgrim's Progress.
5. Talk about the apostle's holding fast.
6. Talk about how truths are knocked from our grasp.

"ABSTAIN FROM ALL APPEARANCE OF EVIL"

"Rejoice evermore. Pray without ceasing. In every thing give thanks: for this is the will of God in Christ Jesus concerning you. Quench not the Spirit. Despise not prophesyings. Prove all things; hold fast that which is good. Abstain from all appearance of evil"-I Thessalonians 5:16-22

Apparently, there were those at Thessalonica who thought they could flirt with the world and "rejoice evermore." But it is evil that brings God's children into the pit of despair; dashes their hopes; diminishes their joy; stops their prayers; makes them unthankful; quenches their spirit; moves them from God's house; and confuses their judgment of right and wrong. You can not hold hands with the devil on Saturday night and hold hands with Jesus on Sunday morning. Our God is a jealous God. If you hold hands with the devil on Saturday night, the best you can do is bring him with you to church on Sunday morning!

Paul's thought is very suggestive. We are to abstain not only from what we know is evil, but from things that even *appear* to be evil. Curiosity has killed the cat and it has slain many a Christian. Satan will have us think that we can look upon that which God has forbidden and we are safe as long as we do not touch. Was that not the opinion of King David as he beheld Bathsheba from his palace roof; or Samson as he flirted with Delilah; or Eve as she looked upon the forbidden fruit and saw that "it was pleasant to the eye"? What would they have gained had they abstained from the "appearance of evil?" What would they have retained?

In his "Holy War", John Bunyan drew the same truth in an allegory. When eye-gate was taken by evil Daibolis , the whole town of Man-soul was in danger. Eye-gate was where Lord Innocence was killed. Then Mr. Lusting was made Lord Mayor. Mr. Forget-good became the town recorder in place of Mr. Conscience. And so the story goes for those who do not abstain from the appearance of evil. Satan knows that a circling fish will soon bite the worm after which all rejoicing is turned to sorrow. The many categories of sin are too numerous for us to mention. We must all search our own hearts and discover the bait that Satan has so cleverly placed before our eyes. He knows your weakness better than you do. Do you know what he knows?

Helpful Hints:
1. Name some evil things that you have abstained from.
2. Talk about the wiles of the devil.
3. Talk about Eve.
4. Talk about Sampson
5. Talk about David and Bathsheba.
6. Talk about the town of Mansoul.

"WHY JESUS CAME"

*"And she shall bring forth a son, and thou shalt call his name
Jesus: for he shall save his people from their sins"*
-Matthew 1:21

Couched in three glorious truths we find wonderful words of comfort. Had mortal man spoken these words, Joseph might have wondered if they were true. Surely, we can believe the words of God's special messenger.

These are shalls from the angelic messenger. They are not perhaps, possibilities, or speculation. The thing is certain, God will have His way, He has predetermined the outcome. Satan and all of his forces could not change even one of these glorious truths. Though Herod would be moved to destroy our darling Christ Child and Pilate would agree to His crucifixion, God's decrees *shall* be carried out.

Most Christians will agree to the first two truths. They will agree that Mary brought forth a Son and they will agree that His name is Jesus. Yet, many become doubting Thomas concerning the third. Doubting Thomas will say that Jesus made man savable. They either doubt Christ's ability or His purpose. Yet, the angel said He *shall* save.

If we were looking for salvation, should we not look to One who saves? What hope could the poor and afflicted find in one who makes man savable and leaves a portion of the task to complete? Are we better than Christ? The comfort is found in the success of the Saviour.

Many times the trophy does not land in the hands of the best nor is recognition given to those who have rightfully earned it. Religion does this to Christ, Christianity does not. Let us not rob Christ of His glory. When our days are done and we stand before the Ancient of days, will we claim a portion of salvation as our own? It is certain that all of the praise, honor and glory will be His and His alone. As one man said, "I did all the sinning. Jesus did all the saving." What is your faith in today? Is it in ceremonies, ordinances or duties? Place all of your trust in His finished works and there leave it.

The angelic messenger is specific concerning who Jesus came to save: He shall save "His people". If I were to say, "that is his car; his house; his business" I must mean that those things belong to that individual. "His people" must mean that Jesus came for something that rightfully belonged to Him. Something lost in the fall of Adam would be regained; redeemed; bought back; restored to its rightful owner. They became "His people" long" ago. According to Paul they were "chosen in him(Christ) before the foundation of the world"-Ephesians 1:4. That is how the angel could say, "His people".

Finally, the angel declared what He saved "His people" from. He saved them from "their sins". It was sin that expelled Adam and Eve from their beautiful Eden. It was sin that brought enmity between God and man. Sin barred the door to glory for "His people". The sins of "His people" were placed upon Him as He hung upon the cross. His blood paid the price that "His people" could not pay. He was wounded for our transgressions, bruised for our iniquities and with His stripes we are healed. He did what the angel declared: He saved His people from their sins. Let all the honor, the praise and the glory be his!

Helpful Hints:
1. Talk about the shalls of the Bible.
2. Talk about particular redemption.
3. Talk about the doctrine of election: His people.
4. Talk about God's foreknowledge.
5. Talk about salvation all of Christ not man's works.

"DISCIPLESHIP, A NOBLE PROFESSION"

"So likewise, whosoever he be of you that forsaketh not all that he hath,
he cannot be my disciple"-Luke 14:33

Being a disciple of Christ is the most noble profession that a person may aspire unto. In God's eyes, it is more important than being a famous movie star, a successful athlete, a corporate executive, a millionaire, a president or a king. While the merits of man will be covered by the sands of time, it is the disciples and their humble testimony that God has recorded in His word, a testimony that will shine throughout eternity.

This word, "disciple", is used to describe the followers of Christ more than any other term in the New Testament. While the word Christian is used but three times in the New Testament to describe the followers of Christ, "disciple" is used over 250 times. This is the word that Jesus chose to depict His most ardent followers. It must be important!

The term "disciple" means *learner*. Therefore, a true follower of Christ is a learner of Christ and His principles.

This term affords me a lot of latitude in my daily walk. It does not give me an excuse for my failings, but it does mean that I have not arrived; I still have a lot to learn. It means that I will make mistakes from time to time because I am yet a learner. I like that. I do not have to put on airs. I am learning to be a better pastor; father; husband; neighbor; employer; and citizen. All of these categories, and many more, are found in the teachings of Christ and in the category of discipleship. His doctrine touches every facet of my life, all of which I need improvement, all of which I have a lot to *learn*.

Once we have established this point, it is easy for us to understand why a woman who has chosen the biblical pattern of being a loving mother and faithful wife has actually chosen the life of discipleship. She is pleasing the Lord. Though "Inc." magazine would not feature her on the front cover and "Vogue" would not publish her attire, she is the backbone of any society. She is the one that molds our future generation.

Likewise, the man who has chosen to be a faithful husband and dedicated father is of far greater value in God's eyes than a chair at the corporate meeting, a big car or a mantle of trophies. As you can see, discipleship is important. Disciples are the most essential building blocks for our nation, our churches and our homes. We do not need programs and laws to strengthen our churches and bring this country back to its Godly heritage. We need disciples!

If you will notice the words of Jesus, His picture of discipleship was far different than what we hear in the world today. He is not saying, "anyone can be my disciple", His encouragement is in the negative, "You cannot be my disciple". He did not send out a survey to find what everyone wanted in a church. He was not devising schemes and programs to attract the multitudes. He was thinning them out. He was not looking for numbers, He was looking for commitment. As one man said, "There is a difference between interest and commitment. When you are interested in doing something, you do it only when it is convenient. When you are committed to something you accept no excuses". Jesus must come first. That is why being a disciple of Christ is the hardest thing a person can do. Being a disciple requires the daily sacrifice of self.

As the multitudes diminished we find a class of people who remained, "Then drew near unto him all the publicans and sinners for to hear him"-Luke 15:1. The scribes and Pharisees departed. They could learn nothing from this man, they knew it all. But for those who felt their condemnation, the world and worldly aspirations had lost their attraction. Their eye was on the Saviour . He was first. They needed Jesus and His principles more than anything. They became the disciples.

Helpful Hints:
1. Name some of Jesus' disciples.
2. Talk about the importance of learning from Jesus.
3. How do we learn from Jesus today?
4. Talk about our commitment to Christ.

"THE TREASURES OF THE SNOW"

"Hast thou entered into the treasures of the snow? Or hast thou seen the treasures of the hail, which I have reserved against the time of trouble, against the day of battle and war"
-Job 38:22,23

In His treatise upon creation, God would ask Job and his friends if they had considered a gift that we all may enjoy: the "treasures of the snow." By this religious exercise, Job and his friends would find their hearts stirred and their actions rebuked as they were reminded of God's wisdom, His majesty, His sovereignty and His power. For just a moment, let us enter with Job and his friends into just a few of "the treasures of the snow."

Among the many splendors of God's creation, nothing is more beautiful and majestic than a snowfall. In just a few moments, the earth is canvassed with tons of beautiful, downy crystals of ice. We are told that no two snowflakes are identical. Who, but God, could invent such a thing. Man must mass produce many objects of the same shape and dimension, but God's wisdom was displayed as we beheld billions of snowflakes, each one possessing its own unique splendor and beauty.

Yes, snow is a product of God's wisdom and His majesty. As the painter would see the object of his creation before he placed it upon the canvas, so God, in His wisdom and majesty, would design the snowflake. Majestic beauty must come from a majestic mind. Consider this treasure and we begin to consider God.

It is true, man has copied a miniscule of God's creation with his noisy snow cannons. But what are a few particles compared to the millions of tons of the downy, silent mass that covers the hills and plains. Truly, this silent display of God's wisdom is one of the most beautiful spectacles of His creation. I see it on canvas, in magazines, on postcards, and on television. While men are applauded for their actions, let us applaud God for His majestic display of wisdom and beauty.

I am sure that man will never discover all of the benefits that these "treasures" will afford him. Perhaps Job and his friends knew more than we do today. It is known that snow will make the earth more fruitful. It serves to purify the atmosphere. It destroys harmful insects. By the little that we do know, we must say, "How complex is God's creation. He has seen to every need. How great is His wisdom. How wonderful are his treasures!"

Who, but God, could create beauty and power in one event. Who, but God, could speak so powerfully, yet so softly. If He had a mind to do so, all of creation could be brought to a standstill by one snowstorm. Planes are grounded, communications are silenced, schedules must halt and man's plans must take a back seat as God speaks to us through His creation. I find a *treasure* in this. Each snowstorm is a silent sermon. The earth must stop for a little while and confess that God is alive and He is not silent. Did your hear Him speak?

While some will blame El Nino for the weather, the believer knows that all of creation is held together and command by El Shaddai, the Almighty, All-sufficient One. Man is always trying to predict the weather. God commands it. He is sovereign. He "hath his way in the whirlwind and in the storm, and the clouds are the dust of his feet"

From time to time, God must remind proud man who is in control of all things and who possesses all power in heaven and in earth. If we forget Him, we can be sure that He will remind us! God has used the weather more than once to remind man of His power and Lordship. It was by a great deluge that God once judged a wicked world. By rain, by hail, by drought, by whirlwinds, God can get man's attention very effectively. Just by withholding the moisture from the atmosphere God can, and has, brought all of creation to its knees. He destroyed the armies of the Amorites and the crops of the Egyptians with hailstones. The weather is God's arsenal. If He desires, He can fight as effectively with snow and hail as man can with his modern weapons of war. His arsenal is always full and His aim is wrought with skill and wisdom. Only God, by His infinite wisdom and Holiness, can possess such power and use it for good. What a treasures we may find in the snow!

Helpful Hints:
1. Talk about creation.
2. Talk about the sovereignty of God.
3. Talk about how God used the weather many times to fight the enemies.
4. Talk about Elijah's prayer that it might not rain.
5. Talk about how God used the weather to fight Pharaoh.

"MAKING MELODY IN YOUR HEART"

"Speaking to yourselves in psalms and hymns and spiritual songs, singing and making melody in your heart to the Lord"
-Ephesians 5:19

Singing "spiritual songs" is a God-ordained part of the Christian's worship service. It is not a time of worship that God winks at, it is worship in and of itself. If we miss this portion of worship we have missed much, for many times the unction of the Holy Ghost may be felt as genuinely during the song service as during the prayer and the preaching. Though we should never replace preaching and prayer for this mode of worship alone, it is important that we understand the necessity of it.

It has been said that there is something wrong with people who talk to themselves, but in reality, that is what we are doing when we sing the songs of Zion. "When you sing", writes Paul, "you are Speaking to yourselves". While many might be offended if a person called them a wretch, sinners will find comfort in speaking to themselves these words: "Amazing grace how sweet the sound that saved a wretch like me". I have heard of some who have changed the word of this old tune from "wretch" to "one". But if God has blessed us with light upon our depravity, wretch is the word that fits our case and brings comfort to the soul as the inner man confesses his condition to the Lord of glory. Such is the benefit of "Speaking to yourselves".

"Speaking to yourselves" also means that we are speaking to one another as we are speaking to God. It is a collective prayer and consent of truth. I know what you are saying and you know what I am saying and as we are saying it, we agree upon what we have said to God. I have personally witnessed a genuine peace come over a congregation as they sang, "Blest be the tie that binds our hearts in Christian love."

"Speaking to yourselves" means that we are thinking upon the words that we are saying. What profit is singing if we do not notice the words nor care for their import? Just like preaching and praying, the mind is exercised by this spiritual mode of worship. This brings us to Paul's next point: what we should sing.

The beautiful book of Psalms was the principal song book of the Old Testament worshipers. I believe it was used by the infant church. But since that time, many beautiful hymns have been written that convey numerous scriptural, practical, and experimental truths that not only comfort the heart, but instruct as well.

They are called "Spiritual Songs" because they are not *carnal*. They do not excite the flesh nor do they stir up the world in the heart. They do just the opposite. They serve to crucify the flesh, encourage the pilgrim, revive the heart and built up our most holy faith. They help to take our mind off our worldly sorrows and cares as they prepare our hearts to receive the preached word.

If they are "Spiritual Songs" they must be scriptural: they must harmonize with the teachings of the Bible. They must contain and agree with Biblical truth. Many times, I have been taught a scriptural truth during the song service. One of my favorites goes:

"Not the labor of my hands;
Can fulfill the laws demands;
Could my zeal no respite know,
Could my tears forever flow,
All for sin could not atone;
Thou must save and Thou alone."
-Rock of Ages

Oh, that all could understand the scriptural principles and experience the grace revealed in this song!

Many times the writer of a song has expressed a prayer of his heart; his experience of grace; of trial; of doubt; or of wonder. These *kindred* experiences have a calming influence upon an anxious heart as we learn that others, many who lived long before we did, have experienced similar trials and tribulations. Yes, these are our people, other believers.

Though the heart is not a musical instrument, it is the place the Lord looks for the melody. It is the instrument that He *delights* in. This is the instrument that places every participant in the spotlight of God's affection. He looks upon the heart. I may not be able to carry a tune in a washtub, but in God's ears, my melody is just a beautiful as the angelic chorus when I sing from the heart. The heart is involved in this mode of worship. I am involved, I am taught, and I feel God's spirit because it is not for show. It is worship because it is "to the Lord".

Helpful Hints:
1. What is your favorite song and why?
2. How does the song service in your church compare to scripture?
3. Do you think of the words as you sing?

4. Why are there instruments in the Old Testament worship and not in the New?

5. What makes up a spiritual song?

6. Describe the difference in the way we feel when we sing a spiritual song and when we sing or hear a worldly song.

7. Can you discern the difference in these two spirits?

"HOW WE ARE BORN AGAIN"

"The wind bloweth where it listeth, and thou hearest the sound thereof, but canst not tell whence it cometh, and whither it goeth: so is every one that is born of the Spirit"-John 3:8

Nicodemus, a ruler of the Jews, has come to Jesus by night making his confession, "We know that thou art a teacher come from God." He came at night, fearing his privileged position among his Jewish brethren. He preferred his seat in the *synagogue* above fellowship with Christ. We have met many such confessors in our own day who have preferred pomp and show above Jesus. But a confused teacher we find Nicodemus to be when Jesus spoke of how one is born from above. Thus, he questions our master: "How can these things be?"

Every expression that we find in the Bible concerning the new birth reveals God's sovereign act of mercy when one is born again. They depict man as passive, dead in sin, unable to make a spiritual movement until the Lord comes with healing in His wings. To Nicodemus, Jesus uses the phrase: "Born again". Yet, to the same truth, Paul uses words like "quickened"(Ephesians 2:1), regeneration(Titus 3:5); and translated(Col. 1:13). All of these terms are used to express the same experience as one who is dead in trespasses and in sin is made alive in Christ Jesus as Christ takes up His abode in the heart.

As Jesus explained to Nicodemus "How we are born again", He used a simple illustration that could be easily understood by all: the wind. From His words we learn about God's sovereignty in the new birth experience and His power over the Devil and fallen man.

Jesus said, "The wind bloweth where it listeth". The word "listeth" means *pleases*. The wind is very *discriminating*. I have seen a tornado lift a roof off of a building and bypass a pot of flowers. Such is God's Spirit. It is *sovereign* concerning where it will blow and upon whom it will blow. It blows effectively upon the objects of His grace and brings them from darkness to light as they are translated from the kingdom of darkness to the kingdom of His dear Son. Surely, this is a beautiful picture of God's love and grace. It struck Saul of Tarsus down upon the road to Damascus and changed his heart from hateful to helpful; it changed the heart and conversation of the thief on the cross; and in his mother's womb, John the Baptist was filled with the Holy Ghost. These examples were given us to reveal God's choice and sovereignty because there were no preachers, no sermons and no evangelists. There were only two present: God and the sinner.

The power of the wind has been demonstrated time and time again by tornados, hurricanes and wind sheers. This sudden and powerful force reminds us of the Spirit's power over man. Man can feel the effects of the wind; he can observe the effect of wind upon other objects; but he has absolutely no power over the wind. He can not command it to come, nor can he resist it when it does blow. This takes the sinner and man's free will completely out of the picture. Jesus has the power to enter the heart when and where that He pleases.

Man can not fathom the power that it must take to regenerate fallen man! It takes more than a preachers voice; a sinners response; or participation in a particular ordinance. According to Jesus, it takes the same power to regenerate as it does to resurrect(John 5:25-29).

Not only can we see the effects of the wind, we can also *hear* the wind, "thou hearest the sound thereof". The wind can make a lot of noise as it exerts its powerful force. So does God's spirit. Though the wind makes an audible noise, God's spirit is spoken of as a "small still voice." But how effective is this voice! It tells us that we are sinners and we need a Saviour; the heart becomes repentant for when we hear of Jesus, there is an affection for His person; we want to call upon His name; and there is a hope that swells in our heart for better things and a better place. Has this spirit blown upon you? Then you have great evidence that Christ has died for you and you shall spend eternity with Him in glory!

The experience of Nicodemus was given for an example. An example of those children of God who are born of God's Spirit but do not understand HOW. If He abides in you heart, let credit be given to the ONE to whom credit is due. Let us cast our crowns at the feet of Jesus!

Helpful Hints:
1. Compare the new birth to our natural birth:
a. Do you remember your natural birth?
b. How do you know the day you were born?
c. What did you do to be born?
d. Were you active of passive in your birth?
2. What scriptures teach us about the new birth?
3. What is the purpose of the gospel?
4. What is the purpose of baptism?
5. Can sprinkling regenerate a person?

"THE SOVEREIGNTY OF GOD"

"And at the end of the days I Nebuchadnezzar lifted up mine eyes unto heaven, and mine understanding returned unto me, and I blessed the most High, and I praised and honoured him that liveth for ever, whose dominion is an everlasting dominion, and his kingdom is from generation to generation: And all the inhabitants of the earth are reputed as nothing: and he doeth according to his will in the army of heaven, and among the inhabitants of the earth: and none can stay his hand, or say unto him, What doest thou?"-Daniel 4:34-35

If we were asked to give a subtitle to the book of Daniel we would quickly write: The *sovereignty* of God." Each chapter reveals how God overrules the designs of angels(the armies of heaven) and men(the inhabitants of the earth) as He brings His sovereign councils to pass. It reveals that history is really HIS STORY unfolding unto an expected and predicted end. Though our text is taken from the confession of a heathen king, we can find no better scripture to depict the sovereignty of God than the one we have before you. Do you believe that God is sovereign?

Many will confess a sovereign God. But when we begin to talk about specifics, I find there are limits placed upon His *immutable* council. It takes a lot for man to acknowledge God's sovereignty. Just as Nebuchadnezzar, we must be humbled and human pride must be forfeited to acknowledge God as sovereign.

Election is a great stumbling-block for many concerning the sovereignty of God. Some say that this doctrine is understood only after we get into the Celestial City, but may I say that this treasure has caused many to sell all and buy the field. Many cast it aside as a doctrine too deep to consider, yet, God has included it along side other sacred truths for our comfort and edification. According to the Bible, God is sovereign concerning who will live with Him in glory, and Paul would have us to know that this choice was made before the world was spoken into existence to prove God's sovereignty in the matter: "According as he hath chosen us in him before the foundation of the world". If God would have made His choice after man was created, man could pat himself on the back for making the choice, which boast we see in many religious circles today. Yes, man will choose his wife, his friends, and even those to rule over him, and yet deny that God has the same right to do so concerning the jewels that will make up His breastplate. Man will allow God to predict and plan the future of the world but not the eternal destiny of children He loves. We must ask ourselves the solemn question: whose hands would he be safer in, the Lord's or our own?

As we read the Bible, man's willful rebellion continually collides with God's will for man. Yet, God always has His way. He is sovereign. It was man's will for Daniel to be devoured by lions. It was God's will for his enemies to fall in that place. It was Jonah's will to flee to Tarshish. It was God's will for him to preach to Nineveh. It was Herod's wish to destroy the Christ child. Whose kingdom still stands? It was Nebuchadnezzar's will to burn up God's witnesses. But whose men were consumed in the flame? It was man's will to silence the mouth of Peter and Paul. Who was really in prison? Whose literature is most read? Who are the most popular authors of the century? Of the millennium? And what about us? Where would we be today if God had turned us over to self? To our own lust? If He had not faithfully chastened us sore for our sins and placed His spirit within us? How could we discern right from wrong, good from evil had He not written His law in our hearts? If we have light, we will praise God for His sovereignty!

There is a great comfort in knowing that God is *sovereign*. When trials and afflictions come our way; when wickedness is all about us; when the headlines are uncomfortable and the future is uncertain it is a comfort to know who is in control. If God is not sovereign every moment, who is sovereign when God is not? When tribulations come our way, it is a comfort to know that God is sovereign. Though He may not have ordained our trouble, He must have allowed it to transpire. Though we may pray without ceasing, it is a comfort to know that God has heard our cries and can bring it to pass *if* it is *His* will. And there we may leave it, in the hand of a sovereign and Holy God who will do what is right. Though it may sound hard, I must say it: "Ask me to believe in a god that is not sovereign and you ask me to believe in a god that does not exist. If God is not sovereign then He is not God!"

Helpful Hints:
1. In your own life, what has God done to overrule your own will?

2. What doctrines of the Bible display God's sovereignty?

3. Why is this doctrine offensive to man?

4. Why did this king Nebuchadnezzar change his opinion of himself?

5. What other places in scripture do we find God's sovereignty revealed?

"THE PURSUIT OF HOLINESS"

"But as he which hath called you is holy, so be ye holy in all manner of conversation; Because it is written, Be ye holy; for I am holy"-1 Peter 1:15-16

The desire to do better, the pursuit of holiness, is an *evidence* of grace. I believe this holy desire is found in the bosom of all of God's children. Some curse it; many try to ignore it; nevertheless it *remains,* it refuses to go away. In regeneration, God has written his commandments upon our heart and they cry unto the conscience day and night: be ye holy for I am holy. This sermon no man can preach for what man is Holy? By this cry we are "convinced" of our sin.

The commandment does not mean that God expects perfection; that we can live above sin for, "If we say that we have not sinned, we deceive ourselves, and the truth is not in us"-I John 1:8. I have met men who claimed they could live above sin but when their doctrine was challenged, they lost their temper and their sin revived.

If we were to wonder what God's will is for each of us we have this answer: to become more like Him; to grow in grace; to increase in godliness; to become better today than we were yesterday; to mature spiritually as we mature naturally: to walk closer with Jesus day by day. Thus, the apostle writes: "For this is the will of God, even your sanctification"(I Thes. 4:3). This means that we have been consecrated for a Holy use; that we are to grow in grace: pursue holiness. Are you changing?

Surely, there is no such thing as a full grown Christian. There are always changes to be made for the better. It is always less painful when we understand this holy will and cooperate than to jump ship to Tarshish. If you are looking for God's will in your life this is it: your sanctification…to become more like HIM!

Change is a very painful process. It takes pain to destroy our lust, to quench our love for the world and to move us to obedience. As the sculptor chips away at a shapeless piece of stone, so God chips away at our hearts and brings beauty out of chaos. Our change is not brought about by comforts, but rather by afflictions; suffering; trials; and pain.

God's first stroke with His chisel is *regeneration*. This is a very real part of our sanctification. When we are born again the Holy Ghost serves as an inward light, revealing our sin. Thankfully, the hand of the Holy Sculptor continues. He does not lay his chisel down here. Chip, chip, chip, by trials and afflictions He hammers away, destroying our worldly comforts. Yet, "no man should be moved by these afflictions: for yourselves know that we are appointed thereunto"-I Thessalonians 3:3. When we know we are to suffer for Christ's sake, it becomes armor for our mind, "Forasmuch then as Christ hath suffered for us in the flesh, arm yourselves likewise with the same mind: for he that hath suffered in the flesh hath ceased from sin"-I Peter 4:1. Suffering kills the desires for sin. Many times God will send suffering our way which will occupy our energies otherwise spent on sinful behavior that would have destroyed us.

Our sanctification is ushered along by the preaching of God's word; by the singing of spiritual songs; by filial communion with the Saints of God and by direct intervention of the Holy Ghost.

Surely, we must look for God's sanctifying hand in every trial, every affliction, every truth, every blessing.........in every thing. For this is His will concerning YOU, even *your* sanctification!

Helpful Hints:
1. Describe your personal history of sanctification?
2. What can you do to cooperate more fully?
3. Talk about this process in the life of the apostles.
4. What are some of the first steps in this process?

"THE OLD HERESY"

"And certain men which came down from Judea taught the brethren, and said, Except ye be circumcised after the manner of Moses, ye cannot be saved"-Acts 15:1

In Acts 15, we find the apostles disputing over one of the oldest heresies among believers: salvation by works. The false apostles had disturbed the flock and taught them, "Except ye be circumcised after the manner of Moses, ye cannot be saved"-Acts 15:1.

This is a dangerous doctrine. It split the Baptist denomination in the early 1800's. David Benedict's, "Fifty Years Among the Baptists", reveals the changes brought into the camps of the Baptists in his day. Prior to this split, there was one Baptist faith in this country. They all embraced the great doctrines of God's grace. To divide God's people is Satan's desire. I find many today who know of distant relatives that were numbered among those old believers. I dedicate today's article to their faith, hoping their posterity will search it out and return to the faith their forefathers once embraced.

It was this heresy that stirred the heart of the apostle to write the great letter to the Galatian churches in defense of God's grace. Barnabus and Paul did not say, "Well, it is the same God that we worship and it really does not matter". They "had no small dissension and disputation with them"-v2. In other words, it was a great dissension and disputation. Grace is worth disputing.

The bottom line to this heresy is simply this: man places himself where Christ should be concerning salvation. Man has placed himself at the top of the bottomless pit throwing the line down to fallen man rather than Christ descending the depths and rescuing fallen man. We must ask, "How did that first man get up there anyway?"

Though names have changed through the years, various works and schemes have been substituted for the "circumcision" in this dispute: "Except ye be _____ after the manner of US, ye cannot be saved". Place what you will in the blank, you will still come up with *works. Man* is at the bottom of it all. And what one man can do, another can't. Thus, another method must be invented for those who never had the chance, for the imbecile, for the aborted and whatever or whoever will not fit into the mold of conditional salvation. We must answer with Peter, "But we believe that through the grace of he Lord Jesus Christ we shall be saved, even as they"-v11.

Verse five is a sad testimony. It tells us that "Certain of the sect of the Pharisees which believed" taught this heresy. Yes, believers rejected the doctrines of God's grace and substituted a system of works. They took the tradition used to identify them as God's chosen (circumcision) and set it up as their saviour. A tradition that was to be done away with at that. Such will be the end of all traditions and ordinances when Christ the Saviour returns!

Why does the creature run to his works rather than trusting fully and wholly in the finished works of Christ? I will give you three reasons: (1) People like to think they are in control of their own destiny. But are we? Do we know that we even have another day here? And if we can not order another day on earth, can we order our days in glory? (2) We are taught all of our lives that we must earn what we get. Our house, our car, our wages, we live by the sweat of our brow. We are programmed for works! But Christ earned what we lost. He paid what we could not pay with His own blood. That is grace. (3) When the Holy Ghost reveals our sin we want to do something….and we should. Let us present our bodies a living sacrifice; let us identify ourselves with Christ by public Baptism; let us endeavor to live accordingly. But let us not usurp Christ's glory. Righteous endeavors done out of a heart of love are well pleasing to the Father, but let us not offer them up in payment for sin for then they become "filthy rags".

Grace is unmerited and undeserving favor. Ezekiel paints a beautiful picture of grace. He shows us where we were when God found us, and what God did for us. "And when I passed by thee, and saw thee polluted in thine own blood(where we were), I said unto thee when thou wast in thy blood, Live; yea, I said unto thee when thou wast in thy blood, Live(what He did for us)"-Ezekiel 16:6. Polluted in Adam's sin, helpless to lift ourselves out of our fallen condition was our case. But the eye of a loving Father passed by and pitied His own. He took us up, washed us in the blood of His own Son and gave us an inheritance among the Saints. That is grace.

Grace is the beggars crown; the sinners comfort; and the devil's curse. It is not a respecter of race, religion, riches, rags, king's decrees or the influence of great nations. It belongs to God. He dispensed it freely. Is your faith and hope of glory in Christ or your works?

Helpful Hints:
1. Describe the difference between grace and works.
2. Talk about some of the "works" systems in religion.
3. How does grace reach those who can never hear the gospel?
4. How should it affect those who do?
5. How do law and grace agree?

"FIVE PHASES OF SALVATION"

"Neither is there salvation in any other: for there is none other name under heaven given among men, whereby we must be saved"-Acts 4:12

When we speak of salvation, we speak of Christ, for in Him we find salvation in every form and fashion. The very name, Jesus, means Saviour: one who delivers; one who *saves*. Whether we are looking for salvation from the evils of this present life, or salvation from the eternal consequences of sin, Jesus should be sought very diligently as the object of our faith because, "there is none other name under heaven given among men, whereby we must be saved"-Acts 4:12.

THE ETERNAL PHASE OF SALVATION

Concerning our eternal destiny, salvation began long before man appeared upon the scene. This phase of our salvation occurred in heaven, in eternity past. Therefore, man was passive in this phase of salvation. It involves God's foreknowledge, election and predestination: "For whom he did foreknow, he also did predestinate to be conformed to the image of his Son, that he might be the firstborn among many brethren." Romans 8:29. According to Paul, God foreknew His people and predetermined their future image. The Christian should count it one of their greatest blessings when they learn that God knew them before they knew Him; that He thought upon them before they thought upon Him; and that He loved them before they loved Him. Before Eden, before Adam's dark transgression that affected all of humanity, God had a purpose and plan to rescue His elect. Jesus carried it out!

THE LEGAL PHASE OF SALVATION

The legal phase of salvation involves redemption, justification, substitution, and the forgiveness of sin. It occurred upon Calvary's cross. When someone asks me when and where I was saved I must reply, "Upon Calvary, two-thousand years ago". I could not represent myself. I needed a mediator. One that could lay hold upon God and man; One that could fulfill the law that I could not keep; one that could reign over death; one who could answer the demands of God's righteous law written against my soul; One in whose veins flowed the precious, sinless blood of a Man-God, the full price of redemption, "In whom we have redemption through his blood, the forgiveness of sins, according to the riches of his grace"-Eph. 1:7.

THE VITAL PHASE OF SALVATION

This phase of salvation occurs in the heart of man. It is when we are brought into vital union with God by the new birth; when we are born of His spirit; quickened from death to life: "and you hath he quickened, who were dead in trespasses and sins"-Eph 2:1. Paul says, "you were dead. God gave you life." Therefore, we were passive in this phase of salvation as well. We are not born again to become God's children. We are born again *because* we are God's children. This spiritual birth brings us into fellowship with our heavenly Father. It gives us the ability to learn of Him; to love Him; to communicate with Him; to feel His presence and know that He exists. Again, we find Jesus active in this phase of salvation, "Verily, verily, I say unto you, The hour is coming, and now is, when the dead shall hear the voice of the Son of God: and they that hear shall live"-John 5:25.

THE PRACTICAL PHASE OF SALVATION

The practical phase of salvation begins with our thinking. Man is *active* in this phase of salvation. The law, written upon our hearts in regeneration, is brought to light. (2Tim. 1:10). In Acts, chapter 15, Paul refers to it as *conversion* as he declared the "Conversion (not regeneration)of the Gentiles". It is not the new birth. How could we hear if we were spiritually dead? When those who have been born again hear of their Saviour there is evidence…. Jesus is there. He alone can open the eyes and ears of understanding!

THE FINAL PHASE OF SALVATION

This final phase of salvation is yet to come. It is when Christ returns to claim His own. It does not occur in heaven; upon the cross; in our hearts; or even in our minds. It will occur all over this world and completely consume every heir of grace as they are glorified and changed. This is when Christ returns and speaks with a voice that will wake the dead: "for the hour is coming, in the which all that are in the graves shall hear his voice, And shall come forth; they that have done good, unto the resurrection of life; and they that have done evil, unto the resurrection of damnation"-John 5:28-29. In this phase of salvation man is passive and Jesus is active. Hallelujah, what a Saviour!

Helpful Hints:
1. Talk about the great doctrines of election, predestination and foreknowledge.
2. Give supporting scriptures.
3. Talk about the complete harmony of the Godhead and their individual parts in our salvation.
4. Discuss each phase of salvation individually.

"THE LITTLE FOXES, THAT SPOIL THE VINES"

"Take us the foxes, the little foxes, that spoil the vines: for our vines have tender grapes"-Song of Solomon 2:15

The Church of Christ is a *noble* vine. It is the place where majestic fruit is born, the tender grapes of God's spirit: "love, joy, peace, longsuffering, gentleness, goodness, faith, meekness, temperance". Since this is a love song, we should know that the fruit that the vine bears is in proportion to the *love* they have for their great Husbandman. In his "Song of Songs", Solomon relates the many earthly distractions that will hinder such fellowship, distractions that rob us of our joy and the fruit that may abound in our lives. Such are the "little foxes that spoil the vines."

The fox is a seemingly small creature. But what mischief such a small creature can cause among the vines. The rascal comes out at night, unexpected, unnoticed, and gnaws on the vines of the tender plants hindering the flow of sap to the fruit. There are many foxes haunting our vineyards! We could sooner count the sands of the sea as we could name them all! Sampson caught three-hundred of them, tied firebrands to their tails, and sent them scurrying among the crops of the Philistines. Though we would never be cruel to animals, such treatment, figuratively speaking, we would encourage to the keepers of our Lord's vineyard to the menaces among their vines. Therefore, let us follow Solomon's advice and "Take us the foxes, the little foxes, that spoil the vines".

Let us take the little fox of *bitterness*. He is cruel. Many times he lurks unnoticed in our own hearts. He lurks in families, between husbands and wives; children and parents; and even among those of the noble vine. Paul found him at Philippi. From his prison epistle, he refers to this church as "My joy and crown". Yet, with the next stroke of his pen, he drives the foxes from their vine, "I beseech Euodias, and beseech Syntyche, that they be of the same mind in the Lord." The epistle arrives from Paul, it is read before the whole church, and two people that Paul loved very much are singled out because the fox of bitterness was gnawing on their vine. Paul didn't side with either party. Taking sides will always benefit the devil. There is only one side: the side of Christ, "be of the same mind in the Lord"; do what Jesus would have you do. That will kill the fox every time.

The fox of *pride* is an evil creature. He was found in Haman's vineyard. Though Haman was a prosperous man, had many friends and a fine family, this fox robbed him of all of his fruit. Haman must get even with one man that had offended him and was finally hung on his own gallows. Though God may bless us with many graces, the fox of pride will eat the tender fruit of it: "Pride *goeth* before destruction, and an haughty spirit before a fall"- Proverbs 16:18

There is another little fox that sneaks into our vineyard: the fox of *anger*. Solomon said, "anger resteth in the bosom of fools". Spurgeon accurately defines anger as "temporary insanity". It arouses the tongue to spew out poisonous venom. A relationship can be destroyed in just a few seconds. This is a mean little fox indeed! Modern psychology will tell you to vent your anger, break things, hit things, whatever feels good......do it. In other words, feed the fox some of your fruit and keep him happy. The Lord knows better how to deal with such foxes for He knows that unrestrained anger leads to sorrow and ultimately depression, headaches, ulcers, sleepless nights, fear, withdrawal, and physical problems. Though the emotion of anger is not a sin, anger's unrestrained reaction is the little fox. Don't feed him, "take him".

Our space is gone and we have many foxes yet to take. Paul exposes the most deadly method of killing foxes in Ephesians 4:31,32. Here the Apostle encourages us to "walk in love, as Christ also hath loved us, and hath given himself for us an offering and a sacrifice to God for a sweetsmelling savour"-Ephesians 5:2. Walking in love is the shotgun approach to killing foxes. One shot of love and many are "taken". Walking in love is maturity. It is a good feeling to know that the Lord sees our faults and continues to love us. To kill the foxes that haunt our vineyards He calls upon us to do the same and "take the little foxes that spoil the vine."

Helpful Hints:
1. Name the fruit of the Spirit.
2. Who do you see them in?
3. How and when do we see them exemplified in the life of Jesus?
4. How can you be a better Church member?

"THE NECESSITY OF PREPARATION"

"And five of them were wise, and five were foolish"
-Matthew 25:2

The parable of the ten virgins presents an honorable occasion as well as a wonderful opportunity. The Bridegroom (Jesus), is paying a special visit to His bride(the church) and her attendants. Five of them were wise: they prepared for His visit. Five of them were foolish: they had not prepared. That was their foolishness. The parable is to the bride of Christ, the church in every age. Let us learn from our Bridegroom the "Necessity of Preparation."

In 1976, the Hoosiers basketball team went undefeated capturing the NCAA title. When interviewed by 60 Minutes, their leader, Bobby Knight was asked, "Why is it, Bobby, that your basketball teams at Indiana are always so successful? Is it the will to succeed?" "The will to succeed is important," replied Knight, "but I'll tell you what's more important......it's the will to prepare. It's the will to go out there every day, training and building those muscles and sharpening those skills."

Most of us understand what these men have learned concerning *natural* things. But Jesus uses His example of the ten virgins to call us to a higher plane. He calls upon us to take this precept into our spiritual life. Prepare for *Him*!

God expects us to prepare.........He *watches* for it. David said, "Now I have <u>prepared</u> with all my might for the house of my God"-I Chronicles 29:2. King Rehoboam did evil, because "he <u>prepared</u> not his heart to seek the Lord"-2Chron.12:14. Kings and priests should seek God's council and direction in all they do. Concerning king Jehoshaphat we read, "Nevertheless there are good things found in thee, in that thou hast taken away the groves out of the land, and hast <u>prepared</u> thine heart to seek God"- 2 Chronicles 19: 3. And we read, "So Jotham became mighty, because he <u>prepared</u> his ways before the Lord his God"-2 Chronicles 27:6.

Preparation is the harbinger of *revival*. The New Testament Church began with Christ's harbinger, John the Baptist, preaching, "Prepare ye the way of the Lord, make his paths straight." A lot of unspectacular preparation he must have made in the wilderness. But his results were powerful and effective. The Lord crowns the efforts of those who prepare.

As I read the prayers in the Bible, some were ejaculatory, offered in a moment of desperate need, but many of those great intercessions were preceded by spiritual forethought. We prepare speeches to men, should there be no preparation of the heart before we speak to God? I find the prayers of Daniel, Nehemiah, and other great intercessors laced with scripture, calling upon God to honor a precious promise. Oh, that people would study the promises of God! Granted, there are times that it seems that our prayers go no further than our heads, but I have found that meditation and preparation before prayer opens the heart and loosens the tongue. Let us prepare before we approach the great throne of grace.

Every minister learns the necessity of preparation. Spurgeon said, "I surely think that if a man does not prepare his sermons he is very blameworthy." Reading the scriptures, meditating upon their truths, communing with God concerning their meaning and the proper way to present them is what we mean when we say *prepare*.

But what about the congregation? Should they prepare? If they come to God's house with oil in their lamps, they must! I remember a preacher talking about his grandfather who laid his clothes out on Saturday night and went to bed early so he would be ready for services Sunday morning. This made an impression on the young child. Late Saturday nights produces empty vessels of oil and sleepy eyes on Sunday morning. And what about Sunday morning? Are we quick to pick up the Sunday paper and find out the latest in Hollywood and the world? Surely this will serve to empty the vessel as well! Fill your vessel with intercession for your pastor's liberty, your brethren's peace and the Spirit's presence. Pray for the message; pray for conversions; pray for laborers; pray for the word to prosper; and pray for your own good spirit. Have a look at God's word. Meditate upon the great opportunity of fellowship with our Bridegroom and enjoy a spectacular season of fellowship with Him. Do you see the necessity of preparation? Lord, we delight in thy visits. Help us to prepare!

Helpful Hints:
1. Talk about spiritual preparation; before church services; during the week; before prayer.
2. Talk about how preparations are blessed for individual areas in the church; the song service;

the public prayer; the message delivered and the congregation as a whole.

3. Why is this so important?

4. Talk about preparing the heart each morning before we go about our daily activities with prayer and devotions.

5. What hinders your/our preparations?

"CLAIMING THE PROMISES"

*"Remember the word unto thy servant, upon which thou hast
caused me to hope.
This is my comfort in my affliction: for thy word hath
quickened me"*
-Psalm 119:49-50

Here we find David in the posture of prayer. From his language we find that his soul has been severely afflicted by *something* or *someone*. But in the midst of his affliction he has found comfort. Hope has arisen in his heart because he has read something in scripture.........."thy word". What was preserved and inspired centuries before suits his particular need: he has found a precious promise and claimed it as his own!

I love God's promises. His word is packed with promises to His children. Peter refers to them as "exceeding great and precious". One man counted them and said that there were 7,487 promises of God to man. Another said that there was a promise suited for every trial and affliction. Among these we will find promises for husbands, for wives, for families, for nations and for children. As Vance Havner said, "His promises are checks to be cashed, not mere mottoes to hang on the wall!" Have you claimed any of God's promises as your own?

Some of God's promises are conditional: we must do something to receive them. Others are free for the taking: all we must do is claim them by faith. Some of them are boldly proclaimed, and whether we know about them or not, they are as sure as the One who made them.

One that I claim most often is, "as thy days, so shall thy strength be"-Deut. 33:25. Here we find a promise for *strength* to face the trials and tribulations of each day. To every heir of grace this promise is made. All we must do is claim it. When the days are long and the nights are short; when hope has failed us; we must return to this promise and claim it as our own. Perhaps it is the one the psalmist claimed?

To our children God has promised, "Honour thy father and mother; which is the first commandment with promise; That it may be well with thee, and thou mayest live long on the earth"-Ephesians 6:2, 3. Here we find a promise with a condition attached. God has promised peace and safety to those children who obey their parents in the Lord. Parents, have you shown your child this promise? Have you given them the Godly instruction they should obey?

To all of humanity, God has promised that he would not destroy the earth again with a flood(Genesis 9:8-17). The beautiful rainbow is a token of this promise. Whether we know about it, claim it, or even believe it, the promise is sure.

Are you weak? Your promise is found in 2 Corinthians 12:9. You must claim it. Are you searching? Your promise is found in Matthew 7:7. Are you in need of forgiveness? Consider 1 John 1:9. Are you beset with sudden fears? Look to Proverbs 3:25. And so His promises go. Surely there is encouragement found in the multitudinous promises of God.

But let me give you another thought concerning God's promises. Couched within every *commandment* we will find a promise. When God says, "Remember the sabbath day, to keep it holy"(Exodus 20:8), do you not observe the fruit manifested in the lives of those who do? It is a commandment, but there is a blessing in the obeying of it. We may approach the 'thou shalts' and the 'thou shalt nots' knowing that a promise is attached. Is He not a rewarder of them that diligently seek him?

The psalmist approached *his* particular promise by *faith*. He claimed it as his own and observed the promise couched within as if it had been personally written to him from eternity past. He did as we must do. Simply observe it as "the word unto thy servant". It fit his particular need and so shall it fit our own.

Claiming the promises of God becomes our *wellspring* of hope: "upon which thou hast caused me to hope". Then David called upon God to remember His promise, hope sprang from his breast as Old Faithful rises to the sky day after day. God rejoices in those who believe Him. He is well pleased when His children claim His promises and call upon Him to honor them.

In his "ALL SERIES", Herbert Lockyer wrote, "The promises of the Bible are like an arranged measure of gems and precious stones and pearls of inestimable value in God's cabinet of spiritual jewels, and which constantly remind the Christian of His true, abiding riches. All of these gracious promises deserve to be 'bound upon our fingers and written upon the table of our hearts." Dear Christian, have you searched the scriptures to find the promises you need today? They belong to you!

Helpful Hints:

1. Name as many of God's promises as you can without the Bible.

2. With the Bible!

3. What promise or promises are important to you at this time?

4. How do faith and hope work together in claiming promises?

5. How does the moral law apply to our lives in promise keeping?

"IN THE VALLEY"

"And Isaac's servants digged in the valley, and found there a well of springing water"-Genesis 26:19

Wells of springing water are seldom found on the mountain top. We must descend into the valley. Such we will find in our spiritual exercises. Though we all love the mountain top experiences, we cannot live there. As one preacher has noted, the air is too thin. I have met those who claim they dwell there all the time. But I can not claim such an experience. Through much digging some water may be found upon the mountain, but "springing water" will be found in the valley. Have you been there?

The mountain is the place for *celebration*, but the valley is the place of *learning*. It is in the valley that we learn most about God, His Son........ourselves. It is a place for spiritual eyesight. No one wants to be in the valley. It is a frightening place. For therein dwell doubts, fears, depressions, guilt and sorrow. But all of these may be assessed accurately and disposed of properly in this valley of vision. The valley was the habitation of the prophets, or seers, in Isaiah's day. Thus he writes, "The burden of the valley of vision. What aileth thee now, that thou art wholly gone up to the housetops?"-Isaiah 22:1.

To this valley of vision, one of the Puritan prayers descends:

"The Valley of Vision":

"Lord, high and holy, meek and lowly,
Thou hast brought me to the valley of vision,
where I live in the depths but see thee in the heights;
hemmed in by mountains of sin I behold thy glory.
Let me learn by paradox that the way down is the way up,
that to be low is to be high,
that the broken heart is the healed heart,
that the contrite spirit is the rejoicing spirit,
that the repenting soul is the victorious soul,
that to have nothing is to possess all,
that to bear the cross is to wear the crown,
that to give is to receive,
that the valley is the place of vision.
Lord, in the daytime stars can be seen from deepest wells,
and the deeper the wells the brighter thy stars shine;
let me find Thy light in my darkness, thy life in my death,
thy joy in my sorrow, thy grace in my sin,
thy riches in my poverty, thy glory in my valley."

The doctors of the world often consider people sick if they journey to this valley. Since the world is one of gaiety and pride, they tell us we must never wear a long face or reveal an afflicted spirit. It is not condoned. Many time drugs, alcohol and entertainment are used to keep people floating on some kind of mountain. The Bible declares the valley to be a place that every child of God must travel from time to time. We must descend into the valley to be *humbled*. We must descend into the valley to be *tried*. We must descend to see and *understand*. The valley reminds us that we are strangers and pilgrims in this world and prepares our hearts to seek a better country, "that is, an heavenly!"

There are things that one will find in the valley that can never be found on the mountain. Sins are seldom revealed on the mountain. We must descend from our exalted position to see into our own heart. Zephaniah wrote, "I will also leave in the midst of thee an afflicted and poor people, and they shall trust in the name of the Lord"(Zephaniah 3:12). "In the midst" of a proud world, such a people will be found; those who have been afflicted by their sin. Surely, they have sojourned in the valley. How else did they learn they were poor and needy? How did they come to trust in the "name of the Lord"? On the mountain they were rich, in need of nothing but in the valley they saw their need and found Jesus, the all sufficient One. He is the well of "springing water", the lily of the valley.

Pride is unobserved upon the mountain. Nebuchadnezzar must be humbled as a beast of the field for seven seasons until he acknowledges the sovereignty of God and the giver of every good and perfect gift. Saul of Tarsus must enter the valley and count all things but dung that he may win Christ. On the mountain Peter denied his Lord, but in the valley he found Him. And though Job was not given to pride, he also found his answer in the valley. Mark ye well this kindred experience! The acute afflictions of the righteous do not come without reward. They have a purpose.

There are many valley experiences. Jesus is the "lily of the valleys", not the valley singular. He may be found in every valley showing forth His majesty and sending out His healing fragrance. Have you found Him there?

Helpful Hints:
1. What have you learned in the valley of vision?
2. How can you encourage others that are in this valley?
3. Describe Christ and His valleys.
4. The Apostles and their valleys.
5. Why are valleys necessary?

"A HAPPY OCCASION"

"I was glad when they said unto me, Let us go into the house of the Lord"
-Psalm 122:1

This beautiful expression is found in one of the short 'Psalms of degrees'. There are fifteen Psalms of degrees thought by many to have been sung by Israel as they journeyed toward the temple in anxious anticipation of meeting Jehovah in worship. Today, let us imagine that we are walking together, tribe by tribe, singing with one voice and one heart: "I was glad when they said unto me, Let us go into the house of the Lord."

To be anxious to meet in God's house is an evidence of grace, a mark of spiritual maturity. Some might say, "I don't know if God loves me or if He even knows that I exist." What wonderful evidences we find in worship! This Holy desire is an evidence of God's love for us. In his love song for the Lord, Solomon wrote, "Draw me, we will run after thee: the king hath brought me in to his chambers: we will be glad and rejoice in thee, we will remember thy love more than wine: the upright love thee"-Song 1:4. Thus we find Solomon, "glad" as well to be ushered into the presence of his Lord. I love the order of Solomon's song: God draws, then we run. God always comes first in the relationship.

We may discover many reasons why David was *glad* when his friends and companions said, "Let us go into the house of the Lord". First, he must have been glad to have such *spiritual* friends. Not only did *they* want to be in God's house, they wanted *David* there as well. They must have loved him. They were interested in the prosperity of his soul. They wanted to share with him the "beauties of holiness".

Evangelism is here expressed: "they said unto me." David was invited! How many have you invited to God's house? As in David's case, we must be faithful to encourage those of like precious faith, but we must also invite the unconverted for the cause to prosper. Our vision must not be only inward, it must be to "every creature". Our Lord's last recorded words were, "and unto the uttermost part of the earth."

Do we not see *anticipation* in these words? The anticipation of sitting together in heavenly places with brothers and sisters of like precious faith; to see their faces and hear their voices once again; to sing some of the wonderful songs of Zion; to approach God's throne of grace in solemn prayer; to feel the unction of the Holy Ghost. As they approached God's house, they must have wondered what the message would be. Where would the priest open the sacred scroll? What scripture would he expound? The closer they got to the dinner table, the more their souls anticipated the meal! Thus we have a heart preparing psalm.

These words must also have served as a simple *rebuke*. What if they sang the words and were NOT glad when they said, "Let us go into the house of the Lord"? Had they left their first love? Had they become cold? Had Baal and the world taken God's place in their hearts? Soul searching words we find here. As our tornado sirens warn us of impending danger, a negative response to this first stanza should send us running to the shelter of repentance from "dead works" to say, "Restore unto me the joy of thy salvation; and uphold me with thy free spirit"-Psalm 51:12.

We may never be invited to sit in the president's cabinet; to meet at Camp David; to have a chair on a prestigious board; or to sit at the meeting of the United Nations. Yet, in God's eyes, this simple invitation is of higher origin than them all, to meet with God in "the house of the Lord". Lord, we thank Thee for providing and preserving this sacred place for us and for an invitation many years ago!

Helpful Hints:
1. Give some scriptural examples of disciples inviting others.
2. List some friends that you can invite to God's house.
3. Allow this question to search our own hearts.
4. What are some stumbling blocks for this happy occasion?

"OUR VICTORY IN CHRIST"

"O death, where is thy sting? O grave, where is thy victory?
The sting of death is sin; and the strength of sin is the law.
But thanks be to God, which giveth us the victory through our
Lord Jesus Christ"-I Corinthians 15:55-57

Our Lord Jesus has never failed at anything He has attempted. We see figures of Him in David as He stood before Goliath; in Sampson as he pulled the walls down upon his enemies; and Moses as he led his people safely to the promised land. Our Lord stood before many cruel enemies. Herod, the high priests, the mob and Satan all sent their poison shafts to destroy Him. But the climax of the battle was ever before Him. He must face death and the grave.

Death and the grave are *cruel* enemies. They are no respecters of age or persons. Death robs the cradle, the home, the hand and the heart. From the tiny infant to the hoary head, both rich and poor, bond and free, death and the grave claim their victims every day, every hour, every moment, leaving a wake of sorrow, misery and grief in their path.

Is not death and the grave man's greatest fear?

Let us take courage in the apostle's words. Though death and the grave are still with us today, though they still rob us of our loved ones, their claim is only for a moment: they have been conquered, defeated, and overcome(1 Corinthians 15:25-26). Though they are real and cause us much suffering and pain, they are only reminders of what we have been delivered from. It is from this blessed truth that we may draw our comfort: Jesus rose from the grave. He is victorious! His victory is our victory!

Paul speaks of Christ's resurrection as a victory. I remember hearing stories about the victory of the United States over Hitler's Germany in W.W.II. There were many American men in secluded areas that did not hear of their victory for many days. Though victory was heralded on the air waves and in the papers, some did not hear of it for months and others for years. There were even those who died as victors before the message reached their ears. But the victory was theirs all the same. They were included in the number.

Christ's resurrection did not make man savable. What kind of victory would that be? Victory may only be claimed when the enemy has been defeated. There may be many who never hear about our Lord's resurrection. But if Christ represented them the victory is theirs all the same. Do you believe in Christ; in His resurrection; in His deity? Then he represented you. You shall rise as well. Did your loved one that has departed the scenes of this life believe in Jesus? Then you shall join them one day in glory where there shall be no more heartache, sin or good-byes.

By Christ's resurrection and victory, we may look at death in a totally different way. We may look at death as a beginning rather than the end. We may see death as a separation from the body of sin; a door we must pass through to a better place where dwelleth rest, peace and righteousness. Rather than looking at death as defeated captives, we may look at it as victors. We may look at our loved ones who have died in Christ with hopeful eyes rather than helpless hearts. We may approach the grave with the anticipation that one day Jesus will return with the voice that will rend the tomb and raise the body from the grave. We may find great comfort that our loved ones are with Jesus and we shall see them again. Let our "thanks be to God, which giveth us the victory through our Lord Jesus Christ."

Helpful Hints:
1. Talk about the coming of Christ.
2. Talk about the events surrounding the resurrection of Jesus Christ.
3. What does His resurrection mean to you personally?
4. Talk about a *bodily* resurrection.

"SETTLED IN HEAVEN"
"For ever, O Lord, thy word is settled in heaven"
-Psalm 119:89

What is *your* opinion of the Bible? Do you question its authenticity? Do you read it with a skeptical eye? Do you wonder if some of the passages have been tainted through the ages or if they are really supposed to be there? Do you feel that some of the statements are archaic, that they do not meet the needs of our present day? I am sure that these questions, and many more, plague God's people as they read the greatest Book that has ever been written. We must not allow Satan to plant seeds of doubt in our minds. Let us approach God's word with confidence and trust knowing that God speaks to us through His word; He has not changed His mind; He is not going to change His mind; what is written is written for our good; the matter is settled in God's mind and it should be in ours as well...... "For ever, O Lord, thy word is settled in heaven."

Though the Bible has many writers, it has but one author: the Holy Ghost. That is why we find such continuity from beginning to end. In his book, "Evidence

That Demands a Verdict", Josh McDowell observes, "It was written over a 1,500 year span. It was written over 40 generations. It was written by 40 different *people*" Some of those include Moses, a young prince brought up in Pharaoh's court; Peter, a fisherman; Amos, a herdsman; Joshua, a military leader; Nehemiah, a cupbearer; Daniel, a prime minister; Luke, a doctor; Solomon, a king; Matthew, a tax collector; and Paul, a Jewish rabbi. It was written in different *places*: Moses wrote in the wilderness; Jeremiah wrote in a dungeon; Paul wrote from prison; Luke wrote during his travels with Paul; John wrote on the isolated isle of Patmos. The Bible was written at different *times*: war, peace, prosperity and famine. It was written by some amidst a mountain top experience and by others in the valley of affliction and sorrow. The scriptures were written on three different continents: Asia, Africa and Europe. It was written in three languages: Hebrew, Aramaic and Greek. It covers a host of different topics which include hundreds of controversial subjects. Yet, throughout the Bible we find harmony as every writer focuses in on one solitary theme: God and the redemption of His people through the sufferings of His Son, Jesus Christ. Only One perfect Author could accomplish such a divine task. We must read it with the eye of faith!

The Bible is an *inspired* book. That means that it is God *breathed*. Men wrote not according to their own prejudices; convictions; or personal whims. They wrote as they were moved by the Holy Ghost, "For the prophecy came not in old time by the will of man: but holy men of God spake as they were moved by the Holy Ghost"-2 Peter 1:21. In other words, God wrote *through* them to His people. What is written is not man's opinion, it is God's declaration. Every word should be viewed as such. I find it contemporary for every facet of life: for the father; the husband; the mother; the wife; the worker; the boss; the child; the workplace; the home; the family and the world in general. Only an *inspired* author could approach life with wisdom that would span the centuries and remain accurate and relevant.

God has *preserved* His word throughout the centuries. For almost two-thousand years, infidels have attempted to refute and overthrow this Book. Yet, today it stands. Bernard Ramm said: "A thousand times over, the death knell of the Bible has been sounded, the funeral procession formed, the inscription cut on the tombstone, and committal read. But somehow the corpse never stays put." No one has ever brought any evidence forward to disclaim or annul any biblical truth! Many monsters have tried to take it out of Christian homes; ban it; burn it; and outlaw it from use. But today, it remains the most purchased, most read Book that has ever been printed. Sidney Collett in , "All About the Bible", says, "Voltaire, the noted French infidel who died in 1778, said that in one hundred years from his time, Christianity would be swept from existence and passed into history. But what has happened? Fifty years after his death, the Geneva Bible Society used his press and house to produce stacks of Bibles." When men fight against the Bible, they fight against God! Whether man tries to physically destroy it or just live in contempt of its truths, God will defend and preserve His word because it is forever settled in heaven.

Helpful Hints:
1. How many books are in the Bible?
2. Who wrote each one?
3. Describe the background of each writer: background, occupations, time and etc.
4. Do some homework on the KJV, how it came to pass and the men involved.
5. Describe the differences in the KJV and modern versions of the Bible.
6. Why is this so important?

"THE FAITH OF
OUR FATHERS"

*"Now faith is the substance of things hoped for, the evidence of
things not seen. For by it the elders obtained a good report"
-Hebrews 11:1,2*

Faith is a *powerful* weapon. It is a part of the Christian armor. Paul refers to it as the "Shield of faith". As the warrior would hold his shield before him as he advanced in battle, the Christian holds his faith ever before him as he marches through this world. Simply put, faith is believing that God will do what He has said. That is why faith is so powerful. It attaches itself to God by one or more of His promises.

This eleventh chapter of Hebrews has been appropriately labeled, "The Faith Hall of Fame". As we read it, we discover that it was by faith that the Saints of old attached themselves to God and obtained a "good report". Let us attempt the same!

"Through faith we understand that the worlds were framed by the word of God"-v3. Faith goes against our natural reasoning. Therefore one must have faith to understand the things of God. In this sense, faith is like an internal communicator. It enables us to understand what God has said through His word and enables us to apply it the head and heart. Man, left to himself, will never understand the biblical account of creation. If Genesis 1:1 is viewed with a skeptical eye, what will be done with the rest of the book? When God spake to the "elders", they took God at His word and acted accordingly. They didn't say, "Are you sure about that, the scientists and learned scholars of our day speak contrary to your report". No, they believed God and obtained a "good report". The student obtains a good report card by learning from the teacher and passing the test. Likewise, by faith we obtain a good report from God by *believing*.

It was by faith, that Abel, long ago, "offered unto God a more excellent sacrifice than Cain." By this we learn that whatever we offer, whether it is our selves or our substance, it should be offered by faith. The faith offering is an offering that expects nothing from God in return except a "well done my faithful servant, enter into the joy of the Lord". It is offering because we love God. It is giving back to God a portion of what He has already given to us.

By this we may also understand that we can give with the *wrong* motive. Those that promise twenty dollars in return for your ten have the heart of wicked Cain. When Cain and Abel brought their offering before God, He looked upon their hearts and saw two different hearts. One heart was happy to offer. A heart of praise, expecting nothing, is never disappointed. God rewards this kind of heart. The other heart was prompted by pride, expecting praise. When Cain did not get it, he was angry with God. Being mad at God is spiritual heart disease. We have a lot of this sickness today.

From Enoch we learn that it is by faith that we *please* God, "for before his translation he had this testimony, the he pleased God." How can a child please his father if he does not believe the things that his father says? Though God has spoken many things to us through His word, things hard to be understood, a childlike faith in those words is pleasing in His sight. Whether it is duty or doctrine, our reliance upon God's word is pleasing to Him. One day, they looked for Enoch and he was not found. God was so pleased with him, that He translated him to glory. How great was Enoch's faith! God took him on up to glory!

Helpful Hints:
1. Talk about the different accounts of faith in Hebrews 11.
2. Talk about faith being the substance of things hoped for.
3. Talk about faith being a fruit of the Spirit.
4. How has your faith been challenged?
5. The power of faith.
6. Pleasing God by faith.

"BUILDING BY FAITH"

"Noah, being warned of God of things not seen as yet,
moved with fear, prepared and ark to the saving of his house"
–Hebrews 11:7a.

Today, let us consider Noah, from whom we will learn that fear and faith work together, moving us to accomplish feats that are, otherwise, humanly impossible. Though many will scoff at God's little children for believing in things that they can not see with the natural eye, the greatest feats that have ever been performed were accomplish by childlike *faith*. By faith, Noah, the amateur ship builder, constructed a boat that survived the greatest storm this earth has ever seen. The Titanic was built by experts and did not survive its first voyage. Noah's first boat repopulated the world!

In his "Body of Divinity", John Gill said, "Faith is to the soul as the natural eye is to the body". Genuine faith is not stepping out into thin air. Faith attaches itself to something that can not be seen with the natural eye or touched with the natural senses...... but just as real: God's word.

One-hundred and twenty years before God destroyed the earth with a flood, He told Noah about His plan to destroy the earth with rain and a flood. To us, that may seem like an easy enough thing to believe, but we need remember…….it had never rained! The fact that Noah feared was evidence enough that he believed what God has said. The earth was watered by vapors and mists. Therefore, Noah, was warned of God of "things not seen as yet" and still believed.

Noah took God seriously. He *believed* that God would do what He said He would do. That is simple faith. Though he had never seen it rain or built a boat, much less an ark of such enormity, he followed God's instruction precisely. This teaches us that we *build* by faith. We build our families; our churches; and our lives upon the things that God has said to us through His word. Though the infidels may scoff, the faithful will build and enjoy salvation.

NOAH PREACHED BY FAITH

Not only did Noah build the ark, he began to warn others of the impending danger. Peter refers to him as a "preacher of righteousness". Day after day, Noah hammered away at this great ark, located nowhere near a body of water, and preached to people about their sin and the impending judgment of God. He told them water would come and the boat would float. People laughed at him, ridiculed him, talked about him behind his back and mocked him. Noah is a figure of Christ. I can just hear the scientists of Noah's day saying, "Noah, you are way over your head. There is no such thing as rain. What you are suggesting is scientifically impossible." But when the flood came the scoffers' mouths were filled with water. It is not for preachers to preach their own opinions. Nor is it their job to tell people what they want to hear. By faith, they just tell people what God has revealed to them. The results are in God's hands. So are the people.

FEAR AND FAITH

From this we come to our conclusion: fear and faith compliment one another. Noah's faith in God's word, kindled by a healthy fear that God would do what He said He would do, moved him to build the ark and preach to others. Genuine faith goes beyond believing. Faith takes *action* in what has been said. James wrote, "Faith without works is dead". Oh, that we saw such fear of God today! Noah's faith was expressed in every nail, every board, every sermon, for one-hundred and twenty years. Noah feared God more than man. He told people the truth as he built the great ark. In one sense, his ark was his sermon. Do you see how fear and faith work together? We are not to become weary in well doing. We shall reap if we faint not. What has God said to you through His word? Let us get our hammers and nails and begin to build our ark upon the sure foundation of God's word!

Helpful Hints:
1. An excellent opportunity to discuss creation and the world before the flood.
2. Talk about the ark and the animals!
3. Talk about the flood, the earthquakes, the foundations of the deep being broken up. Do some homework on the subject!
4. Talk about the people on the ark and the repopulation of the earth.
5. Talk about the population of the earth before the flood.
6. Talk about the wickedness and God's reason for destroying the earth with a flood.
7. Talk about faith.

8. Talk about reverential fear of God and how it should move us.

9. Talk about the rainbow and what it means.

"OBEYING BY FAITH"

"By faith Abraham, when he was called to go out into a place which he should after receive for an inheritance, obeyed; and he went out, not knowing whither he went"-Hebrews 11:8.

Living a life of faith is not a comfortable lifestyle. It was never meant to be. Though we may talk about being faithful, if we are honest, we find ourselves surrounded with many doubts and fears when put to the test. Consider Noah's experience. Abraham was called upon to do something that was very uncomfortable to the flesh: leave all that he knew. The command was given without any additional information as to where he was to go and the people he would meet up with in his travels. If all of this was given up front, there would be no need for faith. This is the essence of faith in a nutshell: doing what our Father has said without asking the usual childish questions like, how, how long, why and why me. The end of faith is not giving assent to the fact that God is God, but rather the simple act of *obeying* His command! When we do not obey, we are really saying that we do not trust the counsel of our heavenly Father.

Imagine that! God called Abraham to leave his home, his dwelling place, his acquaintances, his occupation, and He didn't even tell Abraham where he was sending him. God said, "Get thee out of thy country, and from thy kindred, and from thy father's house, unto a land that I will shew thee: And I will make of thee a great nation, and I will bless thee, and make thy name great; and thou shalt be a blessing"-Gen 12:1-2. I can just hear Abraham asking God, "Where do you want me to go?" And God's reply was, "To a land that I will shew you". In other words, God was saying, "Trust me Abraham, I'll take care of you". Abraham did not know where he was going...but God did!

God does call upon his faithful to do some very *uncomfortable* things. Has God ever called upon you to surrender some creature comforts to follow Him? Have you found some of the things in His word to be contrary to what the world is telling you? Let us take the *uncomfortable* path of faith. Therein the blessing is found.

Faith is not stepping out into thin air. Abraham did not decide upon his own to leave his place. He did not follow a whim, He didn't say, "I shall go off into who knows where and expect God to bless me". His journey was not of his own making. His actions were based upon something solid and sure: God's word. That is not thin air!

Some believe that faith is only for great deeds. They look for some great thing to do for God: live in a foreign country; fast for many days; become a leader like Abraham or Moses; or preach like the apostle Paul. But I find that it is the simple things in God's word that we stumble over the most. We stumble over them because they do not seem big enough. Every day our faith is put to the test in the small, seemingly mundane affairs of life. God's word gives us information for the home; the workplace; God's house; every avenue of life. We may never be an Abraham or a Moses. But if we use our God given faith to overcome our own particular trials and tribulations, we will please God just as much because it takes just as much faith to be a faithful husband or wife, to be a Christian mom or dad, as it did for Noah to build the Ark and Abraham to leave his country. How can we say such a thing? Because God gives us the measure of faith to overcome our own particular challenge. Since I have not been called upon to build an Ark, I should not expect the faith, or even the desire to do so. If called upon to build one, I would expect my heavenly Father to give me the unction from above to accomplish the feat.

From Abraham's experience we learn a maxim in faith: our obedience is in proportion to the faith that we have in God's word. If we believe what God has said, we will obey, for we see the reward of faith. If we allow doubts and fears to keep us from the performance of the His word, our faith is lacking, we miss out on the blessing. If God said it, we must believe it; trust it; act upon it; and live according to it. We can read the Bible one-thousand times over; we can know and memorize all of scripture; but unless we step out on the principles, our faith is dead.

Abraham became the father of a great nation. He was called "High Father" by his people. Paul referred to him as "faithful Abraham". God called him "my friend". Look at his life and consider the blessings so wonderfully packaged in the single fact that he *obeyed*.

Helpful Hints:
1. Discuss the difference between genuine faith and thin air.
2. Discuss Abraham's life if he had *not* obeyed.
3. Why is genuine faith so uncomfortable?
4. What comforts did Abraham give up?
5. Discuss the reason that Abraham was called the "Fried of God".

"SOJOURNING BY FAITH"

"By faith he sojourned in the land of promise, as in a strange country, dwelling in tabernacles with Isaac and Jacob, the heirs with him of the same promise: For he looked for a city which hath foundations, whose builder and maker is God"
-Hebrews 11:9,10

Not only did Abraham's great faith enable him to obey God as he walked away from all that he knew, it altered the way he looked at life. After his conversation with God, Abraham could no longer call earth his home. Sojourn means to reside as a foreigner. Though Abraham enjoyed the earthly promises, his experience with heavenly things began to make him homesick for another world. He no longer saw earth as a permanent residence!

FAITH ALTERS OUR AFFECTIONS

Having been touched by the divine hand and moved by the heavenly call, Abraham's affections and eyesight had been altered. Is it not so? Just one spiritual experience with God changes our whole outlook on life. Thankfully, this world is not all there is. There is something better, much better, which lies before us. God is alive and he has taken knowledge of us. We begin to anticipate that day when we shall dwell with Him on high. One taste of honey desires a second, one experience with the Lord causes us to hunger another, ultimately, the continual and unending fellowship with God on high. All that this world has to offer seems less important. Earth's riches pale into insignificance when compared to heaven's glories.

The word *tabernacle* is very suggestive. It suggests a *tent*, something that is folded up and moved from place to place. As we trace Abraham's life, it seems that he could find no place, even in the land of promise, that could fill his spiritual needs. He could find no place to call home. He could not get close enough to God. He wandered about all of his life pitching his tent from place to place. That is surely the lot of the faithful. As the song goes, "This world is not my home, I'm just a passing through".

A KINDRED EXPERIENCE

Abraham was not alone in his experience. Isaac and Jacob are both mentioned in our text. They experienced their wilderness wanderings and dwelt in their tents as well. The seed of the faithful is here represented. God has always provided Himself faithful witnesses since creation, other faithful men and women, who would not call earth their home.

As they sojourned through the land of promise they confessed that they were strangers and pilgrims(v. 13). A *stranger* is a person away from home and a *pilgrim* is a person looking for a home. Being away from home is a lonely feeling. Such feelings will be experienced by God's faithful. Their inward longing is heavenly. They begin to look for a better place of residence, the lot of the pilgrim. Is that not the hope and desire of every believer, to dwell with the Lord in glory? Surely, all of God's faithful have shared this kindred experience from time to time. The greater the sorrows and afflictions in this world, the more God's faithful are made to look and long for their heavenly abode.

THE INVISIBLE CITY

Abraham "looked for a city which hath foundations, whose builder and maker is God." Unseen by the natural eye, this city is just as real as Chicago or New York. When these cities are gone, God's city will be situated and inhabited by the faithful because it has been built by the great invisible Builder who may only be seen by the eye of Abraham, the children of faith!

Helpful Hints:
1. A wonderful opportunity to talk about heaven!
2. Talk about the many places Abraham went and his experiences there.
3. God's presence in every place!
4. Talk about the two worlds.

"THE STRENGTH OF FAITH"

"Through faith also Sarah herself received strength to conceive seed, and was delivered of a child when she was past age, because she judged him faithful who had promised. Therefore sprang there even of one, and him as good as dead, so many as the stars of the sky in multitude, and as the sand which is by the sea shore innumerable"-Hebrews 11:11,12.

As we continue our study in faith's hall of fame, we find that women have graced the halls of faith with their uncompromising love for God. Several may be discovered in this chapter of faith. Today, let us consider the faith of Sarah, the wife of Abraham. From Sarah, we will discover the *strength* of faith.

THE STRENGTH OF FAITH

Faith is a *powerful* force. The confirmation of this power is observed in this chapter by many amazing feats performed by otherwise weak vessels. The power is not found in the person chosen to exercise the faith. The power is in the One who made the promise. As we read the story of God's dealings with Sarah, we find a *weak* vessel. It is from the weaker vessel that God gets the greatest glory and the strength of faith is demonstrated.

Sarah was weak in *faith*. We find her full of unbelief, full of doubts. When God announced to Abraham he would have a son, and Sarah would be the mother, Sarah laughed(Genesis 18:9-15). Sarah behaved as we do most of the time. She looked upon human means, her own strength, to fulfill the promise.

Sarah was also *physically* weak. She was "past age". Naturally speaking, she was too old to have a child. Abraham was another weak vessel involved in the miracle. So far as fathering a child, he was "as good as dead". Looking upon her own ability to fulfill the promise she found little hope so "she laughed" when she heard God make the promise to Abraham. At first glance, all she could see were two weak vessels trying to make a miracle.

Somewhere between the time that Sarah laughed, and the time that she, "received strength to conceive seed", she must have looked away from self and believed the promise. She must have, as we say, chewed the cud, thought upon what God had said, considered the matter, recognized her unbelief, and slowly, but surely, began to believe what God has said. Faith begins in the mind and is then digested in the heart and is revealed in the hand. She first considered the one who made the promise who also said to her, "Is any thing too hard for the Lord?" Then she began to hope for the fulfillment of the promise. Faith is the substance of "things hoped for". If she hoped, she had the substance of it which is faith. Then the strength was given and the promise performed. That is what it says, "She judged him faithful who had promised." The power of faith is found in the childlike trust that God will do what He has promised. When faith attaches itself to God with a childlike trust and looks away from self the power engages: the strength is found to fulfill the task!

Thankfully, God's promises are not based upon man's ability. If God had chosen a strong young man and a healthy young woman to bear the promised seed they would have needed no faith. Faith is given for the impossible task. It is given to the weak, to the poor of this world, to the needy, to God's children: "God hath chosen the foolish things of the world to confound the wise; and God hath chosen the weak things of the world to confound the things which are mighty; And base things of the world, and things which are despised, hath God chosen, yea, and things which are not, to bring to nought things that are: That no flesh should glory in his presence"-1 Corinthians 1:26-29. Faith is not given to exalt man. Faith is given to exalt the Lord who made the promise. That is why he uses weak vessels.

Helpful Hints:
1. Talk about God's promises.
2. How we are changed by faith.
3. God's omniscience, hearing and knowing our thoughts.
4. Talk about Sarah's change of heart.
5. Talk about the impossible task before them.

"COME APART AND REST A WHILE"

"And he said unto them, Come ye yourselves apart into a desert place, and rest a while: for there were many coming and going, and they had no leisure so much as to eat"-Mark 6:31

The disciples had recently learned of the death of their beloved brother, John the Baptist. They came to Jesus, bearing their burden, telling Him of their heartache and fears. Their burden was heavy and their trial difficult. Jesus knew they needed some *rest.*

In the fast paced society in which we live today, these simple words should remind us all, that from time to time, we need to come apart from our toils and labors and relax or we will come apart at the seams. This is not an encouragement to neglect our families, our duties as parents, husbands, wives, or neglect our jobs and God given responsibilities. Too much of that is seen in our recreational society. Nor are we to make a god out of rest. The words of Jesus demonstrate to disciples everywhere that He recognizes our need of rest, time away from duty and responsibility, to let the brain air out and sweep the cobwebs from our minds.

It seems to me that many fits of depression can result from a lack of coming apart to rest a while in some solitary place where we may leave our cares for just a little while. These "had no leisure so much as to eat." It was not because they did not enjoy their labor among the people. They needed to rest so that they might labor better. The weary hand of the carpenter must rest from time to time or else his project will turn from good to bad: sore thumbs, bent nails and fraying tempers.

Spurgeon rightly noted: "The bow cannot be always bent without fear of breaking. Repose is as needful to the mind as sleep to the body....Even the earth must lie fallow and have her Sabbaths, and so must we. Hence the wisdom and compassion of our Lord, when he said to his disciples, 'Let us go into the desert and rest awhile'......The Master knows better than to exhaust his servants and quench the light of Israel. Rest time is not waste time. It is economy to gather fresh strength.....Fishermen must mend their nets, and we must every now and then repair our mental waste and set our machinery in order for future service. To tug the oar from day to day, like a galley-slave who knows no holidays, suits not mortal men. Mill-streams go on and on for ever, but we must have our pauses and our intervals. Who can help being out of breath when the race is continued without intermission? Even beasts of burden must be turned out to grass occasionally; the very sea pauses at ebb and flood; earth keeps the Sabbath of the wintry months; and man, even when exalted to be God's ambassador, must rest or faint; must trim his lamp or let it burn low; must recruit his vigour or grow prematurely old. It is wisdom to take occasional furlough. In the long run, we shall do more by sometimes doing less.....Let no tender conscience doubt the lawfulness of going out of harness for awhile, but learn from the experience of others the necessity and duty of taking timely rest." To his words we agree most heartily!

One final observation: while they came apart to rest, they were with Jesus. Their rest and recreation were not *divorced* from their Lord. If our R & R were not in moderation, I do not believe Jesus would go with us. Surely, He does not go with those who neglect their families, their church or their duties. Their enjoyment was clean, wholesome, fruitful, and with His companionship and approval, much more enjoyable. It may be on the golf course, in the garden, at the fishing hole, or just walking under the canopy of God's creation. Let us all take the time to come apart and rest awhile but never make a god out of it!

Helpful Hints:
1. Discuss healthy R & R.
2. Plan an outing with your family.
3. Talk how recreation can be made a god.
4. How can this affect families?

"UNCONDITIONAL ELECTION"

"For the children being not yet born, neither having done any good or evil, that the purpose of God according to election might stand, not of works, but of him that calleth"
-Romans 9:11

What does the Bible mean when it declares that election is unconditional? It means that God did not choose a people, love a people, and redeem a people based upon their performance, ability or any good works that He foresaw. It shows us that God chose His people in spite of their sin and redeemed them from their sin. In types and shadows, Jacob and Esau are the examples that Paul uses to teach this magnificent doctrine. As one of my friends said in a sermon, "If you are having a problem with election, just dial 911."

Jacob's name is indicative of man by nature. Jacob means *deceiver*. As the story goes, he stole his brother's birthright with a mess of pottage. He dressed up in a costume, lied to his blind father, and stole his older brother's blessing. Yet, in spite of his lying deceptions, God loved Jacob! So, what does all of this mean? It means that God's electing love is not based upon our performance. God did not choose Jacob because of any good that He foresaw, for until God appeared to Jacob and changed his name there was nothing good to see. Nor did God reject Esau because of any evil that he foresaw. If God's election were base upon merit, He would have rejected Jacob and left him in his deceitful lifestyle.

Surely, this goes against the thinking of man. He chooses up sides and picks the strongest for his team. God chooses the weak, the unprepared, the untalented and even those that are far from perfect. He gives them what they need to do good and He receives the glory. Man has such difficulty believing that election is unconditional. It contradicts our carnal reasoning.

Then what is God's election based upon if it is not righteous ability? Paul tells us: "Jacob have I loved". God's election is based upon the love that He had for His people. Election means "a choice of love". It does not say "Jacob will I love" or "Jacob will I begin to love when he repents". "Have I loved", goes all the way back before they were born. That is why it says, "being not yet born." God's choice was based solely upon the love that He had for His people.

Election is not a doctrine that *limits*. It is bigger than any religion. It includes a people out of every kindred, nation, tribe and family, even people who will never have the opportunity to hear the gospel. Yes, we believe in evangelism. But let our message be one of a successful Saviour who loved, elected and died for His sheep. As Paul wrote, "Who shall lay any thing to the charge of God's elect?"

Some might say, "Well then, who are the elect if it is not based upon our works or repentance? How can we know if we are among the elect?" Paul gives us our evidence in 1 Thessalonians 1:4,5: "Knowing, brethren beloved, your election of God. For our gospel came not unto you in word only, but also in power, and in the Holy Ghost, and in much assurance..." Paul could tell who the elect were and so can we. It was, and is, the people the gospel affects. To many, the gospel comes to them in "word only". The preaching of the cross is to them "foolishness". They hear the word preached but it has no affect upon them. But to God's elect, the Spirit bears witness that they are the children of God. It comes to them in "much assurance." How is it with you? Is the name of Jesus important to you? Do you love Him? If you do, you are of this noble seed, the elect of God!

Helpful Hints:
1. Talk about Jacob' life.
2. Talk about his deception of his father.
3. Talk his reaping what he had sown.
4. Talk about God being with him all of his life.
5. Talk about the stumbling blocks people have with this doctrine.

"BEING PREDESTINATED"

"In whom also we have obtained an inheritance, being predestinated according to the purpose of him who worketh all things after the counsel of his own will:"-Ephesians 1:11

The apostle rejoiced in the great doctrine of predestination. Paul used the term more than any other writer in the New Testament. Why was this? Because the chief of sinners had nothing in his hand to offer God for salvation. Paul's sin was ever before him. He not only put Christians to death, he also tortured them to the point of blaspheming the name of Jesus. Paul could never tip the scales of good works over to his favor. His hope was in the finished works of Christ, predestinated to save all that the Father had given to His son. Those who view their own case accurately will rejoice in this sovereign truth. C.H. Spurgeon once said, "I question whether we have preached the whole counsel of God, unless predestination with all its solemnity and sureness be continually declared."

The biblical words, "predestinate" and "predestinated" are translated from the Greek word *proorizo* which means: "to predetermine or declare before". Surely God is able to do that. If God were not able to orchestrate the affairs of men and angels, how could He bless men to prophesy future events before they transpired; how could Christ have fulfilled the many messianic prophesies concerning Himself? Men will allow the almanac to predict the season to plant their potatoes; look at the Zodiac as a sign for their mate; call upon the gazers of crystal balls to tell them their future and then deny the authority that God has to orchestrate the eternal destination of His people!

PEOPLE ARE PREDESTINATED

When the Bible speaks of predestination, it does not declare that God predetermines every thought, every motion, every event and every action. Though God is not surprised by any thing, he sees the end from the beginning, these verses specify people: "For whom he did foreknow, he also did predestinate to be conformed to the image of his Son". *Whom* speaks of people, not events. Though God can predetermine events, and has orchestrated the affairs of men, the doctrine of predestination concerns the greatest theme in all the world: the redemption of His people. God predetermined for His people to live with Him in glory and brought it to pass by the atonement of Christ upon the cross.

PREDESTINATION COMPLIMENTS ELECTION

The doctrine of predestination *compliments* the doctrine of election. In Ephesians, chapter one, after stating that we are "Chosen in him before the foundation of the world", Paul writes, "Having predestinated us unto the adoption of children by Jesus Christ to himself, according to the good pleasure of his will"- Ephesians 1:5. God literally adopted His chosen people from the fallen family of Adam and placed them into the redeemed family of

Christ. That was predestinated or predetermined before the fall. Predestination compliments election because in the typical adoption process it is the adopter that makes the choice, not the adopted. As with most adoptions, the adopted party is completely passive in the arrangement. The adopted party did not choose the parent, the parent chose the child and many times that is all arranged before the child is born into the world. That is why Paul could write, "according to the good pleasure of his will", not the will of the one adopted.

Predestination also agrees with election concerning our inheritance: "In whom we have obtained an inheritance, being predestinated according to the purpose of him who worketh all things after the counsel of his own will"- Ephesians 1:11. If you have inherited something, someone chose you to receive it. It is the sovereign right of the one who possesses the assets to bequeath it to whom they will. It is not the norm for a king to leave his ransom to a stranger, nor for parents to leave their inheritance to people that they do not love or respect. Almost every inheritance is left to children, flesh and blood offspring, who are loved and cherished. Such is the inheritance of the Saints. The will has been made; the testator has died; the heirs of grace, the elect, shall receive Christ and all of His riches. Satan and all of his host can never change one jot or title of the inheritance because it is *predestinated* of God. In this doctrine we find great reason to rejoice!

Helpful Hints:
1. Read the different places this doctrine is taught and expound.
2.Discuss the difference between predestination and foreknowledge.
3. Talk about prophecy and it coming to pass.
4. Discuss our inheritance.

"PAUL'S AUTOPSY of MAN"

"Their throat is an open sepulchre; with their tongues they have used deceit; the poison of asps is under their lips: Whose mouth is full of cursing and bitterness: Their feet are swift to shed blood:"-Romans 3:13-15

In Romans, chapter three, Paul performs his *autopsy* of the natural man and gives us his forensic report. He begins by saying, "As it is written, There is none righteous, no, not one." No matter what kind of math we use, that is a big zero. This includes the patriarchs, the apostles, preachers, popes and presidents. As Jesus said to the rich young ruler, "none is good, save one, that is, God." Until God places something good in man, Himself, His Spirit, there is nothing good to be found, even by the closest of examinations. You may examine man with an electron microscope, dissect him from head to foot, examine every molecule, every atom and find the blot of Adams' transgression indelibly etched upon every fiber.

By nature, man can not know or *understand* the things of God, "But the natural man receiveth not the things of the Spirit of God: for they are foolishness unto him: neither can he now them, because they are spiritually discerned"-

1 Corinthians 2:14. By nature, man can not *hear* the gospel, "He that is of God heareth God's words: ye therefore hear them not because ye are not of God"-John 8:7. By nature, man can not *believe*, "But ye believe not, because ye are not of my sheep, as I said unto you"-John 10:26. By nature, man can not *please* God, "So then they that are in the flesh cannot please God"-Rom 8:8. What is the Bible saying? It is saying that man, left to himself, is *depraved*!

THE WEAK LINK IN THE CHAIN

I have heard the gospel presented as a rope that is thrown down into a pit where fallen man is found. One man who has been pulled out of the pit now turns and throws the rope down do others in the pit. If the sinner will grab hold of the rope, the man at the top will pull him out of the pit. This sound pretty good at first. After all, we don't want anyone to remain at the bottom of the pit. This man at the top of the pit is doing a noble thing, being at the top, drawing men out of perdition. Yet, there is something wrong with this picture, there is a weak link. It is not the rope, it is the man. We have depravity on both ends of the rope. We must ask this question: Since man is depraved, since he can not understand, hear, believe or please God, how did that first man get out of the pit? The only way the first man could get out of the pit to throw the rope down to others is by God's grace, by Jesus going down into the pit and rescuing him directly......and that is how we all get out of the pit. Until man is rescued from the pit and his nature changed, he will love the pit and what is in the pit so much, he will never grab hold of the rope. Depraved man loves the pit and everything in it. If Jesus rescued the first man from the pit, don't you think He is able to get the others out as well? In the pit of depravity we will find, "Fornication, idolatry, adultery, theft, covetousness, and extortion"(1 Corinthians 6:9,10), among many other notable lifestyles. Until the heart is changed the rope is offensive.

The weak link in this chain of events is man, "For what the law could not do, in that is was weak through the flesh, God sending his own Son in the likeness of sinful flesh, and for sin, condemned sin in the flesh"-Rom. 8:3. The flesh is weak, depraved, unable to keep the law. But thanks be to God who sent His own Son to keep the law for the objects of His grace. He bore their sins upon His cross. He paid for their sins with His own precious blood. He did what depraved man could not do. That is why we say that the doctrine of total depravity is one of the many doctrines of God's grace.

Helpful Hints:
1. Talk about the fall and the doctrine of original sin.
2. Talk about the purpose of the gospel.
3. Talk about the atrocities of mankind and his depravity.
4. Talk about the things you would like to change in your own life.

"LIMITED ATONEMENT"

"She shall bring forth a son, and thou shalt call his name Jesus: for he shall save his people from their sins"-Matthew 1:21

The Bible is very specific concerning who Jesus came to save. He came to save *His people*. When we read the Bible we must also read what it does not say. It does not say that Jesus came to save *all* people. Nor does it say that Jesus came to save *some* people. The possessive word, His, indicates ownership: they belonged to Jesus before He came into this world.

When we speak of limited atonement, we do not mean that God is limited, nor are we saying that the mediatory work of Christ upon the cross was incomplete. Limited atonement means that the atonement of Christ was limited to the objects of His grace, those chosen and loved before the foundation of the world. As the High Priest went into the most Holy place for Israel alone, so Christ suffered for the sins of *His people*.

ATONEMENT

Atonement means to appease or make amends for injustices done. Israel's day of atonement was a type and shadow of our day of atonement. Their day of atonement occurred once, every year, a perpetual reminder of their need for further cleansing, "But this man, after he had offered one sacrifice for sins for ever, sat down on the right hand of God." The High Priest could never sit down, his work was never complete. The atonement of Christ was one sacrifice for ever! We can add nothing to it, and thankfully, we can take nothing from it.

LIMITED ATONEMENT AGREES WITH PREDESTINATION

Limited atonement agrees with the doctrine of predestination. Peter said we were redeemed by "the precious blood of Christ, as of a lamb without blemish and without spot: Who verily was foreordained before the foundation of the world"-I Peter 1:19,20. Before the foundation of the world, the lamb was selected, the sacrifice of God's own Son was planned by the Godhead. John wrote of Jesus as a "Lamb slain from the foundation of the world". Though sin has caused great suffering and pain, the plan to rescue God's elect has always been intact, planned and sure. What great security we find in the doctrines of grace!

LIMITED ATONEMENT AGREES WITH ELECTION

The doctrine of Limited Atonement agrees with the doctrine of election. Not only did Jesus know *why* He was dying upon the cross, He also knew *who* He was dying for.

His eyes were not closed when He freely offered Himself without spot and blemish to the Father. Isaiah wrote, "by his knowledge shall my righteous servant justify many; for he shall bear their iniquities'-Isaiah 53:11. Christ went to the cross with *knowledge*. He is the omniscient God.

By His redemptive work upon the cross, Jesus either paid for all the sins of all people; or he paid for some of the sins of all people; or he paid for all the sins of some people. If He paid for all the sins of all people then all people have been redeemed. If He paid for some of the sins of all people then none are saved. If He paid for all of the sins of some people, these people have been set apart, loved and rescued from their sin and this atonement is sure to all of *His people*.

Helpful Hints:
1. Talk about the types and shadows of the day of atonement.
2. Talk about the offerings of the law service and how they depicted Christ.
3. Talk about the suffering of Christ.
4. Talk about redemption.

"IRRESISTIBLE GRACE"

"Who hath saved us, and called us with an holy calling, not according to our works, but according to his own purpose and grace, which was given us in Christ Jesus before the world began"-2 Timothy 1:9

The grace of God is the most wonderful message to ever be proclaimed by throughout eternity. It baffles the Saints and irritates the devil. How can a holy God bless undeserving sinners? How can God be just in His judgment of sin and bestow honors upon fallen creatures? The only answer that may be given is Christ Jesus. Jesus is the channel through which grace must come. He is truly the fount of every blessing. Through Him and by Him are all blessings given to undeserving sinners.

Grace means unmerited favor; blessings bestowed upon the undeserving. Irresistible means that the objects of God's grace are completely *passive* in the blessings and benefits bestowed. They can neither command them to come nor cause them to go away. It *must* be that way. How else could proud and stubborn rebels ever be brought to the place that they would call upon God and reverence His Son? John Newton, the writer of the beloved hymn,

"Amazing Grace", was arrested by the Holy Spirit while at sea engaged in the ignoble profession of slave trading. He was not attending a church, nor was he sitting under the sound of the gospel when his heart was convicted concerning his sin. That power was *irresistible*. The divine influence of the Holy Ghost convicted his conscience to such a degree that it changed his whole career. He began to seek the Savior and this irresistible influence of the Holy Ghost humbled this man to write, "Amazing grace, how sweet the sound, that saved a wretch like me I once was lost but now I'm found, was blind but now I see."

How great is God's grace! How meritoriously it is represented in Christ Jesus our Lord. We see it in His *death*. Did you ask for Jesus to die for you? Could fallen man have contrived such a scheme to rescue the elect? Would we have thought to ask God to send His only begotten Son into this world to bleed and die for us?

It is equally observed in His *love*. Isaiah knew of it and wrote, "The Lord hath appeared of old unto me, saying, Yea, I have loved thee with an everlasting love: therefore with lovingkindness have I drawn thee." Precious thought! The Lord's love is everlasting! We can do nothing to change it. It is sealed with His covenant, proven by His suffering and ratified by His victory. His love did not change when Adam fell nor shall it change when we fall. If He loved us before, He shall love us still, "For I *am* the LORD, I change not; therefore ye sons of Jacob are not consumed"-Malachi 3:6. It was love that *carried* Him to the cross. It was *love* that endured the afflictions. It was love that drew His elect from death to life; from the drowning waters of perdition to the solid foundation of His inheritance among the Saints. Christian, His love for us is *purer* than ours for Him, it is irresistible and full of grace.

Irresistible grace is equally observed in God's effectual *call*. There is a distinctive difference between the gospel call and the effectual call. The gospel call comes from the mouth of man. It may be refused. It may fall upon the unregenerate ear. It may fall upon those who do not have the mental faculties to comprehend and understand. It can not give life, but it does have great power, "it is the power of God unto salvation to every one that believeth". It affects believers. It convicts us of our sin; shows us our position in Christ; saves us from false doctrine; from false prophets; from the many snares of Satan; and gives us a vision of Christ, His holiness and the world to come. That is powerful stuff and it is all by grace!

The effectual call comes from the mouth of God. Isaiah writes: "So shall my word be that goeth forth out of my mouth: it shall not return unto me void, but it shall accomplish that which I please, and it shall prosper in the thing whereto I sent it"- Isaiah 55:11. Note, "MY MOUTH" and "IT SHALL ACCOMPLISH". That is irresistible grace! As our text declares, it is a "holy calling, not according to our works". It is according to His works. It is referred to as a spiritual resurrection (John 5:25). It is a quickening, (Ephesians 2:1). It is a new birth, (John 3:8). It is an act of creation, (II Corinthians 5:15). Let us rejoice in the fact that God can change the darkest heart; He can turn the proudest rebel; and He can cleanse the foulest sin. Such power is not found in the mouths of mortals. God's grace is irresistible.

When Jesus returns to gather His elect from the four corners of the world *everyone* will be convinced of His irresistible grace. Will Lazarus say, wait a little longer Jesus and I will come out to meet you? No, no. Every knee will bow and every tongue shall confess that Jesus Christ is Lord; that He is truly the Son of God. Satan must declare it and though his army of fallen imps may foam at the mouth, they too shall declare that God's grace is irresistible. Let the tongues of every Christian abound with this theme: God's grace is irresistible!

Helpful Hints:

1. Name some things that God has done for His people that are irresistible.

2. Talk about he new birth and how it too is irresistible.

3. Talk about the resurrection and the irresistible power of God's voice.

4. Talk about the posture of one who is dead in trespasses and in sin.

"A PLAIN PATH"

"Teach me thy way, O Lord, and lead me in a plain path, because of mine enemies"-Psalm 27:11

Here we find David in a fervent posture of prayer. It seems that many decisions are before him and his mind is uncertain as to which way to turn; which road to take; which option to choose. We will all find ourselves in this circumstance from time to time. It may be yours today. Let David's prayer become our own.

The first thing we notice about this petition is David's plea for Godly instruction: "teach me". In his "Treasury of David", C.H. Spurgeon writes, "This prayer evinces an humble sense of personal ignorance, great teachableness of spirit, and cheerful obedience of heart." It is wisdom to realize that we have a lot to learn, and that God may still teach us many things regardless of our age or position in life. From Jehovah's great fountain of wisdom may be found direction for every decision. Our inability to decide is an indication of our need for the arm of our Beloved. It has ushered us into the posture of prayer, and even though our path is not yet clear, there are comforts to be

found in His presence. The decision is no longer ours.....
it is His.

David then asks for "thy way". Here we find *submission*.
David has turned from self-centered desires to the only
One who knows what is best for him. As the old hymn
goes:

"Thy way, not mine, O Lord, However dark it be;
Oh, lead me by Thine own right hand; Choose Thou the path
for me!
Smooth let it be, or rough, It still will be the best;
Winding or straight, it matters not; It leads me to Thy rest.
I dare not choose my lot; I would not if I might;
But choose Thou for me, O my Lord! So shall I walk aright."

If we have genuinely asked for "Thy way", should we
not seek counsel from the sacred *scriptures* for an answer?
Surely, this would shed some light upon our present
plight. In the 119th psalm, the writer found the scriptures
to be "My delight and my counsellors"-v.24. Let the sacred
cannon become our counsellor until the path is plain.
Holy inspiration will always agree with the divine mind
of God!

David then asks to be led: "lead me". We are either
following the Lord's path in our life or walking in our
own light. The blind can not lead the blind or they will
both fall into the ditch. If we follow our own light we
shall walk in circles, lost in a maze of indifference. His
hand is outstretched to weary pilgrims and His grace is
sufficient for the trial. The pressure is off of self when we
follow such leadership. As the woodsman's eye is upon a
sure compass, our eye must be constant upon Him.

"A plain path" is a path that is level, straight and
upright, with great visibility. Though the challenge may
be great, in time it will become the path of least resistance

because it is His way: it is level. A straight path is one that allows the sojourner to see far ahead, the future becomes clear. It is upright in that it is honest and right.

David's enemies must be mentioned because these seem to be the distraction to his plain path, obscuring his vision. These are Satan's adversaries that confuse, scare and hinder our progress. The critical tongue, jealous Saul or the enemies of David's own heart come to our mind. They are the waves that disrupted Peter's vision as he walked to Jesus on the water. As long as his eyes were fixed upon Jesus, the storm had no power and his path was miraculous. Until the path is plain, we must adopt David's attitude which is reflected in the last verse of this psalm, "Wait on the Lord: be of good courage, and he shall strengthen thine heart: wait, I say, on the Lord."

Helpful Hints:
1. What decisions do you have before you?
2. Are there scriptures that address your personal plight?
3. Talk about the things that David did after prayer and the things he did without prayer.
4. Talk about distractions.

"CONSIDERING"

"The ox knoweth his owner, and the ass his master's crib: but Israel doth not know, my people doth not consider"-Isaiah 1:3

Isaiah was called to prophesy against God's people in a very sad time: they no longer *considered* Him. To consider means to understand, to exercise the mind towards. Though the ox had a mind to consider his owner, his gentle commands and the storehouse of provisions that were found in the master's crib, God's people no longer exercised their mind towards their provider and guide. They had forgotten the fount of their blessings!

Considering requires an exercise of the mind which springs from the heart. The infidel will describe the Christian as a shallow minded person who is willing to believe anything and everything without a shred of evidence. God does not hold such an opinion. He did not call upon the infidel or the unbeliever to consider. They were not capable. He called upon *my people*.

Generally speaking, God should be considered every day. Has a day gone by that you did not think upon the Lord of glory? Has a day gone by that you did not approach the throne of grace and ask for His providential hand of protection for your family; your country; your church? Should a day go by that we do not thank Him for His abundant blessings and ask for the forgiveness of our sins? I am sure that these, and many more categories, had slipped the minds of God's people of old. A sad time indeed!

Perhaps many of them had forgotten the Hebrew *method* of prayer. They were to pray at the time of the morning sacrifice, at midday, and at the time of the evening sacrifice. Surely, this was designed as a method of *forced* consideration. If they prayed, they must think upon Jehovah and their relationship with Him. In such a mode of worship, God would be considered daily. Today, many will consider the stock market; the sports events; politics; ad infinitum; but many days go by without considering the great I AM.

God should be considered in every decision that we make. David asked the Lord to lead him in a "plain path" that his decision would be God honoring. Benjamin Franklin had a method for making decisions that is still in use today. He would make a list, placing the pros on one side and the cons on the other side. He then went down the list, striking out and crossing off until the most important issues were remaining. Then he could make his decision. But let the Christian add another column to his page. At the head of this column place GOD: what would He have me to do? Such a method will keep us from many sins and heartaches.

God should be considered in times of adversity. Solomon wrote, "In the day of prosperity be joyful, but in the day of adversity consider: God also hath set the one over against the other, to the end that man should find nothing after him"-Ecclesiastes 7:14. There is nothing wrong with prosperity if it is gotten honestly. And there is nothing wrong with enjoying it: "be joyful". But Solomon had learned that amidst prosperity, adversity would always be found. Utopia can not be found this side of glory. Since the fall of Adam, God has placed prosperity and adversity side by side that man would not forget the source of his blessings. Adversities come in many shapes and sizes. Jobs fizzle out; problems occur in families; health can fail; and life may become a task. But in all of this, did not adversity bring us to our knees, seeking and *considering* the only One who can restore what the cankerworm and the palmerworm hath devoured. Had God not humbled us by adversity, this Sunday, we might be heading to the casino in our motor-home rather than the house of God with our family. Consider this my friend.

Faith calls upon us to not consider some things. When God promised Abraham that he would have a son in his old age, Abraham was not to consider the fact that he was too old to have a child; he was not to consider that his wife was beyond the age that one could conceive: "And being not weak in faith, he considered not his own body now dead, when he was about an hundred years old, neither yet the deadness of Sarah's womb: He staggered not at the promise of God through unbelief; but was strong in faith, giving glory to God"-Romans 4:19,20. Faith calls upon us to look away from the natural to the spiritual; to ignore the hindrances; and consider the One who made the promise.

God's house is a place that we are not only to consider God, but that we are to be considerate: "let us consider one another to provoke unto love and to good works: Not forsaking the assembling of ourselves together, as the manner of some is; but exhorting one another: and so much the more, as ye see the day approaching"-Hebrews 10:24,25. The rebuke is plain. It is considerate to be faithful to God's house and inconsiderate to others when we are not. It is true, the ox may fall in the ditch from time to time and hinder our devotions in God's house. But when that becomes a way of life it is time to mend the fence or sell the ox. Consider God in this matter as well!

Helpful Hints:
1. Talk about considering God in our blessings.
2. Talk about the things you did not consider before you became a Christian.
3. Talk about the things Israel did not consider.
4. Talk about the condition of the world around us and the things they do not consider.
5. How can we be more considerate of God.
6. To one another in our homes.
7. In our Church.

"THE CROSS OF CHRIST"

"Blotting out the handwriting of ordinances that was against us, which was contrary to us, and took it out of the way, nailing it to his cross"-Colossians 2:4

Christian, are there areas in your life that you are ashamed of, areas you wish were not there: sins committed; words spoken; moments wasted in vanity and pride? If so, there is great comfort to be found at the cross of Christ. It was there that Satan received his deadly blow; the place where Jesus suffered for those very things so that we would not have to. The cross of Christ is the place of forgiveness; full pardon; complete atonement and redemption from sin. Let us be ashamed of our sin, but never in the cross of our Lord.

I love the apostle's illustration of the cross. In that day, the writer composed his documents with a quill and ink. When a mistake was made, there was no eraser. The mistake was removed by blotting the ink off of the page. Such is the language that Paul uses as he describes Christ's atonement upon the cross. Our sins were blotted out, no more a part of the legal document written for eternity. Much like the delete key on the computer, press it and all has vanished, "As far as the east is from the west, so far hath he removed our transgressions from us"-Psalm 103:12. No more can Satan accuse us before the Father. The law and all of its legal documents have been shredded, canceled and nailed to His cross.

There have always been legalists that would tell us that we must do something to make the cross of Christ effective. But Paul said, "But God forbid that I should glory, save in the cross of our Lord Jesus Christ, by whom the world in crucified unto me, and I unto the world"-Gal. 6:14. Paul would not glory in an outward performance of rituals. He would glory in the cross alone, for there he saw his sins blotted out. As one man said, "Vanity is fond of ritualism which makes no demand upon the conscience." Man loves his platitudes; his steps; his ceremonies. But Paul found no comfort in these. He would have loved to sing: "Nothing in my hand I bring; simply to the cross I cling".

Some may say, "Was the cross of Christ my cross? Did He die for me? How can I know that He died for me and that my sins were blotted out?" To these questions we would ask, "Is the preaching of the cross foolishness to you or is there a power found therein that comforts your soul?" If it is foolishness, if you have no interest in the cross and the One who died thereon, you will perish in your sin. But if your soul is stirred by One who loved you, and gave Himself for you, His cross was your cross, "For the preaching of the cross is to them that perish foolishness; but unto us which are saved it is the power of God"-Rom. 1:18. As the moth is drawn to the light, so the quickened heart is drawn to the cross. Therein is found light, comfort and full pardon. Your interest is an indication of your guilt and your confession of guilt is an evidence of your calling. Like a magnet, His cross draws our affections from afar. Our interest in His cross is the fulfillment of prophecy, "and they shall look upon me whom they have pierced, and they shall mourn for him, as one mourneth for his only son, and shall be in bitterness for him, as one that is in bitterness for his firstborn"-Zech. 12:10.

The cross is a place that we may visit *daily*. It is the place I take the devil to when he takes me to my sin. His chain goes no further than the cross! The devil hates the very shadow of the cross. As the wild animal hates the trap, the devil hates the cross of Christ. The saint has no excuses for his sin; no one to blame but self; no justifying remarks for his own behalf. But he does have a cross, the place where sins were blotted out.

We all have a cross to bear. Simon was compelled to bear the cross of Jesus…..he did not volunteer. Yet, what a blessing this cross bearing turned out to be. We read later of his son, Rufus, chosen in the Lord! Our cross will not pay for sin. If it would, then the cross of Christ means nothing. Our cross is the place that we die to the world; where we say no to the flesh when Satan tempts us with the lust of the flesh, the lust of the eyes and the pride of life. Our cross is a place of victory as well as self denial. It is where we no longer live to self, but rather for Christ and others. Our example is Christ and His cross!

Helpful Hints:
1. This is a good time to share your crosses and burdens with others.
2. Consider the profitability of your cross.
3. Talk about Christ's suffering.
4. Talk about full pardon.

"SEEKING GOD'S FACE"

"When thou saidst, Seek ye my face; my heart said unto thee,Thy face, Lord, will I seek"-Psalms 27:8

If your heart has been stirred to seek after God you are in good company. Josiah, while he was yet young began to seek after God; Job said, "Oh that I knew where I might find Him"; Solomon wrote, "I will seek him whom my soul loveth"; Ezra prepared his heart to seek the law of the Lord; and Jehoshaphat set himself to seek the Lord. Great blessings were found in their lives and powerful testimonies exhibited in their behavior. The Bible is full of God-seekers. Today, let us join their blessed company and seek God's face while He may be found.

WHY WE SEEK

If you will notice David's language, it was God that made the *first* move: "When thou sadist, Seek my face...". David was *invited* into the awesome presence of God's face. God came first in Paul's experience as well. He was struck down on the Damascus road as he was ushered into the divine presence of Jesus. Peter was not seeking God's face as he washed his nets and Jesus found him; Nathanael would ask Jesus, "Whence knowest thou me? And Jesus would reply, "Before that Philip called thee, when thou wast under the fig tree, I saw thee". The Lord always comes first in our relationship with Him. God seeks us and translates us from the kingdom of darkness into the kingdom of light. Man, left to himself, will not seek after God. To the carnal mind, the Creator God does not exist: "The wicked, through the pride of his countenance, will not seek after God: God is not in all his thoughts"-Psalm 10:4. If you are seeking God it is a blessed thought to know that He is seeking you!

GOD'S FACE

Much may be read and learned from the countenance of the face. God encouraged David to seek His face as David cried with his voice and pleaded for mercy. A face turned in our direction means: you have my attention….. go on, I am listening! It is an indication of favor. Do not our faces turn away from those that we are angry with? Our own children learn much from our faces. When we are upset and angry we talk with our faces unless we hide them. God is saying, "David, I am not angry with you just look at my face." In the face is found character; beauty; and expression. The mouth is found on the face and it would be from God's mouth that David would receive Holy instruction that he so desperately needed.

Many times, I have sought after God only to find myself disappointed. I could not find Him. It was not God's fault. It was my own. I had not sought His face, I had sought his miracles. I was more interested in His gifts than His graces. I wanted something and not Him. Many followed Jesus like-minded, therefore He said: "Ye seek me, not because ye saw the miracles, but because ye did eat of the loaves, and were filled"-John 6:26. The day before, Jesus had fed 5000 with five loaves and two fishes. Miracles were around them but all they saw was the bread because that was their primary interest. Their belly was above their heart. They wanted the bread, not the One with the miracles. Today, people have many material things, yet they starve for spiritual things. His hand has been graciously opened to us and we have forgotten His face. As parents want their children to seek them because they love them, not for what they can give them, so we should seek God's face. Perhaps David was seeking God's power and not His person and the Lord said, "Seek my face". Surely, we have all found ourselves in this position from time to time. Let us not remain there. Let us seek His face, not His hand. His rewards are in His hand and it tenderly opens to those who genuinely seek His face.

Seeking God's face is a most rewarding experience. According to the writer of Hebrews, "he is a rewarder of them that diligently seek him"-11:6. *Diligence* is the key. That means that there is a craving for God's presence which sets the soul to searching. In every pursuit, diligence has its rewards. Athletes who are diligent in their training are the ones who excel; students who are diligent in their studies become high achievers; businessmen that are diligent in the workplace are most successful; and those that diligently seek God's face are those who enjoy His presence the most. That, I believe, is the greatest reward we could hope for: to find Him!

How may we know that we are seeking God's face and not His hand? Notice David's response to God's encouragement, "When thou saidst, Seek ye my face; my heart said unto thee, Thy face, Lord, will I seek". He abandoned his belly for his heart. A sincere searching of the heart is here indicated. Are the things that we are seeking God honoring or for the promotion of self. Are we seeking what He can do for us or are we asking what we can do for Him? Are His presents more important to us than His presence? Are my wants His wants? Are we interested in His hand and not His face? Let us remember, If we find His face we will have His hand!

Helpful Hints:
1. Talk about seeking God's face.
2. Talk about His face vs. His hand.
3. When have you sought His face most diligently?
4. How did you find it?
5. The rewards of seekers. See Hebrews 11.

"HOW OUR THINKING AFFECTS US"

"Finally, brethren, whatsoever things are true, whatsoever things are honest, whatsoever things are just, whatsoever things are pure, whatsoever things are lovely, whatsoever things are of good report; if there be any virtue, and if there be any praise, think on these things"-Philippians 4:8

Though many things have changed since the days of the apostle, some things have not. One of those is how our thinking affects us. Paul gave the Philippians a catalogue of things to think about for their profit. Surely, this list is profitable today for our own edification. God knows it. That is why He inspired the apostle to chronicle such meditations. Satan knows it, that is why he is bending all of his influence to encourage us to think otherwise. Consider with me, for just a few moments, how our thinking affects us.

THOUGHTS ARE SEEDS

It is wisdom when we learn that our thoughts are little seeds, planted in the mind, that produce fruit of their *own* kind. They are the eggs that hatch into actions. Like it or not, our actions are the fruits of our thoughts: sow a thought, reap an action, eat of the fruit thereof. Though it would be impossible for us to live above evil thoughts, we should be as the careful gardener who labors to keep his acreage free from weeds and thorns. Good thinking requires an effort, not only to avoid meditations of sinful lusts, but also to plant the proper seeds.

HOW SATAN WORKS

Though a child may have loving parents, and is brought up in a profitable environment, seeds can be planted that produce an evil kind of fruit. As Paul warned the Corinthians, "Be not deceived: evil communications corrupt good manners"-1 Corinthians 15:33. Sometimes my children will say to me, "Dad, you see evil in everything". But as I researched the effect of music upon the minds of our children I came across this article, "The American Medical Association(AMA) and the American Academy of Pediatrics have voiced concerns about certain lyrics used in heavy metal and rap music. The AMA says that messages in these genres may pose a threat to the physical health and emotional well being of particularly vulnerable children and adolescents. The AMA has identified six potentially dangerous music themes: drug and alcohol abuse, suicide, violence, satanic worship, sexual exploitation, and racism. Both the AMA and the Academy of Pediatrics support voluntary regulation and increased social responsibility in the music industry"(Internet Download). What are the AMA and the Academy of Pediatrics saying? What do the statistics reveal? Simply this: evil seeds planted in the mind produce evil actions: how we think affects us. If Satan has your thoughts, he has your future. Seldom is a suicide attempt a spontaneous action. It is frequently the result of a carefully thought out plan from a little seed sown. Violence in the school has been shown to be a carefully thought out and planned meditation. Hateful thoughts are the beginning of racism. Pornography is the beginning of unfaithfulness. Seeds, powerful seeds, planted in the mind will mature and entangle our lives. Certainly, we do not see evil in everything. But we should see evil in evil. Satan will tell us we can expose our minds to evil with little harm. Can we walk though the rain and not get wet? Can you walk thought a cuckle-briar patch and not bring one or two home?

A BATTLE FOR YOUR MIND

There has always been a battle for the mind. Did not Satan temp Eve to think hard thoughts against God? He started her to unprofitable thinking when he said, "Ye shall not surely die. Ye shall be as gods." It is by slogans and commercials that the public thinking is swayed into a modus operandi. In the past, the Marlboro cowboys would have us think that smoking their brand of cigarette was the best thing we could do. Today, one of them is saying, "Bob, I've got emphysema." Yes, the world wants to tell us how and what to think. If they tell you to march to the beat of a different drummer, you can be sure that the drummer is in their band, playing their score. Let the Christian be found, "Casting down imaginations, and every high thing that exalteth itself against the knowledge of God, and bringing into captivity every thought to the obedience of Christ"-2 Corinthians 10:5. What a bountiful harvest our lives will then produce!

Helpful Hints:
1. Talk about the things we are to think about.
2. Talk about how our thinking leads us to sin.

3. Talk about the devices Satan uses to affect our thinking.

4. Talk about the way the world if affected by it.

5. Pray for better thoughts.

"INNOCENT BLOOD"

"These six things doth the Lord hate: yea, seven are an abomination unto him: A proud look, a lying tongue, and hands that shed innocent blood"-Proverbs 6:16,17.

This article is not to add misery to those who have participated in this sin. This article is to shed light upon how God thinks; to prevent others from making a mistake in ignorance; to bring those who have sinned to a place of forgiveness. If you have participated in this sin, think like God, repent and He will forgive you.

God is love. All love emanates forth from His divine presence. Yet, there are many things that God hates. Seven of those things are given to us by Solomon in order that our thinking may be adjusted to think, not like the world, but like our Holy Father's. Today, we focus our attention upon just one of these principles: the shedding of "innocent blood".

Innocent blood is blood that flows through the veins of people who have committed no crimes; they have slandered no one. Innocent blood is blood that flows through the veins of people who can not speak for themselves; they have no voice; they have no choice; no vote; no platform; no defense. If you will look the world over you will find no blood more innocent that the blood of the *unborn* child.

Infanticide is not a political issue. It is a MORAL issue. It always has been. There is no new thing under the sun. The shedding of innocent blood has always been a *sin*. God punished Israel for offering their newborn babies to the false god, Molech, in the valley of Hinnom. A great brass statue was prepared to this image, heated with fire, into whose hands the baby was placed. The ceremonial drums would beat ever so loudly to drown out the screams of the innocent blood.

Pharaoh had innocent blood on his hands when he commanded the midwives to throw the male Hebrew children to their god: the Nile. Herod's hands were likewise stained with innocent blood. He commanded the death of all the children that were in Bethlehem, from two years old and under: innocent blood.

Today, modern science has made the shedding of innocent blood, not only more convenient, but also less messy. The have invented the abortion pill. I find it amazing that the FDA, an organization that was instituted to protect life, has now condoned a substance to destroy innocent blood. I agree with Solomon: "there is no new thing under the sun." They hide behind rights; choices; and dreams. No, we do not have Molech today, we have THE ECONOMY. Same god, just another name. "For this god", they say in their hearts, "let us shed some innocent blood. "

According to God, life begins at conception. John the Baptist was overshadowed by the Holy Ghost while he was in his mother's womb. I am persuaded that countless others, whose innocent blood has been shed, have been born of God's spirit as well before they were born naturally. In the 13th Psalm, David wrote, "thou hast covered me in my mother's womb". I don't know how many trimesters were involved in that statement, but he was known and loved of God before birth. If David was known as a person before birth, are not all?

It has been discovered that 95+% of all abortions are for reasons of convenience; not incest, not rape, not the physical condition of the unborn, and not the threatened health of the mother. 75% of the expectant mothers said the child would interfere with their lives.

I present to you minority thinking, thinking that is despised by the world at large. We must march to the beat of a different drummer, His name is Jesus Christ. May God have mercy upon our nation(Prov. 14:34). Lord, help us to think like thee!

Helpful Hints:
1. Talk about the moment that life begins.
2. Notice the Lord's response to this sin in the Old Testament.
3. Compare the motive of this sin in the Old Testament with today.
4. Talk about God, the giver of life.

"BROKEN FENCES"

*"For the law was given by Moses, but grace
and truth came by Jesus Christ"*
-John 1:17

Moses stood in a *precarious* position: he stood between God and His people. His job was unpopular: he must give God's people the law. If you will read the law that was given to Israel, you will understand Moses' plight. The law restricted; it laid responsibilities upon their shoulders; it represented a big NO, you can't do that! Who likes that word? Yet, maturity will tell us that NO is a word that protects and gives boundaries of safety. But, even then, it comes across a little *crass*. The law will never make us feel good. It was not designed to do so. It was given in love from a loving Father to protect His children and keep them from harm. When we see that principle we appreciate it. Allow me to illustrate God's law.

A few months ago our family was given a Labrador puppy. He has dug under the fence; ran through the fence; and opened the gate. Today he has a noticeable limp because he wandered into the street on one of his outings.

Here we come to the law. It is like the fence. It says no, "thou shalt not", yet it is for our good and protection.

Today, there are a lot of broken fences. A broken fence is different from those that stand, that we see clearly and purposely cross. A broken fence is one that is unseen. When I was growing up we had a few head of cattle. Our pasture was close by the rail-road tracks. From time to time a tree would fall across the fence and the cows would wander aimlessly on the tracks. We lost a few cows on the tracks due to broken fences. Some of God's fences have been broken today by lofty trees of this world who have forgotten their Creator. Their fallen positions have allowed many of God's people to wander innocently and ignorantly across fences to their own hurt. Let us raise them up again for the good of God's people and for the honor of Christ.

There are many helpful fences in the book of Leviticus. For example, in chapter 18, the word "nakedness" is listed 24 times. Among these fences you will find, "Thou shalt not lie with mankind, as with womankind: it is abomination". Modern psychology and science have joined hands to change the truth of God into a lie. They say that sin is no longer wrong because certain genetic traits make us what we are...we can't help what we do because of what we are. To this we agree, yet, not by genetics, but by our fallen nature. We sin because we are sinners. Adam fell spiritually, mentally, morally and genetically. Yet, there is hope for all sinners. We find God's grace and abounding love more powerful than even this sin. When Paul wrote to the church at Corinth, and "such were some of you", this sin was mentioned which rightly informs us that God is right and the psychologists and scientists are wrong. These had repented and were changed by the blood of the Lamb.

In this chapter, you will also find, "thou shalt not lie carnally with thy neighbor's wife" along with many other fences that Hollywood has broken.

As you drive along the streets you will see many dead animals that either had no fence, or broke out of a fence. You might think that the animals would look along the streets and see their kindred lying around dead and wounded and figure out the danger involved in that black ribbon of asphalt. Do we?

Many questions are raised today concerning God's law and its significance to the New Testament Christian? Are we to keep it? If so, what part, when and how much? To this we answer, "The ceremonial law has been done away with. Yet, all of God's fences remain intact today." God's moral laws, how He feels about sin and what He has said about sin have not changed. These are God's fences, not Moses'.

Today we find a freedom that was not enjoyed in the old law dispensation even though the moral law is till intact: "Grace and truth came by Jesus Christ". We have wandered. We have all been on the other side of one fence or another. Some have been afforded great grace and escaped serious injury. Some are crippled; some have lost their joy in life; some have lost their life. It is wonderful news to learn that even though we have broken the law, Jesus has fulfilled it for us. His righteousness has become ours. That is grace. Our respect for the fence today should not be one of fear, but rather one of love for the One who erected them. Our respect is in proportion to our love. When we cross the fence, we have a throne of grace to find great forgiveness. Today, we do not throw the law at God's people. We kindly raise the fence and make it noticeable. May God help us all to stay on the right side of the fence!

Helpful Hints:

1. Go through Leviticus and discuss God's moral law.

2. Discuss how our society tries to deny these laws.

3. Talk about repentance and the repentant at Corinth.

4. Talk about the impact these broken fences have had on our society, our school, our homes and our country.

"THE ATTITUDE OF PRAISE"

"But ye are a chosen generation, a royal priesthood, an holy nation, a peculiar people; that ye should shew forth the praises of him who hath called you out of darkness into his marvellous light"-1 Peter 2:9

To the scattered strangers, Peter sends words of great *encouragement.* He reminds them, that even though they are scattered and persecuted, they still have reason to rejoice: they are chosen, elected to live with God in glory; they no longer need a high priest to offer sacrifices, they are of royal lineage and can offer spiritual sacrifices themselves; they have been made holy by the blood of Christ; all of which sets them apart from the world in a special and peculiar way. Thus, even in their present plight, they should show the world their riches by their attitude........ the attitude of praise.

This attitude of praise is of great importance to God's people. It is an expression of Christ, what He has done for us and our appreciation of His person and gifts. It is one of the things that the world should see in God's people.

I was thinking about this subject while watching a basketball game a few nights ago. On my way home

I thought, "What do we remember most about a game? Is it the score? Who won? What their mascot was? The color of their uniforms? No, we remember the attitude of the participants." I have seen teams lose who impressed the crowds because of their attitudes. I have seen teams win who seemed that they lost because of their attitudes. As Christians, we wear a uniform. It is observed by the community; our children; the enemies of Christ; and God Himself. The early Christians wore it in the arenas when they were thrown to wild beasts and burned at the stake. In times of discouragement, heartache, offenses, struggles, challenges and yes, even losses, the attitude of praise is the jersey to wear. It must be possible or Peter would never have encouraged such behavior from scattered and persecuted strangers.

Attitudes are *addictive*. The attitude of praise lifts the spirits of those who come in contact with people affected with it. It can go through a crowd; a family; a church. It warms the cold heart and refreshes the spirit. It is a balm of Gilead displayed only by *peculiar* people.

By word picture, God has given many worshipful attitudes for His people to catch: (1) David's positive attitude: I Samuel 17:36; (2) Abraham's loving attitude: Genesis 13:8; (3) Joshua's dedicated attitude: Joshua 24:15; (4) Job's submissive attitude: Job 13:15; (5) Caleb's encouraging attitude: Numbers 13:30; (6) Paul's charitable attitude: Acts 20:35; (7) Timothy's determined attitude: II Timothy 2:3; (8) Paul's long-suffering attitude: Philippians 4:12. All of these, and many more, may be found in the person of Jesus Christ. He alone wears the coat of many colors. If we are to emulate Christ in our daily conversation, it is certain that the attitude of praise must be found. Lord, in every situation, help us to put on Christ and wear the attitude of praise!

Helpful Hints:

1. Discuss areas that we can alter our attitudes: around the house; at work; at school and in God's house.

2. Who do we notice that has this kind of attitude?

3. Discuss ways that we may praise the Lord in our prayer.

4. Read some of the prayers of the Bible and notice the praise used by the attendants.

5. Notice the praise used in the psalms.

6. Study the 8 attitudes listed.

"STORMS"

"And there arose a great storm of wind, and the waves beat into the ship, so that it was now full"-Mark 4:37

Here we find the disciples in circumstances that we will find ourselves in from time to time: they were in a *storm*. Life is full of storms: big ones, little ones, short ones, long ones, dark ones, scary ones and sometimes endless ones! This one was a "great storm of wind". As experienced seamen, they had done all they could do. Panic and fear gripped them. They go for the Master.

The mariner well knows the storm. Even on a good day, a dark cloud can arise and cover the sun in just a few minutes. And though it may be sunny just a few miles away, under the cloud, everything seems black and dangerous. What difference does it make if things are clear and beautiful everywhere else if the lightning is real and the waves are raging under the cloud? The feeling of helplessness creeps in to the best of men! Such are the storms of life. Things become cloudy and dark; the future is doubtful; fearful thunders roar up in our ears and a feeling of helplessness penetrates our hearts.

There is a lot that we may *learn* from storms. That was the purpose of this particular storm, to teach the disciples. A pop quiz you might say. Let us learn with them.

JESUS COMES

There are a lot of storms in the Bible. Jonah was cast overboard in a storm prepared by God. Paul was shipwrecked in the great storm, "Euroclydon". In one place, we find Jesus sitting on the mountain as He watched the disciples toiling and rowing to get out of a storm and here we find Him asleep in the ship with his disciple in a storm. As I consider these storms, there is one principle that I find great comfort in: I can not find a storm in which God abandoned His disciples. The Lord always came to the aid of his disciples!

JESUS SOUGHT AS A LAST RESORT

Do we not see a reflection of ourselves in the disciples? Though they were followers of Christ, they waited until the boat was "full" before they sought the Master. Why did they wait so long? Many reasons may be suggested. Pride can keep us from Him. "We are mariners, we can handle this one", I can hear them say. Strong people, those who say they are strong, are many times weakest in the storm because they try to handle it alone. He who slew Goliath would say, "Have mercy upon me, O LORD; for I am weak: O LORD, heal me; for my bones are vexed"- Psalm 6:2. From life's experiences, David knew the source of his strength. He did not face Goliath alone. Jehovah's hand guided the stone and sped it on its way. An unction from the Holy Spirit gave David his strength.

Perhaps the disciples did not want to trouble the Master with such a *trivial* matter. After all, He was in the ship and they did not want to seem faithless. They would not seek him unless things got out of hand. Many times, that is our case. He is our *last* resort. We may boast that there is nothing too big for the Lord, yet we are prone to forget that there is likewise no matter too *small*. The Lord takes delight in sharing every detail of our lives.

They expected the worse: "carest not that we perish". It is the propensity of mankind to expect the worse. They went from handling it themselves to perishing in a matter of minutes. Yet, who can perish when the creator of the universe is at hand?

They doubted His care: "carest not". Again, this is our own experience. We can see how God would care for the Apostles, for the patriarchs of old, but for us, we wonder. Peter learned that He did care. Later he wrote, "Casting all your care upon him; for he careth for you"-1Peter 5:7. Big cares, little cares, all cares are to be cast upon the shoulders of the great bearer of burdens. His invitation remains to be open to fearful marines of life: "Come unto me".

TALK TO JESUS

Why was Jesus asleep in the midst of the storm? Surely, He was not worried. The storm was His own teaching device. We find Him in a solitary place, asleep. He is always in control, even in the darkest storm. Though we know it on paper, we must remember it in our storm. Lord, help us to remember Jesus in our storm!

Helpful Hints:
1. Share your storms and pray together.
2. Note: these men were disciples, personally with Jesus and yet were afraid.
3. Talk about what they learned in this storm.

4. Talk about the other storms mentioned: the Lord's faithfulness, what was learned by those in the midst of the storms and the results of their ministries upon others.
5. Share personal storms and what was learned.

"UNTO THEE, O GOD, DO WE GIVE THANKS"

(THOUGHTS ON THAKNSGIVING DAY IN AMERICA)

"Unto thee, O God, do we give thanks, unto thee do we give thanks: for that thy name is near thy wondrous works declare"-Psalm 75:1

Years ago, a man received a wonderful gift. His college tuition was paid by an unknown source. Though he had several ideas concerning the source of the gift, he never really knew the identity of the person who cared enough for his future to bestow such a valuable gift. Thus, as the circumstances dictated, he was unable to properly thank his benefactor. God's people are not found in such a circumstance. If our eyes are open and our hearts are in tune to the giver of every good and perfect gift, we know well the source of our blessings and comforts: "Unto thee, O God, do we give thanks".

THANKSGIVING DAY: INITIALLY A WORSHIP DAY

If you have a good encyclopedia and it remains untouched by the evil mind you will find recorded therein: "Thanksgiving Day is a day set aside each year for giving thanks to God for blessings received during the year. They were entirely religious and did not involve feasting." We will also learn that the first Thanksgiving Days in New England were harvest festivals, dedicated to thanking God for plentiful crops. For this reason, the holiday still takes place late in the fall, after the crops have been gathered. Where do you suppose they came up with such an idea, to have a festival, or harvest Thanksgiving? They got it from the Bible!

The third of the great annual feasts that Israel celebrated was called the Feast of Booths also known as The Feast of Ingathering. It was held after the ingathering of harvest, the same time the Pilgrims first observed our Thanksgiving. It was held to thank God for the ingathering of the "fruit of the earth" and their freedom from Egyptian bondage. Thus, the Pilgrims were found thanking God, not only for their freedom to worship God according to the dictates of their own conscience, but also for the provisions they so desperately needed. THANKS!

RIGHTEOUSNESS EXALTS A NATION AND THEIR GOD

How is it, that a group of Pilgrims, with scanty provisions could land in an unknown and uncivilized country and become the most powerful nation in the world? Solomon had it right when he wrote, "Righteousness exalteth a nation: but sin is a reproach to any people"- Proverbs 14:34. The first settlers of this nation were not perfect people, yet, they believed and loved God and His Son, Jesus Christ. Let us not allow modern historians to paint any other picture. These settlers were not successful because of their luck, their physical stamina or even their ability. God, by His kind hand of providence made a way for these people because of *righteous intentions*.

Have you considered that the power and glory of this nation reflect God's sovereignty and His ability to exalt a nation when and where He pleases? It does not exalt man, politicians or even modern technology. It has shown the whole world that God can take a little rag tag bunch of settlers and exalt them to become the most powerful and influential people in the world. Surely, he did that with Abraham's seed as we see the power of David's army and the splendor of Solomon's kingdom. Righteousness exalteth a nation. Let us bow before our great Lord who has exalted Himself in blessing His people and thank Him for His watch-care over us.

At its conception, Thanksgiving was designed to give "thanks" to God for His blessings. Let us teach this great truth to our children lest they rise up and forget the source of their blessings. God's arm and not man's has exalted us. Unto thee, O God, do we give thanks!

Helpful Hints:
1. Read about the beginning of Thanksgiving in our country and how the Lord was honored.
2. Notice how God's people in the Old Testament thanked God for their blessings.
3. Write you blessings down on a piece of paper.
4. Talk about your greatest blessings.
5. Talk about how we can be more thankful.
6. Talk about the Godly founders of our country.

"THE 3 O'S OF GOD"
Omnipresence, Omnipotence, Omniscience

The fundamentals of our secular education used to involve three basic subjects: reading, writing and arithmetic. A basic understanding of these principles provided a solid platform for other subjects. Concerning God, there are three fundamental attributes of His divine person from which we may build a solid platform for our doctrine and practice. These are: Omnipresence, Omnipotence, and Omniscience.

OMNIPRESENCE

Omnipresence means that God is everywhere present and nowhere absent. It means that God not only exists eternally, it also means that He occupies every facet of time and space. There is an old story of a little boy who showed a great interest and knowledge in the things of God. Several of the men of the church decided they would get together and ask the little boy some questions and offer him a reward if he could answer them properly. They asked him, "Where would you say God is right now? If you give the correct answer we will give you this orange." The little boy thought a moment and replied, "If you can tell me where God is not, I will give you two oranges."

This is an awesome thought. Wherever we are, wherever we have been, where ever we shall be, God is. This is exactly what David wrote in the 139th Psalm as he viewed the three positions of God in his life: past, future and present: "Thou hast beset me behind and before, and laid thine hand upon me." Though it is a comfort to be assured of His everlasting presence in times of trials and difficulties, yet it is humbling to know that He is present even when we sin. Surely, this is a thought provoking attribute when we apply it to our own lives.

OMNIPOTENT

Omnipotent means *all powerful.* The Bible begins by describing God as omnipotent: He created the heaven and the earth. That's power! The Psalmist declares that God does what He wants when He wants, "But our God is in the heavens: he hath done whatsoever he hath pleased." He has power to give life and to take it. Christ laid down His life and took it up again! He has the voice to raise the dead; to calm the sea; to convict of sin; to stop the hands of time; and command the forces of nature.

Speaking of Christ, the writer of Hebrews declared that the universe is held together by Him, "Who being the brightness of his glory, and the express image of his person, and upholding all things by the word of his power". He is Omnipotent!

OMNISCIENT

Omniscient means that God is *all knowing*. We can not introduce God to anything. He looks upon our hearts. He knows our thoughts. He knows what is on our tongues. David wrote, "O Lord, thou hast searched me, and known me. Thou knowest my downsitting and mine uprising, thou understandest my thought afar off. Thou compassest my path and my lying down, and art acquainted with all my ways. For there is not a word in my tongue, but lo, O Lord, thou knowest it altogether"-Psalm 139. God knows who is going to heaven. Isaiah wrote, "He shall see of the travail of his soul, and shall be satisfied: by his knowledge shall my righteous servant justify many; for he shall bear their iniquites"-Isaiah 53:11. Jesus did not go to the cross an ignorant God. He knew His *elect*. His is satisfied because their sins have been atoned. Do you see how the three O's affect our thinking? What a wonderful platform for our doctrine and practice!

Helpful Hints:
1. Talk about God!!
2. Consider these attributes in salvation.
3. Consider the complete harmony of the Godhead.
4. Talk about how these attributes affect the doctrine of the Church.

"THE CHRISTIAN'S INNER CONFLICT"

"For that which I do I allow not: for what I would, that do I not; but what I hate, that do I.....O wretched man that I am! Who shall deliver me from the body of this death? I thank God through Jesus Christ our Lord"- Romans 7:15,24,25

Have you ever tried to live up to the law only to find that you can not? Have you found yourself trying to get good enough to merit the blessings of heaven only to realize that if you were given a thousand lifetimes you could never get to a place that you could say, "I have attained, I am ready to stand before the judge of all the earth." As hard as we try, there are still doubts, fears, struggles and frustrations within. If this is your case, you have great reason to rejoice for this is where the apostle Paul finds himself in Romans 7 as he describes "The Christian's Inner Conflict."

CONFLICT

Over one-hundred years ago, Spurgeon said, "Conflict is the principle part of Christianity this side of heaven." I believe every Christian, to a degree, experiences conflict. Yet, even here, we find great consolation. Where there is conflict, there is feeling and where there is feeling there is life. I remember the story of the doctor and the patient who was thought to have lost all feeling in his lower extremities. As the doctor probed the foot with a sharp needle to find signs of life a crutch landed upon his head. His conclusion: life in the patient's foot.... and the doctor's head! Where pain is experienced there is life!

If we will notice the apostle's language, we can identify with his struggle: "For that which I do I allow not". In other words, "I do things that my conscience does not allow. I am not always in control of my mind and my actions". Paul is not saying that he is totally out of control. He is not saying that he gives himself up to his lusts and feelings. He is saying he can't be as good as he would like to be....the perfection he knows to be true he can not attain. Though the Christian mind can think ungodly thoughts, lose control of the tongue, allow pride to rise up in the heart, look upon things that they should not look upon and find themselves cold and indifferent towards God and His people they continue the fight......conflict.

Paul goes on to say, "for what I would, that do I not; but what I hate, that do I". What is Paul now saying? He looks at his duties and finds the same failings. He can't do everything that he should be doing!

WHEN IT BEGAN

There was a time in the life of Paul that he could say, "touching the righteousness which is in the law, blameless"-Phil. 3:6. As a Pharisee Paul saw himself as perfect as a human could be. He was perfectly satisfied with his religion, his friends and himself. He had no inner struggle, even as he put Christians to death. In his eyes, he was blameless. When did all of this come to an end? When he met Jesus! That is when he saw himself in Christ's light. That is when his conflict started. That is when we begin to get better!

CONSOLATION

Paul goes from conflict to confession to consolation. In his inward struggle, Paul came to the place that he must confess, "O wretched man that I am! who shall deliver me from the body of this death?". I do some things I should not do, I do not do some of the things that I should do and I can't keep the law to a jot and a tittle! I have great inward struggle in trying to do so! He was honest. He could not attain(see Phil.3:12,13). Where did he find his consolation? In the person of the great law keeper, Jesus Christ, "I thank God through Jesus Christ our Lord." Though he could not keep the law, his faith and hope was in One who kept the law for him. His writing and preaching was centered around this great truth. Salvation is by the grace of God in the person of Jesus Christ. Have you found Him?

Helpful Hints:
1. Consider this struggle.
2. What things should you do?
3. What things should you not do?
4. Consider the Pharisees!

"THE PEARL OF GREAT PRICE"

"Again, the kingdom of heaven is like unto a merchant man, seeking goodly pearls: Who, when he had found one pearl of great price, went and sold all that he had, and bought it"
-Matthew 13:45-46

While there are many treasures to be enjoyed in the Lord's kingdom, there is One token of delight to be adored above all others…..that is the person of the Lord Jesus Christ. When jewelers fashion a ring, they set the most valuable and brilliant gem in the forefront to catch the attention and praise of the admirer, so Christ is set in His Church. Martha was troubled about "many things", but Mary was focused on "that good part"…..she sought the pearl. Many doctrines, traditions and ordinances are important in the Church, but what are they but lesser stones that garnish the most beautiful treasure. The focus of the kingdom is not all of those things, but rather a relationship, a valuable relationship, a relationship that provides us riches that we could never imagine. Jesus is he pearl of great price!

THE VALUE OF CHRIST IN OUR LIVES

In 1905, a man by the name of Kokichi Mikimoto changed the pearl industry forever. He developed the art of cultured pearls. Before that time only royalty could afford them. Wars were fought over them and kingdoms established by them. Montezuma's hoard of pearls attracted the eye of Cortez as much as his gold. Rumors of pearl treasure in Britain encouraged Julius Caesar to invade. According to one story, Maisie Platt swapped her Fifth Avenue mansion for a large strand of pearls valued at $1.2 million that Jacques Cartier revealed to her. Royals of old kept score among themselves, not by their gold, but by the splendor of their pearls. And in the eighteenth and nineteenth centuries, the necklaces of matched sea pearls worn by the Romanov royal women caused their European cousins to become envious of their treasure. The number of matched pearls constituting one necklace was greatly appreciated by the number of trips it would take to the ocean floor to obtain them. Before the invention of scuba and diving gear, and entire career of a pearl diver could expect to retrieve only four or five perfectly matched pearls. Many of those royal strands contained over 200 matched pearls! When our Lord spoke these words, pearls were of inestimable valuable. Thus we observe the value of our Lord Jesus to His own.

SEEKERS

In our parable, we have a noble person. He is a seeker. He is like many others, something is missing in his life. He has tried on the world and is yet lacking in satisfaction. He has been seeking "goodly pearls", good people who display the fruits of God's spirit, people that set examples for us that we desire to live up to. Or, perhaps, he is seeking something more in his religion. Something is missing and he seeks. Christian, have we not found this to be true? Until we fount the living Christ, something was missing….an aching void that could be filled by no other person, place or thing. This is genuine Christianity. When Christ is formed in the soul and when religion is no more a task, but rather a joy!

Surely, then, we understand what he then did: "He sold all that he had, and bought it". The relationship of this pearl had *priority* in the seeker's life. How is it with you today? Have you sold all to obtain this pearl? Is He more important than the sports events, the entertainment, the lusts and pleasures of this world? Do you place Him above all your traditions and ordinances? His reward is great. When the Lord is first in our lives, we will elevate every other relationship as we become better fathers, mothers, pastors, children, and etc. We must remember His promise: if we seek we shall find. This Sunday morning what will you be seeking? Is there a day that we are prohibited from seeking? Lord, help us to lead others to Thee!

Helpful Hints:
1. Have you found this Pearl? Share your story.
2. What are the things we must sell to obtain it!
3. What would the ordinance and traditions be without Him?
4. Talk about those in the New Testament who found Him and what they sold!

"REJOICING WITH CHRIST"

"In that hour Jesus rejoiced in spirit, and said, I thank thee, O Father, Lord of heaven and earth, that thou has hid these things from the wise and prudent, and hast revealed them unto babes: even so, Father; for so it seemed good in thy sight"-Luke 10:21

Search the scriptures diligently and you will find few occasions where the man of sorrows is found in the posture of *rejoicing*. As the beautiful rainbow pierces the dark sky between storms, Christ's rejoicing colors the darkness of the wrath to come that hovers around Him. A delightful, yet rare occasion, so rare that something very important is being demonstrated. Let us rejoice with Him!

OUR REASON FOR REJOICING

If you will notice, Jesus is thanking the Father for spiritual *blindness* on one hand and for *revelation* on the other! Strange as it may seem, the Father has chosen to hide the person of Christ and His truths from the "wise and prudent" as He reveals the significance of Christ and His cross to "babes". This is *divine* sovereignty!

THE WISE AND PRUDENT

Who are the wise and the prudent? Are they people who make an income over a particular level? Are they those who have impressive diplomas hanging on their wall? Are they people who possess brain power, such as Einstein? No. The Bible does not describe them in this way. They are those for whom the preaching of Christ's cross has this effect upon them: "the preaching of the cross is to them that perish foolishness". That is simple. These wise and prudent see the preaching of the cross as foolishness. They hate the cross of Christ and in doing so they shall perish. They are so wise in their esteem of themselves and their knowledge, and so prudent in their choice of friends, that Christ's cross is silly and absurd. In other words, they are simply left to themselves. They are left where all of mankind would have been left if it were not for God's choice in choosing a people and saving them by His grace. Atonement means nothing to the wise and prudent, their sins have never come up before them and there is no need for a cross; no fear of God before their eyes; no love for their Saviour; no evidence of grace in their lives. They despise "Babes" and hiss at their Lamb. Unknowingly, they are slaves to their dark master as they endeavor to tear down every thing that exalts Christ and His cross. They are above such nonsense, yet they place themselves beneath such wisdom(Mat 11:19).

At first, this seems like a paradox. We are to preach the cross, yet there are those that God will hide our message from. Is God fair to do such a thing? We must learn this…..God does not have to reveal Himself to anyone! He is sovereign in election, in predestination, in redemption and in revelation. It is by design, by His divine wisdom, that He is hidden in His own creation and He will reveal Himself to whoever He pleases(Luke 10:22;Mat. 11:27).

By denying God, they deny the only power that can open their eyes and demonstrate what they are by nature. They reveal themselves and make God out to be the only true and wise Creator. Paul wrote it this way, "the world by wisdom knew not God". Man, can neither prove nor disprove the existence of God by telescopes, space ships, test tubes, chemicals, digging, diving or any other natural means. God designed it this way so that man could not, nor will ever, boast that he came to know God by himself. God reveals Himself!

Simply put, a "babe" is a child of God, one to whom God has revealed His wonderful person unto. The cross has meaning to them because it is the means to and end: the salvation of their souls.

Helpful Hints:
1. Notice the different responses to Paul's messages.
2. Notice the biblical accounts of the wise and prudent in the sect of the Pharisees, Sadducees and the Roman powers.
3. Consider the sovereignty of God in His revelation of Himself.
4. In election!

"THE PRAYER OF THE AGED BELIEVER"
"Now also when I am old and grayheaded, O God, forsake me not;"-Psalm71:18a

Much is said today about the youth, yet, in the midst of tutoring our young we can make the grave mistake of forgetting the backbone of many of our churches, those faithful ones who have witnessed many seasons in God's house: the "old and grayheaded."

It seems to be a universal thought among the young that the hoary head has it all together, they have no problems; no struggles; no worries; no fears; and no confusion of face. Yet, the psalmist presets the truth of the matter: when natural strength is waning, when the nest is empty, when pipe dreams are past, when the looking glass is less kind to features, when friends are dispersed into their various places, when many loved ones have passed on to the other shore, the companionship of God is needed more than ever.

Yes, companionship is the psalmist's most urgent cry: "Forsake me not". Many are the companions of youth, yet to the aged, their own dwelling place can seem like a prison. Poor health and lack of strength are the bars and loneliness is the warden. Only He that dwelleth between the Cherubims can fill the aching void.

Apparently, the psalmist had been in this prison and his pen exposes many keys of comfort to unlock the prison of the aged believer. The first verse of this psalm discovers a great trap that Satan will set for the aged believer and the psalmist petitions Jehovah for deliverance from its snare: "Let me never be put to confusion". Surely, it is confusion to think that God has forsaken His beloved child. As one old preacher said, "This is the sharpest arrow in Satan's quiver". What could be worse, especially for the aged believer. Yet, it is a common experience for every age. Our Lord experienced the shaft as he cried, "My God, my God, why hast thou forsaken me?" His disciples experience it. Yet, as the old preacher went on to say, "That, my friends, is a barefaced lie". The promise to his chosen is, "I will never leave the, nor forsake thee"-Heb. 13:5. God's never is NEVER, even in old age.

The word *hope* is mentioned twice in the psalm. Hope is the balm of Gilead to the aged believer. Hope is the expectation and anticipation of a promise made. It was hope in the bosom of Abraham that gave him strength to continue as a stranger and a pilgrim in his wilderness wanderings as he "looked for a city which hath foundations, whose builder and maker is God." Though still in the wilderness, his eye anticipated a better place.

This psalm is pregnant with prayer and praise. These are the themes of a jail cell. Consider Paul and Silas. Even the aged believer can forget to feed his own soul by prayer and praise.

And finally, the eye is turned from inward affliction to outward testimony: "until I have shewed thy strength unto this generation, and thy power to every one that is to come". God's honor and Zion's future became the psalmist's most urgent plea. The outward testimony of the aged believer is an encouragement to all, sure evidence of God's faithfulness and His power to uphold us, even in old age.

Helpful Hints:
1. Consider the challenges of the aged in your family and church.
2. How may we help them?
3. Name some faithful disciples among them.
4. Consider some of them in the Bible.

"A FATHER'S ANSWER"

"Hear, ye children, the instruction of a father, and attend to know understanding."- Proverbs 4:1

Many are the answers that a father must give. Some are difficult. Some will challenge dad to find *acceptable words* that will not only instruct, but will convict the conscience as well. I was recently blessed to hear a father give a heartrending answer to a well beloved son who asked his dad the following question: "Dad, what is so wrong with tattoos and body piercing." Here was his reply: "Son, you know that I love you. You are special gift from God. You are made in the image of God(Genesis 1:27). There never has been, nor will there ever be another person just like you. You are a very handsome boy. There will never be another person that looks just like you. Your soul is unique. This gives you a unique personality that is different and diverse from any person who will ever live. God has given you a good mind. Millions of people do not have that. You have a healthy body, you are able to enjoy many activities. Many people do not have a body like that. Millions of people are born without arms or legs. When you stop and think about it, God has blessed you far above millions of other people. Not only that, the Bible says that your body is a temple of the Holy Ghost(1Cor 6:19). That means that God's Spirit abides within you. It also says that your body is not your own. It was bought with a price, the blood of Jesus. He has asked you to not only honor Him with your spirit, but also with your body(v20). God is very interested with what you do with that temple. Now, Satan knows all of this. He sees all of the special blessings that your Lord has showered down upon you that you may use to represent Him. He sees the loving and kind favor that has been extended to you from a loving Father. Satan also knows that one of the best ways that he can get you to spit in God's face for all of this kindness is to encourage you to defile the very temple wherein He dwells. How would you feel if you woke up tomorrow morning and someone had taken a can of spray paint and marked up our house or hammered a few spikes in it? God loves you and has highly favored you. For all of His kindness and favors, He asks you to honor His temple."

The instruction was biblical. It made me think of the Baal worshipers in the old testament and how they affected God's people with the same fads. Truly, there is nothing new under the sun. The instigators of these evils are well aware that the root of their activities are from dark days when God would warn His people, "Ye shall not make any cuttings in your flesh for the dead, nor print any marks upon you: I am the Lord." The Lord would not have His people identify themselves with the Canaanites. Their marks and cuttings identified the god that they served. Surely, many have followed the fad in ignorance. Today, we identify the source of it all for those who would honor God in spite of popularity. I witnessed the effect that this loving message had upon the child. The boy was evidently a born again believer who wanted to honor God.

Helpful Hints:

1. Talk about how body piercing and tattoos resemble the worshipers of false deities in the Old Testament days.

2. Talk about our bodies being the temple of the Holy Ghost.

3. An excellent opportunity to talk about abortion.

4. Peer Pressure!!

5. Shining our light!

"A LIVELY HOPE"

"Blessed be the God and Father of our Lord Jesus Christ, which according to his abundant mercy hath begotten us again unto a lively hope by the resurrection of Jesus Christ from the dead"
-1 Peter 1:3

Many years ago, a battle was fought. It was the greatest battle that had ever occurred since the world began. The captain of one army evaluated his enemy, a great opposing force. He looked at his own army and knew there was no chance for his army to win. It would be like sending little children to fight giants or matching swords and spears against a nuclear arsenal. So, one day, unknown to his own troops, he marched off to battle and faced the enemy alone. Though he was just one warrior, the enemy used every diabolical device in their arsenal. They knew the death of this great champion would mean certain victory for them. As they had hoped, the warrior was killed. As his body was laid to rest the enemy smiled, considering the millions of captured souls that would become their dupes and slaves. But something unexpected happened. Just 3 days after the great warrior was placed in his grave…..
he arose, walked about, spoke to his soldiers, comforted

them, reassured them, and gave them the greatest treasure that can lie in the bosom of any soldier: hope, a vision of a great and certain victory with an anticipation of the full reward of it. That great warrior was Jesus Christ. As we write, He continues with His comforts, spreading the news of victory throughout his ranks. If you have read the last chapter of His book, you will find Him revealed as the enthroned King, victorious over His enemies, with all of His soldiers around him!

Paul blew His victory trumpet as he wrote: "O death, where is thy sting? O grave, where is thy victory?" Death's stinger has been spent. A bee whose stinger has been used may scare us, yet do us no harm. His poison has been used on another. He must fly away and die himself. Death's stinger has found its place in one who rose from the grave, a conqueror over his venom. The grave has no victory for the Captain of our salvation nor for the least of His soldiers. Though they face the monster death, it has no hold upon the redeemed possession. It shall….it must, follow its Commander home.

There have been many great commanders of conquest: Alexander the Great, Washington, Patton. Yet, none of their men could say of their leader what Paul said of Christ: "We are more than conquerors through him that loved us." How can one be more than a conqueror? First of all, Jesus has "loved us". He knows us personally. Thus He is cognizant of our needs. Though these men were great soldiers, the frailty of their humanity could not love or care for their soldiers as individually and personally as Christ cares for His.

Secondly, none of the soldiers of Christ have been lost in battle. At the victory celebration we find them all present and accounted for as the book is opened and the roll is called. Finally, the most interesting part of being "More than a conqueror" is the fact that the victory was won entirely by the Captain. He trod the winepress alone.

"A lively hope" gave Peter the strength to go on. It is greatly needed by the soldiers of Christ's today as much as ever. Not only at the hour of death, but during the hours of life. Much opposition is around us and the knowledge of our resurrected captain encourages the weary and war worn soul that our battle has an expected end. When our focus is on our Captain, our hope remains lively.

Helpful Hints:
1. Consider the Captain of our salvation!
2. Talk about the value of hope.
3. Talk about how faith and hope work together.
4. Consider the complete victory believers have in Christ.

"FATHER: THE SPIRITUAL LEADER OF THE HOME"

"And if it seem evil unto you to serve the LORD, choose you this day whom ye will serve; whether the gods which your fathers served that were on the other side of the flood, or the gods of the Amorites, in whose land ye dwell: but as for me and my house, we will serve the LORD"-JOSHUA 24:15

The primary responsibility of a father is to be the *spiritual leader* of the home. This was Joshua's theme, the focus of his life. When his life was over, his greatest desire was to leave this world with children who would become salt and light.

Not too long ago, a survey was conducted with over 700 high school students asking their thoughts on the ten most desirable qualities of a father. At the top of the list was found, owning a good looking car. The list went on like this in descending order: being prominent in social life, making plenty of money, never nagging their children about what they should do and respecting their children's opinions.

Answers similar to these would probably have been found in Joshua's day had they taken a poll of their children. As I read over the survey I could not help thinking how easy that we, as fathers, can either forget or neglect our primary role in the home and the answers to the survey are, in reality, the fatherly role image projected in the eyes of many children. It is easy to fall into the trap of trying to make children happy with *things* rather than God. This is the challenge of a "spiritual leader".

If you will carefully notice Joshua's words you discover that Joshua must get his priorities right first: "As for me". Ah, Joshua must first serve the Lord before he can lead his own family. There are many fathers who desire their children to live godly lives. They would like for their offspring to confess Christ and walk in righteous paths. Yet, the image they project is a contradiction to their own lifestyle. I have known some that would say they are embarrassed to talk to their children about Jesus Christ and not flinch as they sat with their children and watched ungodly acts on television while drinking an adult beverage. Surely this is evidence of their own love for Christ. "As for me" must come first!

If a father is the spiritual leader of his own house he must know something about the word of God *himself.* To the father's of Ephesus Paul instructs: "And, ye fathers, provoke not your children to wrath: but bring them up in the nurture and admonition of the Lord"-6:4. People nurture their plants, their gardens and even their dogs. What about their sons and daughters. *Nurture* means *under the care of.....*under the care of the Lord. *Admonition* means *calling attention to.....*calling attention to the Lord and His word. Thus, for the spiritual leader he may say to his children: "it is not my opinion, it is God's." Apparently, the men of Corinth were shirking this responsibility as many fathers do today. It seems that the fault is universal to fatherhood. Fathers would rather be worshiped by owning nice cars, by their wealth or even by their macho accomplishments than to be known by their offspring as spiritual leaders. Paul rebuked the men by saying: "Quit ye like men"(I Corinth. 16:3). That means, "act the part of a real man." Television and popular advertisements give the idea that being a man is drinking, fighting, hunting, fishing and carousing abound. But a real man is not under the control and power of these things. God's man is a spiritual leader. I am persuaded that this role is the most difficult feat that any real man can accomplish. In the eyes of God it is greater than becoming a king or a millionaire. It is available to every believing father, yet it may only be achieved by the grace of God. Let us pray for fathers today and ask God to help us fulfill our God given role as the "spiritual leader" of the home.

Helpful Hints:
1. **Talk about this responsibility of fatherhood.**
2. **How may we do better???**
3. **How may our families help us?**
4. **The impact upon our society!**
5. **What children really need.**
6. **Discuss Joshua's plight.**

"WHEN I WAS IN DISTRESS"

"Hear me when I call, O God of my righteousness: thou hast enlarged me when I was in distress; have mercy upon me, and hear my prayer"-Psalm 4:1

Distress may come in many ways. Break the word down and its end is *stress*. Pressure, worries, fears, disappointments, heartaches sickness and fear have always been the soul hunters of God's people throughout the ages. Some come from our own sin and neglect. Others are the byproduct of a depraved society. Surely, these are not new. David had experienced his portion in the land of the living. His pen speaks of present and past experiences of distress. Yet his pen is not one of surrender. It paints a vivid picture of hope and encouragement.....even in times of distress. As he considered his present plight, and called upon God to hear his complaint, a former experience came to light. As he spoke, God sent him a kind reminder of a miraculous event that occurred the last time he approached the most High in such a state: He came out of it "enlarged"!

Naturally speaking, prosperity should come when the birds are singing, the sun is shining and everything seems to be going our way. So far as natural prosperity is concerned, this is usually the case. Yet David sets before us a paradox. He has been enlarged and his borders have grown at a most unlikely time....."when I was in distress."

How was David enlarged? When we are in distress it seems we are losing ground, wasting precious time and opportunities. The dark clouds and rainy days seem to be wasted days that could be better spent in some sunny corner of the world where cares and troubles do not exist. Yet, how needful is the rain which may only fall from dark and thundering threatening skies. His enlargement was of a spiritual nature. He grew closer to his Lord.

Seldom will we find one enlarged *spiritually* when the barns are full and prosperity knocks at the door. Though no one will ask for it, want it or enjoy it, distress is the pruning instrument in the hand of the husbandman. No matter how good the vine may be, it must be pruned that it may bring forth abundant fruit. When do we find ourselves most on our knees? Is it not in times of greatest distress? The ship must begin to sink in the storm before the disciples will remember their Master asleep in the hold. The example is figurative of our inattentive behavior until times of greatest need. Jesus desires to be on deck with us at all times and many storms are sent our way to renew our fellowship with the one who can calm the sea and the wind with just a word. Perhaps some distress or storm has left an indelible and lasting impression on our heart and even in our lives. Yet, most who have traveled the valley of the shadow of death have found that the benefit outweighs the pain. We have been enlarged spiritually and reminded that the Shepherd is near, our head is anointed and our cup truly runneth over.

Enlarged borders offer us some precious advantages. Our opportunities to minister and witness to others has grown. We have more compassion on others in distress. The borders of Zion are enlarged as we lead others to the source of our strength and comfort. David's thought is endless in opportunities and encouragement as it sets our hearts to seeking God's will in times of distress.

Helpful Hints:
1. How is our prayer life?
2. Consider what we have learned in distress.
3. Consider answered prayers.
4. Unanswered ones to our benefit.

"ETERNAL LOVE"

"For I am persuaded, that neither death, nor life, nor angels, nor principalities, nor powers, nor things present, nor things to come, Nor height, nor depth, nor any other creature, shall be able to separate us from the love of God, which is in Christ Jesus our Lord"-Romans 8:38,39

Christian, do you know and understand the *eternal* love that God has for His people? The understanding of God's love was Paul's greatest comfort and joy because he felt himself to be the chief of sinners. He knew he was capable of falling into gross sin (1 Corinthians 9:27). He knew he could not live above sin and that sin plagued him every day (Romans 7). He struggled with fears (2 Corinthians 7:5). Yet, he was persuaded that God was faithful (1 Thessalonians 5:24). We have heard the doctrine of saved today and lost tomorrow. Perhaps this false doctrine is taught to keep people on the straight and narrow. But we believe as Paul. To one who has had a genuine experience of grace, the Love that God freely bestows upon undeserving sinners is the most powerful force to keep our feet on the straight and narrow. Let others preach works, we will be as Paul and stay on the love of God as our theme. Yet, knowing that the soul is cast down from time to time and the weary worn pilgrim is made to doubt their experience, Paul writes of the eternal and unending love that our heavenly Father has for His children. Paul's list is exhaustive, showing us that there is nothing, absolutely nothing that could sever this love. If the great apostle was "persuaded" that God's love for His people is eternal, that it could never be severed, should we not be persuaded as well? Just look at the list that Paul has given us.

"Neither death".…..No matter how one might die, God's love can not be altered. I read an ancient story about the persecution of the early Christians. One of the evil designs of their enemies was to torture the Christian until they were in such agony and confusion of mind that they would deny their Lord. The very instant the words came out of their mouth down came the axe. Perhaps some of the church membership at Rome had died such a death. Even Paul caused the Christians to "blaspheme" as he wasted the Church of God. Yet, he too, learned of God's eternal love for His people and comforted others in it. The tiny infant who will never see the light of day is just as secure in this love as the greatest Saint recorded in God's word. Death has no power to alter God's love!

"Nor life".…..Here we find Paul painting a broad stroke with his brush. Yet, it is just as true as death. If it were not so, then let us die today that our eternity might be secure! It would be a contradiction for us to believe that God's love is eternal for the infant who dies, yet deny the same for those who face the tempter in the trenches of life. In the *life* of God's children, whether long or however brief, nothing can be done to change His love. Will sin alter this love? It was for sin that Christ died! David's sins were great and he paid for his mistakes in his life, yet, to deny God's continual love for him would be to deny the

Bible. Our mistakes can not change God's love. The Lord's promise is, "I am the Lord, I change not; therefore ye sons of Jacob are not consumed." Yes, many things can and are done to dishonor our Heavenly Father, yet we must realize that the Father's love is as constant as His very being. It is a sad thing, yet we know of some of God's little children who have become so hopeless in life that they have taken their own life, as king Saul did of old. Yet, this hopeless act can never sever God's love for His chosen: Nor life.

Nor angels. No, not even the fallen angels who left their first estate can alter God's love for His people. Though they may persuade good men with their apostate lies and send out false prophets to overthrow the faith of some we must agree with Paul: "Nevertheless the foundation of God standeth sure, having this seal, The Lord knoweth them that are his"2 Tim 2:19a. False doctrine injected into the world can never change God's love!

"Principalities and powers" are with us today. The great rulers of nations who have taken Bibles away from Saints and forced their religion on God's people will never by their cruel devices cause God's love to change. The old doctrine reads thus: "The LORD hath appeared of old unto me, saying, Yea, I have loved thee with an everlasting love: therefore with lovingkindness have I drawn thee." Herod can murder children and take away homes yet God's eternal abode is waiting for those He loved before the foundation of the world!

Should we go on, as Paul did, and tell you about things present, things to come, height, depth, or other creatures of malice? The list is exhaustive. Whatever time, place, creature or plan that Satan and all of his host might contrive, God's love is as eternal as He is Himself. Christian, be persuaded in your own heart and find the peace which passeth understanding!

Helpful Hints:
1. Compare God's love to man's.
2. Consider the impossibilities.
3. Talk about failure and forgiveness.
4. The prodigal's father.

"I HAVE PRAYED"
(September 11th)

This week, our nation has witnessed the most horrific act of terrorism this country has ever known, the destruction of the World Trade Center in New York. Even in our little town, it seemed like a pandemonium as people raced to the gas stations in fear of what tomorrow might bring. In the midst of chaos, what a great comfort it is to know that Jesus Christ sits at the right hand of God the Father and is still in control of all things. In the panic of it all I observed something very interesting: people on CNN were actually talking about prayer and God! As we read the scriptures, it was catastrophe that, many times, brought God's people back to Him and many times their first act was prayer.

Not only should we be praying for the victims and their families, we should also be praying for our president and those around him, that God would grant them the wisdom and strength they need to make the right decisions for our land. Paul reminded Timothy of the importance of prayer for the leaders of lands: "I exhort therefore, that, first of all, supplications, prayers, intercessions, and giving of thanks, be made for all men; For kings, and for all that are in authority; that we may lead a quiet and peaceable life in all godliness and honesty"-1 Timothy 2:1-2. I must confess, I was far along in my adult life before I knew this was in the Bible and that it was my duty be praying such prayers. I was like many today, I took it all for granted.

This encouragement to pray for leaders of lands was not just for a young preacher, it is an encouragement for us all. Every day, the prayers of the righteous should ascend unto God requesting his blessings upon those who make decisions that will affect our homes and families. From the president, even for those at a local level, from those that sit upon seats of judgment, to those who patrol our streets, let us all follow the apostles admonition as we approach God's throne each day.

Solomon wrote, "When the righteous are in authority, the people rejoice: but when the wicked beareth rule, the people mourn"-Proverbs 29:2. Even during the times of wicked kings, Solomon and Paul recognized the importance of righteous leaders and the need to pray for such. The reason is obvious, "That we may lead a quiet and peaceable life". As we exercise our right to vote, this should be the benchmark of our hearts. Who is the most God-fearing candidate? Political party is unimportant. We do not cease to be Christians when we vote. This holy calling should be placed above economy and all other issues as we prayerfully approach the voting booth. How could we pray for a leader to make Godly decisions if we did not at least try to put the most Godly candidate in office? What is their position on abortion, upon marriage, upon prayer and the many Christian liberties our wonderful country was founded upon. In the midst of it all, there is a comfort we may take in our hearts. Just to know that we did not take God's blessings of peace for granted and that we can faithfully say, "I have prayed".

Helpful Hints:
1. Talk about praying for our leaders.
2. Talk about voting for the most godly person.
3. Talk about the values of the political parties.
4. How does this affect our families and schools?
5. How often we pray!

"PERSPECTIVE"
(Biblical Response to September 11th)

It has been over a week since the tragic events transpired in New York and Washington. Many questions are before the eyes of America today. Why? Will it happen again? If so, where? What should we do about it? How should we do it? Why did God allow it? Were the people in the towers greater sinners than others? From liberals to conservatives, from country to country, even from the core of America we seem to have conflicting signals to many of these questions. Yet, the real question, the only question that needs to be asked is this: what is God's perspective?

GOD SCREAMS AT US THROUGH PAIN

C.S. Lewis wrote something like this: "God whispers to us through prosperity and he screams at us through pain". Though the Old Testament has been labeled by modernists as a book of fables and legends, it was by affliction and pain that God brought His people back to Him. More than once, God used a wicked nation to afflict and punish His own people, "O Assyrian, the rod of mine anger, and the staff in their hand is mine indignation. I will send him against an hypocritical nation, and against the people of my wrath will I give him a charge, to take the spoil, and to take the prey, and to tread them down like the mire of the streets"-Isaiah 10:5-6. God did not move the Assyrians like puppets to afflict His people, He gently removed His wings from over Israel's heads and let the wicked world come in upon them. Something they took for granted was removed: His restraining grace. If it were not for God's restraining grace there would be no laws, we could own no property, there would be no peace nor safe havens. It would truly be survival of the fittest: an animalistic world. When God's people turn from Him, that restraining grace is removed.

When the tower of Siloam fell and killed 18 people. Jesus asked this question: "Suppose ye that these Galilaeans were sinners above all the Galilaeans, because they suffered such things?" Notice His PERSPECTIVE: "I tell you, Nay: but, except ye repent, ye shall all likewise perish." In other words, the people who died were no better nor worse than you. They are a cross section of your people who reject Me and my authority. My restraining grace is being removed and more will come that will affect you unless you repent and turn back to the fountain of living waters. Perspective, God's perspective is what we must seek.

> **Helpful Hints:**
> 1. Talk about the book of Judges and how God's people turned from Him only to be persecuted by their enemies.
> 2. What brought them back into God's favor?
> 3. Talk about Christian values in our family and nation.
> 4. What is our part?

"ENCOURAGEMENT AT DEATH"

"And Abraham stood up from before his dead, and spake unto the sons of Heth....And Abraham stood up, and bowed himself to the people of the land, even to the children of Heth.....And after this, Abraham buried Sarah his wife in the cave of the field of Machpelah before Mamre: the same is Hebron in the land of Canaan"-Genesis 23:3,7,19

Abraham was loath to leave the cave at Machpelah where his precious Sarah was buried. Many were the years of their pilgrimage together as husband and wife. Sarah was the mother of his beloved son, Isaac, and had been his faithful companion in days of prosperity and great adversities. It was here that their earthly pilgrimage had ended, and for now, Abraham must say goodbye to his faithful helpmeet. Yet, in the midst of Abraham's great loss, the Holy Ghost has been faithful to record solemn words of encouragement for others who would walk this way, leaving the precious remains of their loved one in caves, cemeteries and sepulchers. By divine inspiration it is twice recorded that Abraham "stood up".

To *stand* in the day of adversity and loss is a great advantage. Sometimes it is all that one can do...... and all that God expects. Even in this, just to stand, we must "Put on the whole armour of God, that ye may be able to stand against the wiles of the devil." His threats of loneliness, depression, guilt and fear are great during our time of loss. We must look to the Rock of Ages to find our comforts and remember that our God is the God of the living. All of His children live with Him whether in life or in death.

What a wonderful and Godly testimony Abraham displayed before the sons of Heth. Descendants of the Hittite nation, their god was not Jehovah. Their god was fashioned and made with hands and must be carried about from place to place. Afterlife was a mystery to them and their god. Where did their loved ones go when the spirit departed from the body? Surely, they did not know as they cut their bodies and let out their own blood to reveal the pain they held for the loss of their loved ones. As Abraham "stood up" he declared his faith in the living God and his hope that his beloved Sarah was with the Lord and at peace. I love the story a preacher told of one of the sisters in his congregation when she lost her beloved husband. The caretakers came in to offer their condolences and medications to alleviate her grief. To their surprise she seemed to be at peace and remarkably calm. They asked her how this could be and she explained her great faith in a living God who watches over His own and how she knew that her husband was with Him now and that she would one day be with him in glory. As the pastor summed it up, "There is nothing wrong with acting like a Christian at the time of death".

As Abraham stood up from before his dead, he demonstrated his faith before the sons of Heth, his faith in our God who has conquered death. His posture is recorded for God's people today as an encouragement that we, too, must go on when we lose our loved ones. To other husbands that have lost their Sarahs I hear him say, "Stand up, show your faith, she would want you to go on. You have been given precious days of life. Use them to God's glory and be an encouragement to others." To the faithful wife who has lost her husband, his words are much the same, "You, too, must go on. There are grandchildren to care for. Your strength will be seen by many. It is God's testimony of faith. I will hold a special place in your heart, yet, I would not have you waste your days in grief. You must go on." To children who have lost their parents I hear him say, "You have a life before you. There are challenges you must meet, worlds you must conquer and a family you must care for. Stand up, go on with your life." So faithful Abraham says to all who have lost love ones. Children, grandchildren, husbands, wives, friends and family: Stand up before the unbelievers and make the most out of the days you have been given. We are just around the corner.

Helpful Hints:
1. Talk about faithful Abraham.
2. Talk about death and dying.
3. Talk about loved ones who sleep in Jesus.
4. Talk about the value of the Christian life in times like these.

"HUMILITY"

"And being found in fashion as a man, he humbled himself, and became obedient unto death, even the death of the cross"
-Philippians 2:8

Among the Christian graces that are pleasing to our heavenly Father, we will find *humility* at the top of the list. Much is written about the subject in scripture for this reason: it is the grace that is the most difficult to attain. Our Lord Jesus is the ultimate example of humility.

HUMILITY IS NOT WEAKNESS

To the Greeks and the Romans, humility was a form of weakness, a moral flaw or a glitch in the character of real men and women. Perhaps that is the reason that Jesus gave us so many lessons on humility. When He spoke of John the Baptist, Jesus asked the people, "What went ye out into the wilderness to see? A reed shaken with the wind". In other words, "Did you go to see a weak man blown about by the world?" They all knew that John was not a weakling looking for the applause of men. Jesus gives him this compliment: "Among them that are born of women there hath not risen a greater than John the Baptist". The strongest of characters are humble ones who are valiant for the truth.

OUR NEED TO BE HUMBLED

Humility is not a virtue that comes naturally for us. We need to be humbled from time to time. Thankfully, our Father loves us enough to accommodate us. This may be accomplished by tragedy; financial setbacks; sickness; injury; and just plain old embarrassments. We tuck our tail between our legs and crawl off in some corner, lick our wounds until we are ready to show our face again in public. When we do, we are of a much humbler spirit. Surely, this is for our profit and gain. As one of our church members said after preaching on the subject, "People couldn't stand me today if God had not humbled me".

WE FORGET THE LESSON

As we forget what we read in yesterday's newspaper, we many times forget the lessons that God has taught us in humility. I have visited in the hospital and counseled people with problems who promised faithfulness to family and church in their hour of greatest need. But when their problem was gone and forgotten, so was their promise. No true repentance here, nothing learned, nothing gained from the lesson. Let our experience humbles us as it did Nebuchadnezzar who once boasted in himself, but arose from his experience with God to say, "And all the inhabitants of the earth *are* reputed as nothing: and he doeth according to his will in the army of heaven, and *among* the inhabitants of the earth: and none can stay his hand, or say unto him, What doest thou?"

OBEDIENCE TO SCRIPTURE IS HUMILITY

Though one may seem humble, true humility is discerned by obedience to God's word. From our scripture, we read that Jesus "become obedient". From His own mouth He declared, "I came down from heaven not to do my own will". He was obeying the Father's will. Therefore, humility is not discerned by a particular mournful look, expression, disfigured face or even from one's words. It is observed in a willingness to conform to what God has said.

WE ARE HUMBLED BY GRACE

God's children are most humbled when they learn about His amazing grace. It is then, and only then, that His word is sought out very diligently. A look to the cross at the One who did no sin, yet suffered in our place brings every heir of heaven to a posture of humility. When we see Jesus as our full atonement we are made to cry out, "Men and brethren, what shall we do?" Though the law might condemn us for a while, grace wins the final battle as it conquers the heart. It brings true repentance and sets our sins before us as towering mountains ready to fall upon us. It is told that President Roosevelt, when taking in the night air with a friend, enjoyed the beauty of God's vast creation. As he viewed the millions of sparkling stars he made the comment, "I'm small enough now, lets go in". With such an attitude, let us enter the kingdom!

Helpful Hints:
1. How has God humbled you?
2. Talk about how God humbles His people.
3. Give some scriptural examples.
4. Enlarge upon the humility of Christ.

"FOCUSED"

*"And it came to pass, when the time was come that he should
be received up, he stedfastly set his face to go to Jerusalem"*
-Luke 9:5

Our Lord led a *focused* life. His purpose was always
before Him. Even as a child He would say, "I must be
about my Father's business." He came to redeem His
people from their sins and nothing moved Him from His
purpose till the atonement was made and the captives set
free. To be focused means that we have a goal in life, a
God honoring purpose and that we are moving towards
that purpose in a determined way. As our Lord's face was
stedfastly set to go to Jerusalem to die upon a cross for
our sins, let us set our face before our calling and lead a
focused life as well.

Remaining focused upon our responsibilities in life is
a challenge. Whether it is our jobs, or our families, we can
be sure the devil will use all his power to distract and
divert our attention from those things that are not only
pleasing to our heavenly Father, but also most rewarding
to ourselves as well. From a host of biblical examples, I will
give you a few examples of people who lost their focus,

why they lost their focus and the resulting consequences of their actions. Let us glean from their mistakes and hopefully, lead a more God honoring, focused life.

In the morning of time, the first wife and mother *lost her focus.* Eve was not focused on the family when she began her dialogue with Satan. Her eyes were wide with the world and we may all read the results in the headlines of God's word. She let a lot of people down. She was to be Adam's "help meet" as all wives are to be. She was to set an example for her children. What great anxiety she brought upon herself and her family for her worldliness.

What about king David? He was greatly blessed, anointed of God, yet at the "time when kings go forth to battle", David looked upon Bathsheba and lost his focus. He was a husband, a father and a leader. Though we may own castles and riches, loss of focus causes grievous and permanent wounds to the soul. That sin haunted David all the days of his life. We read of his pain in the 51st psalm.

As we have already noticed, losing our focus can bring great pain, not only to ourselves, but also to the people around us. Jabez realized that and part of his prayer ran thus, "....keep me from evil, that it may not grieve me". Our own personal evil can cause lifelong pain to self and our loved ones.

The prodigal son was a teenager who lost his focus. He wanted his money and left home with his pockets jingling. As one good preacher said, "He left home looking for a party and didn't have one till he got back home".

Joseph is a good example of a young man who *kept* his focus on his God. He was sold into slavery by his brothers, unjustly accused by Potipher's wife and thrown into prison: he remained focused upon God. He didn't carry bitterness in his heart against those that had misused him. He went on with life doing the best he could knowing that

God was still with him even though the world was not. We read of his exaltation in Egypt. Remaining focused has great rewards.

We all lose our focus from time to time. Not only by sin, but tragedy, family problems, loss of loved ones and just the mundane affairs of every day life can cause us to become distracted with our purpose and callings as fathers, mothers and spouse. Christian, what is your focus in life? Where your heart is, there will be your focus!

Helpful Hints:
1. Share your focus in life: church, family, job and education.
2. Discuss the examples given, those who kept their focus and those who lost their focus and why.
3. Talk about how we can keep our focus.
4. Discuss the many ways we lose our focus.

"PETER'S EXPLANATION OF ELECTION"

"Elect according to the foreknowledge of God the Father, through sanctification of the Spirit, unto obedience and sprinkling of the blood of Jesus Christ: Grace unto you, and peace, be multiplied"-1Peter 1:2

When the Apostle Peter explained election he began with God's perfect *foreknowledge*. He makes it crystal clear: God foreknew His people before they knew Him…. before they were born. Before there were any denominations, doctrines, creeds, church ordinances or traditions, God knew His people. This takes us back to the beginning of our election: God Himself who sees the end from the beginning.

SANCTIFICATION OF THE SPIRIT

The elect are brought into a vital relationship with the Father not by ordinances of men, but rather through "sanctification of the spirit". Sanctification of the Spirit means that one is set apart and cleansed by the Holy Ghost. For Paul, it was on the Damascus road. For John the Baptist, it was in his mother's womb. This is when Christ takes up His residence in the heart, "Christ in you, the hope of glory". This is when God writes His laws upon the heart. The new creature hungers and thirsts for righteousness, God and His word. That is what sanctification does for the elect.

OBEDIENCE AND SPRINKLING OF THE BLOOD OF JESUS CHRIST

As Peter explains election, he does not exalt the sinner. He exalts Jesus Christ and speaks of *His* obedience. We have heard some people say that God looked down through time and saw the sinner obey and accept Christ and God elected them on that basis. Peter didn't explain it that way. Until sanctification occurs, the sinner rejects Jesus and His word...even the doctrine of election. The obedience Peter speaks of is completely Christ's: "And being found in fashion as a man, he humbled himself, and become obedient unto death, even the death of the cross"-Phil. 2:8. His obedience was salvation to the elect.

SPRINLKING OF THE BLOOD

Finally, Peter alludes to the Old Testament "sprinkling of the blood" as he explains election. As the high priest sprinkled the blood of the sacrificial lamb upon the book and the people, the figure became real for His people at Calvary. The high priest did not sprinkle blood upon the whole world. Election agrees with Christ's blood that was specifically shed for those the Father foreknew in love... His elect.

Helpful Hints:
1. Talk about the doctrine of election.
2. Compare it to other doctrines of the world.
3. Note the places in scripture this doctrine is taught.
4. Why do you think we do not hear more about it?

"THE IMPORTANCE OF THE CHURCH"

"But if I tarry long, that thou mayest know how thou oughtest to behave thyself in the house of God, which is the church of the living God, the pillar and ground of the truth"-1 Timothy 3:15

Truth is a rare commodity in the modern marketplace. Whether we speak of religion, politics, science, or medicine, we find conflicting sentiments. When answers are supported by substantial evidence we find peace in our hearts. There is a place of peace, a place where truth may be found and for our spiritual searching to end. That place is the Church of the living God, the pillar and ground of the truth.

The words "pillar and ground" are figures of speech. They are indicative of the supporting *foundation* and *beams*. The Church did not *make* the truth, it *supports* the truth that God has given man through His word. Therefore, the Church is not to invent any new truths. The Church is to pray to understand the truth of God's word, believe it and proclaim it. If any truth exists today concerning God and His people, it will be found in the Church because this is the place that God has chosen to dwell among His people.

Today, we see the evidence of an unchurched society. Basic, fundamental truths are unknown. Man's doctrines that Paul refers to as "seducing spirits, and doctrines of devils"(1 Timothy 4:1) are embraced. The psychiatrists' offices are full. Medications for depression are top sellers. People have more possessions than their forefathers ever dreamed of having and yet something seems to be missing. It must be something that our forefather's possessed for they were not so. May we suggest that that something is God, His Church and the blessings of truth which we all need so desperately today.

When we talk about the *truth*, we are speaking about doctrines that keep our thinking straight, truths that give genuine Godly wisdom, expose sin and exalt Christ. They lead us in a *plain path* and give us peace. These truths give the heart a foundation to rest upon, where one can say, "That is what God said about it and I will rest upon that sentiment, do or die". The truth embraces subjects from creation to rearing our children. It includes how we are to conduct ourselves in our marriages as well as our workplace. The truth reveals sin and gives us authority to say, "That is wrong, not because I or the Church are sitting in judgment, but because God says so." It brings us to a place of repentance and change for the better. The truth will expose error and the false prophet. The truth will comfort God's people in their greatest trials as it exalts Jesus Christ, who He is, and what He has done for His people. It displays God's grace to undeserving sinners and allows them to look at life through the window of God's word. Personally speaking, the Church and her truths have been a great blessing to me in all of these areas, such a great blessing, that I want to share it with you.

Yes, we live in a day when we are taught that there is no absolute truth. Yet, God is truth, His Church must proclaim it and we must not compromise the truth to please mankind. That is the most interesting and dynamic character concerning the truth: it will never change. The winds of time; cultural thinking; political overtones; and whatever country has the biggest gun will never alter God's word, "For ever, O LORD, thy word is settled in heaven"-Psalm 119:89. His word is truth.

Helpful Hints:
1. What does the Bible say about the truths we mentioned at the beginning of our article that oppose humanistic thinking in our day: creation, science, history, psychology and etc.
2. Expose some false prophets with truth and how they try to change it.
3. Discuss the importance of preaching and the teaching of truth.
4. Talk about the reasons that man wants to change the truth.

"GOOD MEDICINE"

"A merry heart doeth good like a medicine: but a broken spirit drieth the bones"-Proverbs 17:22.

This is one of my favorite scriptures. It demands something of me, an attitude, a posture that should be displayed in the house of God. It reminds me of what people around me need, even when I do not feel merry myself. This good medicine needs to be dispensed in abundance if we want to see happy Christians.

Every leader must have a merry heart. Who wants to follow a sad man. As the saying goes: "Smile and the world smiles with you, frown, and face a frowning world." A sour, negative, leader will produce followers of the same gender. Sure, we all have down times, times of struggle, times of loss and tragedy, yet there should always be enough "good medicine" around to lift our spirits and guide us through those dark days. How would a nation feel if their president went around with his head down complaining of the circumstances that surround his life and our country? We may all become physicians of cheerfulness when we display a merry heart because the merry heart is good medicine for all around us.

In our church, in our homes and even on the job, the one with the merry heart is the person we all want to be around. This balm of Gilead rubs off on others and sends them on their way with a better outlook on life. Why is this so? Because the merry heart encourages. It has the tendency to elevate our spirits as it provides an enjoyable environment. Indeed, a joyful heart is "Good medicine" for the soul.

These words remind us that it is not a *sin* for Christians to *smile*. The Pharisees disfigured their faces as they fasted, yet Paul and Silas sang praises unto God while imprisoned. Who were the genuine lovers of God? A merry heart *demands* a smile. Who wants to go to a church where everyone wears a frown? One would wonder, "Is there something wrong with their Lord; their doctrine; or their brethren?" I have seen people smile when their toes were stepped on by the gospel. Surely, that is the sign of a *merry* heart. I remember as a child, seeing a brother laugh during a sermon. I turned to one of my parents and asked, "Is that man laughing at the preacher". "No", was the whispered reply, "he is enjoying the sermon." That was the first time I had ever witnessed anyone smiling in church. Today I know that was the sign of a merry heart. We frequently see Mr. Doctrine wearing a frown and Miss Spirituality bubbling over, talking about herself and her spirituality, but we see Christian with a smile of confidence trusting in His Lord.

Not only is a merry heart good for those around us, it is equally good medicine for our own selves. Yes, we have a lot to do with making our own day rather than allowing our day to make us. We are dispensers of this medicine for self as well as others. A merry heart indicates fellowship with the Lord. From experience, I know this to be a truth. My down times are usually spawned from a focus on the world, times that I have ignored God for a season, times I have avoided study and prayer. We leave our "first love" and our visits to God's house become drudgery rather than edifying. When we find the Lord we find our good medicine for He is the maker of the merry heart.

Helpful Hints:
1. Talk about people in your church who display a merry heart.
2. Talk about how it affects you.
3. What are some things we can think on to make us merry?
4. Talk about how it is good medicine.

"STRENGTHENING THE MIND"

"Wherefore gird up the loins of your mind, be sober, and hope to the end for the grace that is to be brought unto you at the revelation of Jesus Christ"- 1 Peter 1:13.

The world would have us to think that the mind is like a wild horse without a bridle: it runs when it wants, it stands when it wills and it feeds upon whatever is pleasant to its own particular needs. Yet, we find a contrasting mindset in God's word, a mindset which distinguishes regenerate man from a brute beast. We are reminded, as well as encouraged, by the fact that the mind of God's people is like a muscle, it can be strengthened, disciplined and armed for battle. The allegory Peter uses is thus stated: gird the mind, discipline the mind and prepare for the battle that every pilgrim will face.

Because of the loose garments worn by the Orientals, the waist was belted, or *girded*, before engaging in any physical activity. Thus, the warrior prepared himself for battle by strapping a leather girdle about his waist, from which his dagger, his sword and other weapons of his warfare were hung. Have we not found that our greatest struggles begin with loose *thoughts*? We must take the truth of God's word, and belt it around our minds, "Casting down imaginations, and every high thing that exalteth itself against the knowledge of God, and bringing into captivity every thought to the obedience of Christ" (2 Corinthians 10:5). Surly, this requires as much effort and discipline as that of the athlete who trains and prepares daily for the championship. Yet, this crown is not an earthly one, it is purely spiritual! The contrast is extreme. As Jesus said, "For what is a man profited, if he shall gain the whole world, and lose his own soul? or what shall a man give in exchange for his soul?" Matthew 16:26. Which is the most important, earthly trophies, or those which have to do with soul prosperity?

The quickened soul will soon discover that the mind is a battlefield. Who will win the territory? Who will possess the mind? Peter encourages us, because he had been given to wrong thinking when he denied His Lord. He well knew the battlefield and the importance of mind strength. Today, the battleground is the same. The beast and the false prophet are as hot as ever after the territory of men's hearts and souls. They use books, television, music and even schools to promote their agenda and overthrow our thoughts. We must sharpen our sword and engage!

Soberness is the Christian *discipline*. This means to be careful, to watch for trials, temptations and the pitfalls of Satan and sin. The roaring lion walks the street with the false prophets and seeks the unwary mind. Many of God's people, drunken with worldliness and ignorance, are devoured. Keep this in mind today: the whole world lieth in wickedness; there is evil about and the arch enemy is out to destroy. Think soberly.

It is so easy to continually think negative thoughts, things that have not gone right, mistakes we have made, past memories that may haunt our souls, people who have injured us and forget any good thing or person that is around us. This can begin a downward spiral into a pit of depression so dark that we can not see the blessings we DO have. I am sure that many of God's children have hit the bottom of the pit because they have lost hope and forgotten their blessings by focusing their attention on their losses and failures. Some of God's children have gotten so low that they have taken their own lives in a hopeless moment. Let us not allow Satan to cloud out the good in our lives, blessings that we may have overlooked. Let us search every nook and corner of the people and things around us and find something to be thankful for and think on these things.

I remember the story of a mother who continually encouraged her daughter to look on the positive. Coming from a poor family she told her daughter, "If you dwell on the negative it will destroy you." The daughter loved her humble mother greatly and heeded her advice. The older she got, the more she realized the value of her mother's advice. As she matured, she came to know her mother better and the reason of her advice. Her mother had suffered abuse as a child. Yet, by focusing on God and the blessings she did have, she became a loving, caring gentle mother of a wonderful family. The mother did not speak harshly of her past because she did not dwell on it. The daughter discovered it from others. Yes, the past could have destroyed her. She could have passed it down to the next generation by a continual life of complaint. She overcame it by giving thanks and thinking good thoughts.

Christian, gird thyself with hope, firm unto the end. Hope is a grand thing. It is when the mind sets itself upon a promise and begins to anticipate it with joy before it is actually in hand. Peter's "unto the end" means *without wavering*. If God has promised blessings for all of His children, each in a special and distinct way for every heir of grace, who or what can prevent it from occurring. Hang your belt today with the blessings which flow freely from our Lord Jesus Christ, the found of every blessing!

Helpful Hints:
1. How does the enemy try to conquer our minds.
2. Talk about how we can get control of it.
3. Talk about worries, fears, depressions, guilt and handling them in a biblical way.
4. What should we hang on our belt?

"KEEP ME FROM EVIL"

"And Jabez called on the God of Israel, saying, Oh that thou wouldest bless me indeed, and enlarge my coast, and that thine hand might be with me, and that thou wouldest keep me from evil, that it may not grieve me! And God granted him that which he requested"- 1 Chronicles 4:10.

Jabez was "more honourable than his brethren". As we read the words of his prayer we understand why. We feel to know much about the man, about his character, and even his vision by the words that ascended from his lips as he approached the most High. Among those we find a noble petition: "Keep me from evil."

It is wise to ask the Lord to keep us from evil. This is an honorable request for all, especially the leaders in God's kingdom! When the disciples asked Jesus to teach them to pray, He encouraged them with language of the same sentiment as Jabez: "Lead us not into temptation, but deliver us from evil." Without the presence of God, we are no match for Satan. He has been around a long time, observed the greatest warriors of God in battle and he knows our greatest weakness. He will sift us as wheat and bring much pain into our lives if we fight him alone.

It is evil that causes so much pain in our world. That was the reason of Jabez's petition: "that it might not grieve me".

At first glimpse, the request might seem *selfish*. It seems as though Jabez would protect only his own honor and conscience from grief. Yet, we see more to his words than a selfish request. Jabez knew that evil in his life would not only wound his own soul but also inflict pain upon the people around him, people that he loved. Children and family, those that would look up to him, trust him and depend upon him would be grieved by any evil actions on his part. Therefore as we examine his request, we will discover blessings to those around him as well as blessings upon his own head.

TO THOSE AROUND HIM

Yes, evil hurts those around us. Many a mother and father have suffered body and soul from the evil of their own offspring. Son, daughter..... your evil will harm the hand that cared for you more than you will ever know. Many a child has suffered from the evil of their own parents. Gambling casinos and racetracks injure not only the person robbed of their wages, but also the families back home who relied upon their parents income for food and shelter. Drugs, alcohol and lust send their fiery serpents to every member of the family, biting and destroying life and limb. I am sure if we asked the fragile child the source of their greatest joy they would answer, "Godly parents and a Godly home". Jabez realized that his lifestyle was not his own. It would impact others for good or for evil. Society in general, is molded by good or evil. Perhaps Jabez had been injured himself. To those who have been injured by the evil of others, we encourage you to seek the great physician who cares for wounded souls. Read His book. It has the answer to unravel many messes. For the sake of others, let us approach the throne of God's grace with this petition today.

A PERSONAL BLESSING

Some of the greatest pain known to man is the recognition of injuries to people we love. Sleepless nights and hurting heads are many times the malady of self inflicted injuries. Let us not turn to drugs, alcohol and sin to mask the pain, use rather the remedies of repentance, forgiveness and confession. I have heard some preachers talk of personal preservation and perseverance with a boastful spirit. They compare themselves among themselves and think the child of God can not sink to such a state. The latter end of Lot will not agree with such a doctrine. Paul said that he could become a "castaway". John 15:5 speaks of branches that men gather and burn, branches that were once a part of the Holy Vine. Surely, they are a picture of what evil can bring upon God's children to silence a good testimony. Jabez's prayer was a sober one. He was wise enough to realize his potential to sin. Therefore, he sought strength from above. Let us do so as well! Lord, this is our prayer today! May we be answered like Jabez: "And God granted him that which he requested".

Helpful Hints:
1. Talk about our responsibility to those around us.
2. Discuss how sin affects our families, our nation… our church.
3. Discuss how David's sin affected his family….Eve's as well.

4. Turn it around and talk about people being blessed because of another's righteous acts....Christ.....the apostles....godly parents.

5. Do you know of those who have caused much pain?

"SPIRITUAL MATURITY"

"But grow in grace, and in the knowledge of our Lord and Saviour Jesus Christ. To him be glory both now and for ever. Amen"- II Peter 3:18

Spiritual maturity is what pastors love to see in God's children. That is why they labor. They love to see spiritual growth in the flocks they nurture because they know that it is here that Christ Jesus gets the honor. Spiritual maturity is observed and measured in many ways. It should be the ardent desire of every Christian to grow in grace.

One way we measure spiritual maturity is by *knowledge* of scripture and the God given ability to rightly divide the word of truth. The old fashioned method of reading scripture and faithful attendance to preaching is the only way one may become wise. Worldly Wiseman was full of quaint saying and "tips for the day" to make one happy and prosperous. But when the winds and rain came, his house fell because it was built upon shifting sand. Gold is not found lying around on the ground, one must dig for it. There is a goldmine is God's kingdom and in His book.

Spiritual maturity is equally measured by *ministering* to others. A cup of cool water in honor of Christ reflects the simplicity of ministering. Here we find a balance in our maturity. As one preacher has said, "We can be straight as a gun barrel doctrinally, yet just as empty spiritually." Doctrine without kindness to others, especially to those of God's house, is legalistic. Christ not only taught, he ministered. This Christian grace speaks as loudly as doctrine. When we say to our friends, "Come and see", their acceptance of our invitation is based as much on our ministering to their needs as our doctrine.

A dissection of our *prayers* would also serve as an insight into our spiritual maturity. Not only what we ask, but how we ask reflects the true relationship one has with their Lord. Is there any praise for the giver of ever good and perfect gift? Is there a fervent effectual request that the kingdom will come with revival and power? Are there intercessions for others: brethren, family, friends and country? Is there a proper giving of thanks for every prayer answered? All of this is indicative of soul maturity.

Though giving of one's carnal things is many times wrongly taught and abused, it has always served as an indicator of one's spiritual maturity. A dollar for a soul..... give and people live, twist the arm and make people feel guilty, are not methods we find in scripture. The biblical foundation for giving has always been an act of worship, a sacrificial giving back to God what is rightfully His. The widow's *mite* is Christ's illustration to show the shallow religion of the Pharisees and the maturity of this poor woman who trusted not in riches, but in her God who would never leave or forsake her.

Who can say they are fully matured in these graces? Our desire to become more mature should not be a legalistic spirit or boasting. Growth is the byproduct of a tender heart that desires to walk closer with the One they have come to love. Only in this spirit will we truly mature!

Helpful Hints:
1. Give some personal experiences in your own growth as you have come to know Christ better.
2. Enlarge on each of the examples given: knowledge, ministering, prayer and giving.
3. Discuss ways that each of you might grow.
4. Discuss the showy use of these graces.

"A MINISTERING CHURCH"

"But so shall it not be among you: but whosoever will be great among you, shall be your minister: And whosoever of you will be the chiefest, shall be servant of all. For even the Son of man came not to be ministered unto, but to minister, and to give his life a ransom for many."- Mark 10:43-45

Like the diamond, Christianity has many facets. Whichever way one turns the stone, light is reflected and its value is observed in the eye of the beholder. Like Joseph's coat of many colors, the many splendors of Jesus are observed in the numerous gifts He has vested in His Church. These gifts are all given for the building up of Zion and her cause. If we were to survey the categories of gifts found in the New Testament, we could easily place them under one heading and that heading would be ministering to others......and that is what Jesus came to do, He came to minister to others.

What is ministering? The simplest *definition* we could give for ministering is this: "Doing something for someone else expecting nothing in return". Is this not a beautiful picture of Jesus? He spent His time here doing wonderful things for undeserving sinners expecting nothing in return. No, our Lord did not become flesh to be pampered and petted by men. Though He could have enjoyed king's palaces and the lifestyle of the rich and famous, He chose the most humble life of all: the life of a servant. He expected nothing but a cross and to be despised and rejected of men. His ultimate ministration was the ministration of death: "to give his life a ransom for many."

Is ministering something that only preachers and pastors do? We all have this tendency to make Christianity difficult. Many times, we view the things that we are to do as Christians as difficult things that only highly spiritual people, like the apostles, can do. Let me give you a simple *illustration* of ministering. Since we have been married, my wife has demonstrated some wonderful ways to minister. On many a morning, she has left me a little note by my coffee cup with an encouraging, "I love you, hope you have a great day", on a napkin. Sometimes, I have felt like a king as she brought me my coffee in bed! Every day that I come home from work, she greets me with a smile, no matter what has happened that day. Are you beginning to see how easy it is to minister to others? According to Jesus, just a cup of cold water in the name of a disciple has great rewards! So, what do you think happens when such unselfish activity begins to take place? Why, even grumpy old disciples begin to smile and the next thing you know, they are bringing the coffee and encouraging others around them. Ministering is not only simple, it is contagious!

At this point, you might be saying, "That's great for some people, but I don't think I have that kind of gift. I'm pretty shy and I really don't feel comfortable ministering to other people." I am sure that is just what Satan wants us to think so he can keep our light under a bushel. According to Peter, every member of the Church is gifted and this gift of ministering is one gift that every Christian possesses. This is what he says, "As every man hath received the gift, *even so* minister the same one to another, as good stewards of the manifold grace of God."- 1 Peter 4:10. A steward uses what another person has entrusted to them. Our gifts and abilities to minister to others have been entrusted to us by Jesus. These gifts cost Him His life: "When he ascended up on high, he led captivity captive, and gave gifts to men". What a thought! God has taken notice of us and given us a gift. Every Christian should be seeking ways to minister to others expecting nothing in return. The day I preached this message to my home church, I ordained every member as a duly ordained minister of Jesus Christ! Every member is a minister!

This brings us to the mindset of ministering. As our former president, J.F. Kennedy once said in a speech, "Ask not what your country can do for you, but rather, ask what you can do for your country." Can you imagine what would happen in this country if people quit asking the government for handouts and tried their best to put something back in to this great country in which we live? Can you imagine what would happen in many churches if its members were replacing that word "country" with *church.....pastor......deacon.....brother....sister*? Paul said in the latter days, people would be lovers of themselves. That means they will become self centered. Ministering is just the opposite of this. It is a look away from self to the needs of others!

While I was preaching a series of messages on this subject, my wife bought me a card and put it on my desk. Perhaps you have read the words that I found written above a picture of a pan of water and a wet towel, depicting the servants scene in the upper room that night. The card read, "Preach Christ.....if you must, use words". I can not tell you how pharisaical that made me feel. I remembered the times that I had beat someone over the head with doctrine when I could have won them better by ministering to their needs. Yes, doctrine must come in somewhere along the way, but as one man said, "We can be straight as a gun barrel doctrinally, but just as empty spiritually. A church without doctrine is like a car without a steering wheel. A church without ministering servants is like one without gas. Many times, the best way to get the attention of others, the best way to preach Christ, is to show them Christ in our own hearts and do as Jesus did: go about doing good. Ministering to their needs is one of the best invitations to God's house!

If you will allow me, I would like to put in a word for the pastors of churches. Many of them are overworked, underpaid (monetarily), they have little time for their families and would truly like to spend more time in God's word and at the feet of their Savior. We must ever remember that these men are not *Chaplains*. What I mean by this is that they are not to spend every waking moment in a hospital, a nursing home and at the bed of the sick. Surely, all of these are things that pastors must do and love to do. Yet, if the church is functioning as she should, the pastor's job is to equip the saints so they can learn to minister to one another. This was the reason the deacon's office can into being. The widows were neglected in the daily "ministration". They needed to be ministered to. They chose out spiritual men who would see to these needs and free the hand of the apostles and preachers. What did these men do then? They gave themselves to prayer and to the ministry of the word. There is the primary ministry of the pastor: the word of God! And notice the result: "And the word of God increased; and the number of the disciples multiplied..." Since we have studied this at our church, there have been more phone calls, more cards flying though the mail and more visits by the membership to the beds of the sick and to those who fall by the wayside than I have ever seen. It has allowed me to begin a radio broadcast, work on a devotion book and even write this article. As a pastor, I say, "Thank you for our ministering servants".

If you will notice, the infant Church was blessed to have many of these ministering servants. As a matter of fact, this kind of person is the one that is mentioned most in scripture. Read the list of servants at Rome in the 16th chapter. As you read of these brethren, remember that the word "servant" and "minister" come from the same word. That word is *diakonos*, from which we get the word deacon. You will find this spirit of ministering all though the bible, but you will especially find it in the New Testament. Paul mentions Epaphroditus, Timotheous, Erastus and Onesimus who ministered to him in prison. Luke mentions the names of many women who ministered to Jesus (Luke 8:2,3). We even find angels ministering to our Lord after His temptation. Of course, you will find Jesus ministering every where that He went. He healed the sick, raised the dead, opened the ears of the deaf and restored sight to the blind. He had a kind word to say to those discouraged and His friendship to those around Him was as faithful as His Father's love. Did it catch on? You bet it did! Harlots were washing His feet; publicans were inviting Him to dinner; maniacs from the tombs were begging to help Him; fishermen were leaving their nets; Zealots were preaching; runaway slaves were ministering to preachers in prison; and men who once argued who would be greatest in the kingdom, began to wash one another's feet!

Perhaps you still need a little nudge to venture out and begin your own personal ministry. Here is a little acronym that might help you to focus in on your own personal ministering skills. The acronym is E.T.O.A.

Think of it as a flight time: Estimated Time Of Arrival. Of course, the airport leaves the O off, but we need it. And remember, we have not arrived as mature Christians until we begin to look away from self and minister to the needs of others.

E. Stands for Experience. What have I experienced in my personal life that may be of value to others? Have I been through a divorce? Have I had a financial disaster? Have I gone through a serious illness? Have I lost a loved one? Have I suffered from severe depression? Have I had problems with my children? We can easily snuff a self-righteous nose in the air when others have these problems. Yet, is this emulating Christ? Did He do that? If you have experienced hardships, your hardship has been the teacher to enable you to minister to others who are going through the same thing.

T. Stands for Time. How much time to you have to minister anyway. One of my preacher friends shared with me the story of counseling with a family and his wife called him and said, "You don't want to lose your own while you are minister to others". Wives have a way of keeping our feet on the ground! Yet, this is so. We must keep our ministering in perspective and keep the most important things first. Surely, the Lord would not have mothers abandoning their own children to minister to others. If you have lot of time on your hands use it to the cause of Christ and minister.

O. Stands for Opportunity. I believe that the Lord places of opportunity to minister to the needs of others in the pathway of life. Remember the good Samaritan. He was riding along and in his path was the stranger half dead. He took of his own substance and minister to the man. He even left some money for the innkeeper to minister to the man's needs after he had left. He expected nothing in return. Or Simon, a man of Cyrene, a passer by, who was in the right place at the right time to have the blessed opportunity to bear the cross for Jesus. Surely, our ministering should first begin at the house of God, "As we have therefore opportunity, let us do good unto all *men*, especially unto them who are of the household of faith."- Galatians 6:10. But it should not end here. The world is full of people in need.

A. Stands for Assets. What do you have? Perhaps you are blessed with wealth. Use it to minister. Perhaps you have a talent to cook. Perhaps you have a garden. The ideas here are endless. Search your own soul and ask what God has given you by His grace to use for others.

Yes, ministering is a look away from self to the needs of others. The ultimate ministration is the example of Christ upon the cross, the ministration of His death. This should be the mind of every Christian for it is the mind of Christ. "⁵Let this mind be in you, which was also in Christ Jesus: ⁶Who, being in the form of God, thought it not robbery to be equal with God: ⁷But made himself of no reputation, and took upon him the form of a servant, and was made in the likeness of men: ⁸And being found in fashion as a man, he humbled himself, and became obedient unto death, even the death of the cross. Philip. 2:5-8 By this we might say, "Every minister is a martyr, dying daily for Jesus."

Have you ever wanted to do something personally for Jesus since He has done so much for you? Perhaps, be as those women who ministered to His needs? You can. As a final note of encouragement, let us remember who we are ultimately ministering to when we serve others. "And the King shall answer and say unto them, Verily I say unto you, Inasmuch as ye have done *it* unto one of the least of these my brethren, ye have done *it* unto me."- Matthew 25:40

Helpful Hints;

1. Discuss the balance of doctrine and ministering.

2. How can you become a better minister for Christ?

3. Discuss those you see in scripture that reflect Christ in this way.

4. Those in your church.

5. What trials have you experienced that will enable you to minister to others?

"TOO SMALL FOR GOD?"
"Casting all your care upon him; for he careth for you"
-I Peter 5:7

Recently, a child shared a burden with his father and his father encouraged his son to give it to the Lord. The son's reply was, "Isn't that too small to bring before God". To the child, God was so awesome, so important, so great and powerful, that surely this little matter from such a little person could be of little importance to Him. To the great encouragement of the child, Peter's words were explained like this.

First, the word "all" was explained: "My child, every one of us struggle with the same feelings as you have. We all have difficulty believing that Jesus cares for *all* of the troubles of *all* of His people. It seems too much for any One person to know or handle. Yet, we must see Him as *God our Father.* God is able to care for all of His children in a separate and distinct way. Each of us may approach Him as the only child He knows or cares for. Not only that, but we must always remember that the word 'all' is inclusive. It is a blanket that covers all distractions of the soul: small, medium, large. It includes cares about life, death, money, relationships, cares about the past, the future, things that seem impossible to fix, things that embarrass us, things we are ashamed of and things that can not be changed in this life. There is no category that this word "all" does not include. Remember, He is God, He can handle it.

The words, *your care*, contain a personal invitation to each and every child. They display a personal, "one on one" relationship with Him. It means that even though many cares are common to all, every individual is different and important to the Lord and so are their own specific cares. It is not the size of the care, whether great or small, that concerns the Lord. It is the *your*, the person, the object of His affection, that He is concerned with. All cares are the same size to God, from moving mountains to the ghostly fears of the tiniest child. Though it is true that, as a child, you do not carry the burdens of the president or a king, you are not expected to, your care is proportional to your own station in life. If they are important to you, if they upset you, in God's eyes *your cares* are just as enormous and important. I am sure these words of Peter were recorded just for you today.

'Casting' is another wonderful truth. It means to throw something heavy into the hands of one who is stronger and able to carry the load with ease. We must trust Him with it or we will never give it to Him. He rejoices when one of His children casts their weight of care into His hands and leaves it there. Now walk away and forget it. That requires faith. You have done all that the Lord expects you to do about the matter so cast you care upon Him. If you find it in your hand tomorrow, give it to Him again.

Helpful Hints:
1. Discuss the many categories that "all" includes.
2. Discuss how the Lord knows every one of His sheep personally.
3. What must you give to Him that you are carrying?
4. How have you found Him faithful in the past?

"LOVEST THOU ME?"

"So when they had dined, Jesus saith to Simon Peter, Simon, son of Jonas, lovest thou me more than these? He saith unto him, Yea, Lord; thou knowest that I love thee. He saith unto him, Feed my lambs." -John 21:15

As our Lord questioned the heart of Peter, let Him equally question ours today. Self examination is the purpose of many scriptural recordings. Let us imagine that Jesus is sitting next to us and spoken the same words as He did to Peter: "Lovest thou me?"

Jesus' question was not to a nominal follower of Christ. Peter was of the highest office in the Church. It must be a question for us all. Those who have sacrificed much are not exempt from the question for Peter had "Left all" to follow Jesus. Even the most zealous are subject to the inquiry. If we pressed the question to the point of being painful, we could not be censured, for Jesus asked Peter until it "grieved" him. It is good to comfort God's people, but many times heart searching grief is the ointment of the apothecary for our fickle hearts.

As our Lord asked Peter the question, He called him by his unconverted name, Simon, reminding him of what grace had done for him. The question is fraught with suggestions and gets right down to what Christianity is all about. Lovest thou me?

Loving Jesus is the funnel through which all of Christianity must flow. It is the splitting of the atom which explodes into Christian activity. Jesus didn't say, "Are you sorry for denying me? Have you repented? Nor did He ask Peter what his future plans were. If Peter truly loved Jesus all of this would fall into place. He didn't ask Peter if he loved the Church, the ordinances, the music or even the doctrine. Genuine Christianity is a relationship with a person. It is possible that we could love the wedding and forget all about the bridegroom; we could love the sanctuary and ignore the Light of it; we could love the feast and not hunger for the Bread of Life. Yes, to all of the Peters who read this, preaching, praying and doing must be based upon our Love for Jesus.

Our love for Christ is the *root of our love* for other Christians. No person is a Christian who does not love other Christians for "If a man say, I love God, and hateth is brother, he is a liar"-I John 4:20. The apostle of love saw this to be true of the first Christians. Loving other children of God is one of the greatest evidences of our calling for "We know we that we have passed from death unto life, because we love the brethren." It has been recorded that the persecutors of the infant church would say, "See how those Christians love one another." Is there a hand we can not shake or a soul that we can not plead for........ ...lovest thou me?

Our love for Christ is the wellspring for all true *obedience* "For this is the love of God, that we keep his commandments"-I John 5:3. Our love is measured by the degree of our obedience, or better said: walking in the light we have been given. Our good works can never pay for our sin, only the blood of Christ can do that. Those who truly love Jesus will be sure to obey Him out of love.

Jesus knew that Peter loved him before the three fold answer was given. Yet, he allowed Peter the opportunity to tell Him to His face. And knowing that Peter loved Him thus, He knew that Peter would want to do something for Him who had done so much for Peter. Thus He replied, "Feed my sheep". He has given all of His Peters churches to attend, songs to sing and brethren to love. Lovest thou me?

Helpful Hints:
1. Take about love vs. duty.
2. What more can you do for the object of your love?
3. Talk about loving other Christians.
4. Talk about how we express this love to one another.

"A JOYFUL NOISE"

*"Make a joyful noise unto the Lord, all ye lands. Serve the
Lord with gladness: come before his presence with singing"*
-Psalm 100:1,2

Music has a profound *influence* upon the soul. It affects
our emotions, our feelings and has the power to change
our mood in a heartbeat. Just by adding music to the score
of a movie, producers can dictate how the audience should
feel about a particular scene. A song can take us back in
time to people and places long forgotten. Music can lift us
up and it can bring us down. Yet, there are different kinds
of music. There is noise and there is "joyful noise". There
is music and there is *worshipful* music. There is music that
affects the flesh, the natural emotions, and there is music
that moves the spirit within the born again child of God.
The latter would be classified as worshipful music. To
God it would be called "a joyful noise".

It is a sad reflection upon Christianity when worship
music resembles worldly music; when it stirs the flesh
and not the spirit; when it sounds like the music on the
juke box only with the words changed; when it attracts
the world and not the elect. There IS a difference. To this

same schism in his day, C. H. Spurgeon said in a sermon: "God's house is meant to be sacred unto himself, but too often it is made an opera house, and Christians form an audience, not an adoring assembly. We come not together to amuse ourselves, to display our powers of melody, or our aptness in creating harmony. We come to pay our adoration at the foot stool of the great King, to whom alone be glory forever and forever"(17.663). He also said, "Singing should be congregational…..when your heart is full of Christ, you will want to sing." To his sentiments we must agree!

In God's ears, the joyful sound is not produced by a musical instrument. It is not even produced by a beautiful voice or by the harmony of many voices. He who constantly enjoys an angelic chorus is not impressed with human ability. The only instrument that will ever produce a joyful noise in God's ears is the *heart*……a quickened heart that resonates with love and affection for its Redeemer. That is the reason Paul focuses in on the heart in Ephesians 5:19 and Colossians 3:16, the only two scriptures that teach us about singing in the New Testament Church. Every child of God possesses this instrument. It is said that the greatest sound to a violin makers ear is the music produced from an instrument of his own making. Surely, if the Lord quickened the heart and created it anew, it would give Him the greatest pleasure to hear it echo His praise. The heart is the focus of New Testament worship!

Addressing the heart, Paul wrote, "Speaking to yourselves in psalms and hymns and spiritual songs, singing and making melody in your heart to the Lord"(Ephesians 5:19). Notice, the focus is the heart…not an instrument, not a voice. Though a person may not be able to carry a tune in a wash-tub, just reciting the words with a heart in communion with God is just as beautiful in God's ears as Placido Domingo or Luciano

Pavarotti. None are spectators in this kind of worship! In I Corinthians 14:15, Paul gives the recipe for heart worship, "I will sing with the spirit, and I will sing with the understanding also". Spiritual understanding is heart melody. The natural man can not play this instrument(I Corinthians 2:14). It is possible for one to sing "Amazing grace" ever so beautifully, and never recognize that they are a wretch in need of God's grace!

Spiritual songs are both experimental and doctrinal. They agree with the Bible and teach it in song. That is the modus operandi of "teaching and admonishing one another in psalms and hymns and spiritual songs." The heart gives assent to the truth offered up to God. Spiritual songs are sermons sang from breast to breast in the solemn assembly.

The born again heart is the fulfillment of the Old Testament types and shadows. The many instruments in David's choir were only shadows of many quickened hearts in the New. If I could paint a picture of the assembly joined together in song, I would paint a picture of a troubadour, seated beneath the balcony of his love. His heart is afire with one desire: that his love would present herself for just a little while. Christ is the great love of the Church. We should sing that He would present Himself for just a little while in our services. "Come thou almighty King!"

Helpful Hints:
1. Discuss the difference between Old Testament worship and worship in the New Testament Church.
2. Talk about the difference between a performance and worship, between an adoring assembly and an audience, between a fair show in the flesh and true worship.
3. Talk about the excess we see to day in so called Christian music.

"ENCOURAGEMENT FOR THE BEREAVED"

"But I would not have you to be ignorant, brethren, concerning them which are asleep, that ye sorrow not, even as other which have no hope. For if we believe that Jesus died and rose again, even so them also which sleep in Jesus will God bring with him"- I Thessalonians 4:13,14

One of the greatest sorrows known to all is the loss of a loved one from this life. The Christian's greatest encouragement at this time stems from a knowledge of Jesus' death, for if we believe that Jesus rose bodily from the grave, we should also believe that our loved ones will rise as well. Jesus is the firstfruits of them that slept.

As an encouragement to every Christian, Paul has given a glimpse of that monumental event when Jesus returns to open every grave and empty every tomb. From his language, we understand that Jesus is not coming alone. He will bring all of those who sleep in Christ *with Him.* Yes, we will see them again! It could be tomorrow or even next week. What a day that will be when all the disembodied souls of the Saints that presently sleep with Jesus, come back with Him to reclaim their redeemed and resurrected bodies. It is always good to remember that the best is yet to come for God's children. When Mary and Martha lost their brother Lazarus, Martha said to Jesus, "I know that he shall rise again in the resurrection at the last day"-John 11:24. Though her loss was great, her knowledge of the resurrection gave her great hope. We can be as Martha. We can view the resurrection as doctrine without the person of Christ. Jesus reminded her that "I am the resurrection and the life." Her hope was realized sooner than expected as Jesus commanded the body of Lazarus to come forth from the tomb. This is just a glimpse of the wonders we shall behold on resurrection day!

Our belief that "Jesus died and rose again" is the anchor of the soul when a loved one passes from this life. The loss of a loved one would be a hopeless experience if it were not for our knowledge of Jesus who was triumphant over death, hell and the grave. Just to know that King Jesus reigns triumphant over all things, death included, instills hope that our loved ones continue to live in another place far better than this.....and they are with Jesus! Paul wrote, "Which hope we have as an anchor of the soul, both sure and stedfast, and which entereth into that within the veil; Whither the forerunner is for us entered, even Jesus..."- Hebrews 6:19-20. When the soul is tossed to and fro in a dark storm of sorrow, there is no greater anchor than hope. Paul's language is very figurative. The forerunner was the ship that escorted the heavy laden vessel into the harbor and carried its anchor into the safe haven and dropped it. Jesus is our forerunner. Our anchor is within the veil(heaven), firmly attached. His elect are firmly attached to Him by the solid chain of His everlasting love which has no weak link. Surely, God's promises give great consolation and instill hope in the heart of the believer.

Paul did not say that we should not sorrow at all. Sorrow is a spiritual exercise of the soul. It is the God prescribed means of venting a loving heart exploding with sorrow. Even Solomon wrote, there is "a time to mourn". That time is best spent in communion with the Lord who made the promises; the one who safely keeps our loved ones in His beloved company. Let us go to Him with our sorrow and speak of the resurrection as Martha did. He will have compassion. "Jesus wept".

Helpful Hints:
1. Talk about resurrection day.
2. Talk about the resurrection of Christ.
3. Consider the comforts we find here.
4. Talk about the "others" and what they miss out on.

"BENEFITS"

"Bless the LORD, O my soul, and forget not all his benefits"
-Psalm 103:2.

David wrote a song for his people to remind them of the many benefits to be enjoyed by the worshipers of the true and living God. David was wise, he knew quite well that the very people that God favored might look at the world and begin to envy those who knew not their God and turn from His temple. Let US not forget the Lord's benefits!

Today we would pose a question to all: "Is there a benefit in serving God; is there a benefit in going to God's house; is there a benefit in reading His word; is there a benefit in prayer; in private devotions; to Christian living? How do you feel about it? What is your opinion?" We pose the question not to condemn those who would answer in the negative. Rather, we pose the question as an encouragement to those who feel in their hearts that there is a great benefit in serving God. There are times of wonder and amazement when we notice, as Job did, that, "The tabernacles of robbers prosper". In times of wonder and trials let us not become discouraged and forget the Lord's benefits.

In this psalm, the first benefit David calls our attention to is dear to us all, "Who forgiveth all thine iniquities; who healeth all thy diseases"v.3. There is no greater topic to the Christian than the forgiveness of sin. This is the benefit most cherished. Worldly treasures found in the tabernacles of robbers will never compare to this benefit for they all else perishes with time. God's gifts are everlasting. Forgiveness is the out-flowing of redemption, the cross, the blood of Christ, the covenant of grace. As the preachers have noted: "There are only two kinds of sinners: those who know they are sinners and those who know not." Those whose eyes have been opened appreciate the benefit. Let us not forget it. Let it be as sweet to us today as when we first learned that Jesus is the friend of sinners.

All benefits suggests a plurality of blessings. From temporal to eternal; from providence to predestination; from healing of the flesh to healing of the spirit, His blessings are beyond imagination. Every germ of sin that stands between the Good Shepherd and the least of His flock has been taken care of by the great Benefactor.

There are further benefits for David continues to write, "Who redeemeth thy life from destruction; who crowneth thee with lovingkindness and tender mercies"v.4. Kindness is appreciated from all of society, but lovingkindness is a benefit from one who knows His children well for therein is found the word *love*. Love always connects with something or someone. Lovingkindness is the motivation behind redemption. It is the crown the great King places upon the head of all of His children that Paul spoke of, a crown equal for all and boasted by none but the Giver. Surely, it is a tender mercy, a benefit that we should remember daily.

He also wrote of the Lord's daily benefits, :"Blessed be the Lord, who daily loadeth us with benefits, even the God of our salvation. Selah"-Psalm 68:19. Every day, there are benefits both known and unknown to God's people. If we only knew how many times we or our loved ones have been saved from an accident, a disease, or some wickedness, we would be surprised at the *daily* benefits.

Though we may see the fun and frolic in the lifestyle of the rich and famous, yet, in the Christian home I see benefits of far greater value. Yes, there is great benefit in serving God. He is "a rewarder of them that diligently seek him." Today, we encourage all who call upon the name of Jesus Christ our Lord to press into the kingdom, fight the good fight of faith, contend for the faith once delivered to the saints, and endure hardness as a good soldier. Our King is coming back and His reward is in His hand! Think upon His benefits and ask, "What shall I render unto the LORD for all his benefits toward me?"-Psalm 16:12.

Helpful Hints:
1. Let us share our benefits with others.
2. Consider the latter life of the Christian and that of the worldling.
3. Consider the utter end of each.
4. What shall we render?

"KEEP YOUR NETS MENDED"

"Now I beseech you, brethren, by the name of our Lord Jesus Christ, that ye all speak the same thing, and that there be no divisions among you; but that ye be perfectly joined together in the same mind and in the same judgment"- I Corinthians 1:10

When Paul wrote to the Corinthians, he wrote to a house divided. Corinth was plagued with many problems causing a rift among God's people. In his opening remarks, Paul beseeched the brethren to "be perfectly joined together in the same mind and in the same judgment(1:10)." The words, "perfectly joined together" were words the Corinthians well understood. They were words that referred to the mending of torn fishing nets. Paul was saying to them, "If you want to catch fish, keep your nets mended."

Division is Satan's greatest tool......it always has been. Since he is no match for the King of Kings, Satan cowardly divides families, nations and God's people by lies, deceit and whatever fleshly motive he might generate. Every military leader well knows the phrase, "Divide and conquer" as well as "United we stand, divided we fall." If an army can be divided, they are weakened and ultimately conquered.

One of the saddest statements in the Bible is I Kings 16:21, "Then were the people of Israel divided into two parts". It would only be a matter of time before they would hang their harps on the willows before a chiding enemy. God divided the light from the darkness, but He never divided light from light. He will one day divide the sheep from the goats and put His sheep in one fold. Division is the most used, most effective weapon of our sworn enemy. Let us keep our nets mended.

When the Pharisees accused Jesus of casting out devils by the chief of devils, Jesus said something that should be a constant reminder to net mending. He said, "Every kingdom divided against itself is brought to desolation; and every city or house divided against itself shall not stand". This principle applies in a church, a marriage, friendships and wherever God has stamped the word "unity". If parents do not agree in the home, the house is divided and desolation invades. The enemy is always looking for the little lamb without a home or parent. Many fall prey to his schemes of division. Teenagers are prone to divide themselves from the home. Satan may use people, songs, television, the internet, to instill harmful ideas in the mind. These are all loaded with the forked tongue of worldly wisdom to separate children from loving arms. Young people, be wise to Satan's divisions.

At Corinth, Paul knew at least four reasons their Church needed to keep their nets mended: (1)God will not honor a divided house because it is a contradiction to Christ; (2)Corinth would lose their ability to judge and make decisions that would honor Christ; (3) Division would bring reproach upon God's people in the minds of the people around them; (4) It would weaken their testimony.

Among the many causes of division at Corinth, it seems that pride was their first and foremost problem. How well Solomon's words applied: "Only by pride cometh contention"-Proverbs 13:10a. Some were proud of their knowledge, some their name, some the person who baptized them, some of their standing in the community. They had forgotten they were nothing without Jesus. In Him they were all equal: "joint heirs".

How do we keep our nets mended? By keeping Christ first! By keeping His cause, His principles, His authority, His purpose first in our lives. In the first chapter of this letter, Paul used the word Jesus or Christ 18 times. He beseeched them by the name of Jesus, "If you will not do it for Paul who gave his life to preach to you, will you do it for Jesus who died for your sins?"

Mending nets was a tedious, tiresome and never-ending process. Each day, when the ship returned to harbor, the nets had to be checked for tears and mended for the next day when they would, once again, venture out to sea. That is what Peter, Andrew, James and John were doing when Jesus called them to follow Him. It took a lot of time, yet it was necessary for the success of their occupation. Let us prepare at once for tomorrow. Our success depends upon it!

Helpful Hints:
1. **Discuss the problems at Corinth and how they apply today.**
2. **Talk about negative remarks and how they divide churches.**
3. **Talk about our enemy and his devices.**
4. **Discuss methods for the encouragement of harmonious fellowship.**

5. Talk about how television and music place false ideas in children's minds that divide their hearts from God and family.

"COME THOU WITH US, AND WE WILL DO THEE GOOD"

"We are journeying unto the place of which the LORD said, I will give it you: come thou with us, and we will do thee good: for the LORD hath spoken good concerning Israel"
-Numbers 10:29.

One of the greatest joys in life is sharing the things most dear to our hearts with people we love. To the Christian, it is the Lord, His house and the fellowship of the saints. Grateful, thankful, excited about God's presence among his people, full of love for the Lord, Moses wanted to share his experience with others. To his brother in law, Hobab, he made the invitation.

An invitation to sojourn with God and His people has always reflected a kind concern for the spiritual health of another. "We will do thee good" carries the thought of: "I want to share something with you that I hold dear to my heart. It has done me good and I want you to have the blessing as well."

Surely, this sentiment is found in the Christian invitation. Our invitations may be to one who has gone astray; perhaps to keep one from going astray; it might be to one who is strong and could be a great blessing to the cause; it could be to a friend whose company around the throne of grace is sought after; it could be to help a marriage; a child; or a simple opening of a door for a seeker. All of this and much more is found in the word *come*.

It was nothing in or of himself, or even the chosen people of God, that moved Moses to invite Hobab. His confidence was solely because "the Lord hath spoken good concerning Israel". God's promise, not Moses', was the foundation of his hopeful invitation. The Lord has promised to go with us, tabernacle with us, protect us, feed us, water us, love us and finally receive us unto Himself on high where He dwells with the Cherubim and the redeemed family of God. When God blesses us, you will be blessed. Come with us, Hobab, we will do thee good.

Surely, this must be the driving force behind every true preacher and evangelist. They have tasted the goodness of the Lord in the land of the living. They have savored his mercy, his grace and his loving kindness. They are like Jonathan who said, "see, I pray you, how mine eyes have been enlightened, because I tasted a little of this honey"-1 Samuel 14:29. If they are sincere, they are not after your money or to add another number to their list of admirers. They want to share what they have found to be the greatest blessing in their lives, something sweet, the glory of the Lord. This is the true spirit of evangelism. It is not expensive, yet, it is dynamic. It is not selfish. As one preacher put it: "It is one hobo inviting another hobo to dinner."

The world will invite God's children to "come with us" but they have no intention of doing thee *good*. Misery loves company. If friends of the world can make an acquaintance as miserable as they are themselves, they are happy. The credit card companies say, "come with us" . Will they do thee good? The race track and the gambling casinos will say, "Come with us" while we take your savings and the money to feed your family. Will they do thee good? On Sunday morning the world is screaming, "Come thou with us". Who will really do thee good?

The greatest blessing to a mother, a father or a grandparent is sharing the Lord and His house with their family. This blessing will eclipse all others in our earthly pilgrimage. To be present in the Lord's house and share the message of Jesus Christ and Him crucified, to feel His presence in the song and prayer is the best of the best. It is the oasis in this desert that many have sought after and are seeking today. To those hungry and thirsty we will say, "Come thou with us, and we will do thee good."

Helpful Hints:
1. Pray about those that you can invite to God's house.
2. Discuss how we can do them good.
3. Ask the solemn question: "How many have I invited?"
4. Who invited you?

"EVIDENCE"

"For God so loved the world, that he gave his only begotten Son, that whosoever believeth in him should not perish, but have everlasting life."-John 3:16

The Christian's faith is greatly strengthened when they discover evidences of their calling. A prayer answered or a genuine feeling of God's presence serve as "handfuls of purpose" to increase our strength and revive our hope. Precious texts from God's word also provide many evidences of our calling that are even stronger than experience, for many times, our experience can be tainted with fleshly emotions. Sprinkled amidst the numerous verses of scripture, the Lord has given abundant proofs of our calling that serve to be just as dynamic as prayer answered or miracles observed. Sometimes, they are so simply stated, we might overlook the evidence. One of the most powerful is John 3:16.

When Jesus quoted John 3:16, He was not presenting a condition for sinners to meet to be born again or to become part of the world He spoke of. One who is dead in trespasses and in sin does not have the ability to change their fallen nature. Life, whether natural or spiritual, may only be given by the Lord. Man did not invent life and man has never had the ability to take either up by his own power. Yet, there are many *evidences* of life.

When a baby is born, the most wonderful sound in the mother's ear is the cry of the infant. The cry did not give life…. it was an evidence of life. Like the infant's cry, prayer is an evidence of spiritual life for who would call upon One in whom they did not believe? This evidence was given to Ananias, when Jesus sent him to Saul of Tarsus, a man that Ananias greatly feared: "for behold, he prayeth." As an evidence of God's grace and calling Paul would later write, "ye have received the Spirit of adoption, whereby we cry, Abba, Father."

As one preacher said, "I can not go back far enough into my experience to a time that I did not call upon God nor believe in Him." These are not the words of a fool for "the fool has said in his heart, there is no God." Who can remember the time of their natural birth or their first words to their parents? The same may be said in the spiritual realm.

John 3:16 presents evidence that is simple for the believer to discover, yet impossible for the infidel. "Whosoever believeth" is not something that *everyone* can do. It is evidence for one world and a condemnation to another, "he that believeth not is condemned already, because he hath not believed in the name of the only begotton Son of God." Only one world can believe, the world of God's elect. We are not confused when we say this, we just need to identify which world Jesus died for. It was not terra firma, the earth. Jesus did not shed His precious blood for frogs, trees and flowers. It could not be the world of all creatures, for Satan and the fallen angels have no redeemer. It could not be every human being or Jesus would be a failure for "all men have not faith" and some continue to say, "there is no God." Caesar decreed "that all the world should be taxed" and this certainly was not the world that Jesus died for. Concerning this world, John wrote, "Love not the world, neither the things that are in the world". Obviously, the world means many things in scripture. It is sad to see preachers treat it so flippantly. So, the question arises: what world did Jesus die for? Was it a particular band of believers? Does it hinge on a certain ordinance? Must a certain phrase be quoted to obtain it? Is the giving of this special world placed in the hands of certain men? How can we know? Only by looking at the evidence. Do you believe in Jesus? If you do then you have the evidence and the answer: Jesus died for the world of believers and if you believe in Him you are of that chosen world. The evidence is in your own heart, given freely by God.

Jesus knew that the journey is long and that if we are honest, many times we are made to wonder and doubt the awesome majesty of God and the Spiritual world. There are times that our hope grows dim and we are made to cry with the apostles, "Lord, increase our faith." At times like these, let us go to John 3:16 and ask, "Do I believe in Jesus, that He is the Son of God; that He died for my sins upon the cross; that He rose victorious over the grave; that He is seated at the right hand of the Father today; that I am a sinner and all my hope of heaven is in His finished work?" The question should not be, "Do you accept Jesus" for that is nowhere to be found in scripture. The question should be , "Do you believe in Jesus?" If we can answer in the affirmative we have firm evidence that He died for us and one day we will be with Him.

> **Helpful Hints:**
> 1. Consider your evidence and why?
> 2. Talk about the worlds.
> 3. What are other evidences?
> 4. Talk about God's everlasting love!

"REMEMBRANCE"

"And he took bread, and gave thanks, and brake it, and gave unto them, saying, This is my body which is given for you: this do in remembrance of me"-Luke 22:19

The time of communion is a time of *remembrance*. It was in the upper room that our Lord first instituted this ordinance in the New Testament Church. From the bitter herbs of the Old Law service, to the bread and the wine that represented His body and blood, the eyes of the apostles were lifted above the law and the tables of stone, to view the now revealed mystery of Jesus Christ and Him crucified for their sins.

Jesus said, "This do in remembrance of me", as they brake the bread and passed the cup that symbolized His body and blood. Those who love Jesus best, those who appreciate His death and sufferings most, are those who attend the solemn service. They attend the words spoken about their loved One, consider the sacred emblems of His body and blood, and desire a parting embrace from their family members. As John leaned on Jesus' breast, Judas departed.

This time of remembrance is one that we both revere, yet anticipate with great joy. We revere it because it is a time that we remember Jesus' death and the pain He suffered upon the cross when our sins were placed upon Him. Once again, our tongues are unworthy of the occasion. Surely, the merits of His death deserve an eternity of memorial services. One day we will enter the unending praise! We also dread it because we know we could spend our whole life preparing ourselves for this service and yet find ourselves undone and unworthy to drink the cup and break the bread. Yet, let us rejoice, for we, as sinners, have been greatly honored. Jesus has personally invited us to His memorial service. This is the only time that the One that died has arisen from the grave and invited His family to His own memorial service. We approach the solemn service with joy because of the merits of His death and resurrection: our reproach is taken away; our sins are atoned; and Jesus, our conquering King is seated at the right hand of our Father making intercession for us even unto this present hour. Surely, there is a lot to remember when we remember the death of Jesus!

It was that same night, in the upper room, that Jesus knelt at the feet of His disciples and washed their feet. What a scene! The perfect One, humbled Himself at the feet of sinners, and washed their feet. We are made to wonder how so One, so perfect, knowing all thoughts, seeing all sin, could even look upon their face. This must be one of the things that the "angels desire to look into". How poignantly this thought is expressed as the golden Cherubims, with wings outstretched, looked upon the mercy seat. Love, mingled with mercy is abundantly experienced in the memorial service. Why would Jesus adore sinners over angels? As He did so, Jesus said, "Ye ought also to wash one another feet". The hard heart and the bitter spirit is dissolved in this service. That is why

He began it. If the perfect One could bow before the feet of sinners, surely we should forgive the imperfections of brothers and sisters in Christ's family. Though some may say that they can be right with God and at variance with their brethren, this service denies it. In this service, we see both a relationship with our Lord as well as humility before our brethren. "This do in remembrance of me."

Helpful Hints:
1. Talk about the importance of this service.
2. Talk about the emblems of Christ's body and blood and what they represent.
3. Talk about the feet washing service and what it represents.
4. Talk about the reason this service was closed to the world.

"LIGHT AFFLICTION"

"For our light affliction, which is but for a moment, worketh
for us a far more exceeding and eternal weight of glory"
- 2 Corinthians 4:17

Afflictions will come in all shapes and sizes. Physical problems, financial disasters, family problems, heartaches and depressions are all common to man. Rich and poor all meet together in the furnace of affliction, none are exempt. As Job has said, "Man that is born of a woman is few days, and full of trouble" and again, "Man is born unto trouble, as the sparks fly upward". As we grow in grace, it is important that we look for God's hand in the midst of our afflictions.

It has occurred to me that this is one of the most perplexing experiences known to man. We have a tendency to judge others and justify self when it comes to afflictions. When they come our way we might say, "It is just a fluke, a chance of life," not realizing that if God did not bring it, He must have at least allowed it. Yet, when it comes to others, we wonder what deep, dark sin they are hiding and why God is punishing them for it. The veil of affliction is removed when we learn they are not always a rod of correction. Most afflictions come our way not to punish, but rather to bring us closer, to make us more reliant up the Lord, to turn our heart away from the world and make better disciples of us. In this, God gets the glory! We can sit around perplexed about it all or we can be as Job when he said, "The Lord giveth and the Lord taketh away, blessed be the name of the Lord." He saw the Lord in it all and grew closer!

The book of Job is an illustration of God getting glory by a faithful man who is afflicted. It is another book which displays the sovereignty of God. Perplexing it was, even to his best friends. They came to comfort him and did a pretty good job when they sat silent. But they became full blown Pharisees in the end, accusing him of some sin: "Come on Job, cough it up, confess it, what have you done in your secret life to bring all this on your own head". That was the sentiment of their comforts and Job was right when he labeled them, "Miserable comforters." It was perplexing to them because Job's afflictions were not the result of sin. God allowed Satan to vex Job. In the midst of it all, God received the glory for Job's faithfulness, Satan was judged, Job learned a lot about God, himself and the people around him. His friends learned that they did not know as much about God as they thought they did. We need to be careful how we judge other people's afflictions and spend more time dissecting our own. Perhaps the Lord is molding one of His children in the furnace for their good and His glory.

It is wisdom when we learn that afflictions are actually good for
us: as Paul writes, they work "for us". James agrees with his, "My
brethren, count it all joy when ye fall into divers temptations".(James 1:2).

We feel that we need no afflictions. I am sure if you took a survey, few children and teenagers would admit they needed any discipline or direction whatsoever. Yet, without it, a life is wasted and the arrow falls short of the mark. In the Lord's eyes, we are always "children" and need afflictive guidance.

The biblical perspective of affliction is given in many places. It is the fire which consumes the dross and refines the silver and gold. Dross is worldliness or sin. Worldly wisdom denies the existence of such things….God continues to afflict. When the Lord gets ready to begin His refining, He turns the heat up. Surely, this can occur with our knowledge of what He is doing…..or without it. Wisdom is to understand God's purpose in it. Affliction!

Paul speaks of these afflictions as "light afflictions". They are not "light" by measurement of pain experienced. They are light compared to the time we experience these as compared to an eternal weight of glory. Compared to an eternity with the Lord, earthly afflictions are just for "a moment", a wink of the eye or a flash in the pan. Whatever our circumstance may be, let us look for the Lord in the furnace and say with David, "It is good for me that I have been afflicted; that I might learn thy statutes"-Psalm 119:71.

Helpful Hints:
1. Consider personal afflictions and their profit.
2. Discuss the difference between Job's afflictions and David's punishment for his sin.
3. Consider the common purpose of both.
4. Why?

"MOTHER"

"Who can find a virtuous woman? For her price is far above rubies.......She looketh well to the ways of her household, and eateth not the bread of idleness. Her children arise up, and call her blessed; her husband also, and he praiseth her"
- Proverbs 31:10,27,28.

Laura Ingalls Wilder said, "The older we grow the more precious become the recollections of our childhood days, especially our memories of mother. Her love and care halo her memory with brighter radiance, for we have discovered that nowhere else in the world is such loving self-sacrifice to be found; her counsels and instructions appeal to us with greater force than when we received them because our knowledge of the world and our experience of life have proved their worth. Dearer even than mother's teachings are little, personal memories of her, different in each case but essentially the same-mother's face, mother's touch, mother's voice..."

Thou he lived thousands of years before, king Lemuel would agree with Laura Ingalls. He, as well as God, placed a lot of emphasis on the mother. I see a great sadness in our society today. It is a kind of bitterness toward motherhood, as if this were some mundane lifestyle that only the boring and uneducated are forced to enjoy. Yet, I find the true blue mother, the one who knows her calling and seeks to do a good job, accomplishing things that movie stars and those appearing with the rich an famous seem to miss. It is this kind of mother that sets this example of *virtue*.

Virtue is more than good morals. Though it does mean that, in scripture, it adds the dynamics of *force* and *power*. It takes a god-given force to give children the correct answer, in the right spirit, at the right time and model the answer. It takes a force unknown to the world to be the heart of a home rather than the attraction of the world. This is Christ-likeness, a self denying principle that has been spited by politicians and worldly women. Their view of motherhood has had an adverse effect on many mothers leading them away from their source of joy and the superstructure of any society........the home. Their problem is not with motherhood in general, it is with God and his intended purpose for mothers. As the angels left their first estate, so have many mothers. I have never heard a mother say on her deathbed, "I wish I had spent less time with my children and family and more time at the job, at the club, at the sports event, at the shopping mall, at the card game, with the soap operas and trying to look like a model."

To the child, one of the greatest things about mother is the security found in knowing that mother is there, on site, ever present for the largest and smallest needs. Just the presence of a mother sends worries and cares packing to unknown places. Whether it is the need of a band aid, or a problem as big as the world, mother provides a sounding board, an ear to hear, undivided attention with a voice that cares and loves, placing the child on a pinnacle of her heart above every other thing in the world.

Though the mature Christian knows that God is ever present, the child needs mother. This same security, joy and comfort is found in a mother's loving arms. In one sense, the mother is the stepping stone to the Lord Himself on whom we come to rely. All of what I have said is found in the Bible in these few words that speak of a mother, "To be discreet, chaste, keepers at home, good, obedient to their own husbands, that the word of God be not blasphemed"-Titus 2:5. The rewards of such mothers are all around us: "Her children arise up, and call her blessed; her husband also, and he praiseth her". While some women love the praise of the world and a throng of admiring spectators, the virtuous woman is most interested in the praises of her own family.

The following encouragements will produce joy and meaning in a mother's life: Pray *over* each child every day. Pray *with* each child every day. Ask the Lord what they need and how you can fill the void. Have at least one meaningful conversation with each child every day. Tell each child you love them every day. Turn off the phone and TV. and get to know them. Share their daily experiences with them when they come home from school. Talk of the Lord and His blessings often. Let them know He is your source of strength. Live what you tell them. Do things with them however small. Prioritize their existence, be present when they are home. Pray for God's assistance! When one begins this God given calling, other things will become less important and the true joy of motherhood will be found.

I believe that in the heart of every mother is the same cry: "I need my mother", even when mother has departed the scenes of this life. "But what kind of mother do I need?", should be the obvious reply. The answer to that question should pierce the heart and become the looking glass for every mother to look into for her own children.

Helpful Hints:
1. What are some of your favorite memories of mother.
2. Consider the import role of mothers in our society.
3. How can you be a better mother?
4. If your mother is living, how can you show your appreciation for her?

"THE TELLER"

"He telleth the number of the stars; he calleth them all by their names"-Psalms 147:4

How great is our Lord, who telleth the number of the stars. As man sends out his cameras to discover new stars, the Lord watches with perfect knowledge of their number and placement. I have heard of people who have attempted to count the stars, but all attempts have been in vain. Only He who created them knows that number. Surely, this contrast should provide a glimpse of God's knowledge and wisdom compared to man's.

The Lord knows every nook and cranny of the universe better than man knows what is in his pockets. It is a vain attempt for man to dethrone the Lord. Yet, that is what he tries to do when he says that the Lord did not create the universe. This one verse should show how silly man is as he makes such statements. Today, we will ask those who advocate this idea of evolution tell us how many stars there are in the sky. We do not want an estimate, we want perfect knowledge. Then, tell us the secret of every star. Tell us the gasses, the molecules, the atoms and every chemical reaction that brought about its being.

Only the Great Teller has this knowledge. The Lord does not speculate, He demonstrates. He demonstrates His existence by His very creation. This wisdom may only be discovered by children of light.

As we gaze into the vast expanse of the sky we gain some insight into the greatness of our Lord and His beautiful majesty. Yet, with all this beauty we find something that is equally wonderful: we find a personal Lord: "He calleth them all by their names." I love this thought for it reveals the loving character of our Lord. The gods of the heathen, the gods that man has made up in his own mind might be depicted as strong and powerful, but the One and Only true God is the One who has named every individual star. As a boy might name the marbles in his bag or a girl her dolls, the Lord places names on those twinkling orbs in the sky. Perhaps the way they twinkle gives them their peculiar name or the placement they have in the sky. Whatever it is, it will be wonderful to know when we get to glory.

Yet, there is more to this telling, this naming, than just star power. Surely, this is written for the encouragement of His people. If the Lord knows every star, if He has a name for each one, surely He knows His people and has a special, caring, loving name for each one. These names of His people are continually before His eye, as the prophet has said, "Behold, I have graven thee upon the palms of my hands; thy walls are continually before me"-Isaiah 49:16. Whatever the Lord stretches forth His mighty hands to accomplish, His people are continually before His eyes.

It also tells us that heaven is going to be a big place. The Lord told Abraham, "And I will make thy seed to multiply as the stars of heaven, and will give unto thy seed all these countries; and in thy seed shall all the nations of the earth be blessed"-Genesis 26:4. This promise must have been in the Psalmist's mind as he wrote of the Lord telling the stars. It embraces all nations, all tongues, all families and all people of the earth. It is a sad attempt for man to give out the exact number of those going to heaven….. as if he knew. We should ask those who attempt to do so to tell us the number the stars.

The great "Teller" knows all, created all and will one day tell the secrets of the universe to His own. Today, let us rejoice in our Lord who "Telleth the number of the stars."

Helpful Hints:
1. Talk about the subject of creation.
2. God's omniscience.
3. God's personal knowledge of His people.
4. God's promises.

"GOD'S TEMPLE"

"Know ye not that ye are the temple of God, and that the Spirit of God dwelleth in you?"- 1 Corinthians 3:16

Corinth was a city of sin. The temple of Aphrodite was there, a temple dedicated to their goddess of fertility. Over one-thousand consecrated temple prostitutes plied their trade among the inhabitants and visitors of Corinth and it was here that the Lord placed one of His candlesticks to shine a light in the midst of the darkness. To shine their light, this church must not conform to the world. Worldly wisdom had permeated their ranks and there were those who were advocating that it really did not matter how a person lived or how they used their bodies. Fornication was the chief sin of Corinth, people living together outside the bonds of sacred matrimony, husbands and wives unfaithful to one another and sexual misconduct in the grosses terms. Such would be expected from the world but not from professing Christians, so Paul writes his letter to them and brings before them a truth, a theological perspective that they needed to know. He brought it before them in the form of a question: "Know ye not that ye are the temple of God, and that the Spirit of God dwelleth in you?" Aphrodite is not God's temple, you are!

Here we find a Christian perspective, a world view that may only be experienced through the light of a spiritual mind: A person who is born of the spirit of God is not an isle unto themselves, God dwells within them, their body is God's temple. The Lord is vitally concerned with what goes on with His temple. This truth should be contemplated by every Christian every day, every moment. I am sure that it would become a safeguard to our spirit and a guide for our carnal appetites.

Paul taught this truth to most, if not all of the churches with language like: "Christ in you, the hope of glory"(Col. 1:27); "And if Christ be in you, the body is dead because of sin"(Rom. 8:10); "For it is God which worketh in you both to will and to do of his good pleasure"(Phil. 2:13); "I will dwell in them, and walk in them; and I will be their God, and they shall be my people(II Corinthians 6:16)." If we are a child of God, your body has been purchased with the blood of Jesus Christ. As Paul said again, "You are not your own, you are bought with a price". What happens to and with the body is God's business.

A great deal of time and money is spent on our bodies. We worry about its health; we build it up; fix it up; repair it; primp it; pluck it; paint it; feed it; entertain it; amuse it; feed it; cloth it; water it. We want our bodies to look better than anything else in the world. What a difference it would make if we spent as much time contemplating the fact that our body is God's temple as we do fixing it up. Sure, we should strive to keep it healthy, clean and commendable. Paul wanted the brethren to know that their body was God's temple, that the Lord dwelt within them, that they carried the Lord with them wherever they went and that they should be cognizant of His divine presence at all times.

Though Hollywood does not publish this in their movies, misusing God's temple has consequences. Much depression and anxiety of heart comes from abusing God's temple. If we are honest, we would have to say that our greatest pain has come from the misuse of God's temple. I find the happiest people in the world to be those who live with this knowledge: "Your body is a temple of the Holy Ghost."

Helpful Hints:
1. Talk about abortion.
2. Talk about sexual conduct and marriage.
3. Abuses such as tattoos, body piercing and etc.
4. Substance abuses.

"CONSIDER THE MIRACLE"

"For they considered not the miracle of the loaves: for their heart was hardened"-Mark 6:52.

Today, our message centers around the spiritual subject of miracles. I say spiritual, because that is what a miracle is. It has to do with Jesus Christ. A miracle is a Holy Hand in an unholy world. It is when the Lord performs or achieves something that man can not do; when He reaches in and changes things; alters the normal course of nature; makes things happen that would never have occurred naturally. A miracle is not luck, chance or accident. It is on purpose and for a purpose. It may be the answer to a prayer, mercy performed for one of His children, a rescuing angel sent unawares, a gift bestowed by grace, or something done to bring about a predicted historical event predetermined of God. Though God is actively involved in every aspect of creation, a miracle is above and beyond what is normally and usually expected and seen. Or we might say it like this: "God is omnipresent, yet at times He is *manifestly* present. This is what we call a miracle.

I believe in miracles and I believe miracles are performed by the Lord every day by the billions. Yet, we are like the disciples. We consider not the miracles, because our hearts are hardened. Yes, even the disciples, who had just witnessed the miracle of Jesus feeding over 5,000 with five loaves and two fishes had forgotten His miraculous power. So, a few days later He reminds them again by feeding another 4,000. We would think that, by now, the lesson was learned, that Jesus could take care of their bread problems, yet, when Jesus said, "Take heed and beware of the leaven of the Pharisees and of the Sadducees", they thought He was talking about bread they did not have. The world had already crept in. Jesus and the spiritual realm was all but forgotten and once again, they saw the world void of Jesus and His miracles.

Today, let us consider His miracles! As we do I must confess that I am not an expert on miracles. I also know that many of His miracles are unseen and unknown. Like the car that could have swerved, but didn't; the timing changed to alter our course; the weather that changed the outcome of a battle; good advice given in the nick of time; the encouragement given when our ship was ready to sink; the love bestowed when our hopes were near gone; the job opening; the things lost for the best; even unanswered prayers that would have resulted in our own ruin are all found in this category, though often hidden by the blanket of our worldliness. If the Lord had not informed us by His word, we would have attributed the calming of the disciples storm to mere chance or fate. Daniel's rescue from the lions would have been the result of some sick lions and the parting of the Red Sea was a freak accident of nature. Miracles are revealed in the Bible to expose God's power and His care for His people, to remind the hard heart that He is a miracle worker and in control.

Now, what about us? Have we enjoyed miracles in our lives? Every child of God will experience at least one miracle and that is the new birth. As Paul wrote, "If any man be in Christ, he is a new creature." Do you enjoy good preaching, are you hungry and thirsty for spiritual things? This is an evidence of spiritual life, you have had an experience with the Holy Ghost. This is truly a miracle. As Paul wrote, "Knowing, brethren beloved, your election of God. For our gospel came not unto you in word only, but also in power, and in the Holy Ghost, and in much assurance." This is a gift, a desire given from above that not every mortal enjoys. It is a miracle just to understand who Jesus is and have a desire to be with Him.

Life itself is a great miracle. All life emanates from God and the fact that you are alive is a miracle of His grace. You are not a chance, an accident, an animal without a purpose, you are created of God, a miracle. As the spiritual hymn goes: "Here it is I find my heaven, while upon the Lamb I gaze; Love I much? I've much forgiven; I'm a miracle of grace". Sin forgiven is a miracle. The work of Christ was the greatest miracle this world has ever seen. Love bestowed upon undeserving sinners is a miracle. Creation itself, is a miracle. It is not an accident of evolution, it is a creative miracle of God, just like your life. When I hear a bird sing or a hummingbird zip from flower to flower, when I see the sun rise and the beautiful sunset I see a miracle from God. If it is not so, let man paint his own sky and raise his own sun. All of these miracles glorify God. Let us consider them today!

Helpful Hints:
1. Talk about miracles you have experienced.
2. Talk about the miracles in the Bible.
3. Consider the power.
4. Talk about the reasons the world tries to discredit God's miracles.

"FATHER, HAVE I EVER SEEN A CHRISTIAN?"

"And if it seem evil unto you to serve the Lord, *choose you this day whom ye will serve; whether the gods which your fathers served that were on the other side of the flood, or the gods of the Amorites, in whose land ye dwell: but as for me and my house, we will serve the* Lord*"-*Joshua *24:15*

There is the story of a little boy who asked his father what a Christian was. After the father had given his explanation his little boy looked up into his face and asked, "Father, have I ever seen a Christian?" The question pierced the father's heart as we would imagine, but the illustration is good and serves as an exercise of our own conscience as fathers.

According to scripture, being a father is a high calling of God which carries with it many responsibilities. The greatest of these callings is to teach our children about the Lord Jesus Christ and to nurture a genuine faith in Him and a love for His principles. As with Abraham, Isaac and Jacob, the ardent desire of the father should be to hand biblical principles down from father to son for future generations. As the psalmist has written: "Give ear, O my people, to my law: incline your ears to the words of my moth. I will open my mouth in a parable: I will utter dark saying of old: Which we have heard and known, and our fathers have told us. We will not hide them from their children, shewing to the generation to come the praises of the Lord, and his strength, and his wonderful works that he hath done"-Psalm 78:1-4. In their day, the writings of Moses, conquests of their people, the parting of the Red Sea, the manna in the wilderness, the mighty works of God were among the tutorial challenges of the fathers.

The heart of the father can be easily sidetracked concerning this calling. He can become more interested in teaching the child sports and human knowledge than Christ and Him crucified. It seems that this kind of man, the spiritual father, is all but forgotten in our culture today. Yet, some of the strongest men in history were lovers and worshipers of God. Joshua, whose sword drove out the Canaanites said, "As for me and my house, we will serve the Lord." Here is a real man that we would all desire to live up to. He was not a puppet to lust or pleasure, he was strong in the Lord. I believe in the heart of every child is the desire to have a Godly father. Though the feeling may be difficult for the child to express, it is here they find confidence and stability.

By a father's actions, the child is taught. Every father should come to this sober judgment of self: he should be a living example of what he wants his child to be. He must call evil, evil, and good, good. If the father lives apart from God, he can expect his child to do so. We realize there are great instances of grace, as with Abraham who was called away from the idolaters in his family, or Gideon who was raised up to tear down his family idols. We also know that some of the best parental efforts have been thwarted by the devil. Yet, that does not take away from responsibility. One day, the crop will mature. Let us not say "I did it my way." Let us say, "I did it God's way." When your child looks into your face, what do they see?

Helpful Hints:
1. Talk about the role of fatherhood and its biblical responsibilities.
2. Fathers in the Bible.
3. Children and fathers in the Bible.
4. The joys of fatherhood.

"FOUNDATIONS"

"If the foundations be destroyed, what can the righteous do?"
-Psalm 11:3

Today, our message centers around the recent decision handed down by the appellate court that we may no longer say, "One nation under God". Thankfully, we have seen many leaders of our land rise up in protest to this attack upon God, the foundation of our great country.

Though the pens of historians and journalists are doing their best to change the truth into a lie, this country was founded upon God's word, by men and women seeking religious freedom. They were seeking a place that they could worship the Lord without government interference. This can not be questioned. On our coins we read, "In God We Trust"; when we read the words of the early lawmakers, their language is pregnant with the name of God; we hold our hand on the Bible in court and solemnly swear to God; the word "pray" is used on most forms of legal titles and notes ….the evidence goes on.

From the *mouths* of our founding fathers we continue to hear their thoughts of God. George Washington said, "It is impossible to rightly govern the world without God and the Bible". Abraham Lincoln said, "I am profitably engaged in reading the Bible. Take all of this Book upon reason that you can, and the balance by faith, and you will live and die a better man." Herbert Hoover said, "The whole of the inspirations of our civilization springs from the teachings of Christ and the lessons of the Prophets. To read the Bible for these fundamentals is a necessity of American life." J. Edgar Hoover said, "The Bible is the unfailing guide which points the way for men to the perfect life. The lessons of charity, justice and equality which enrich its pages should be learned well by all men in order that greed, avarice, and inequity can be blotted out." This is our foundation!

It is without question that these men were not perfect.….nor was Peter, Abraham or Moses. Those who try to destroy our foundations search for the mistakes of these leaders and highlight them before the eyes of the public rather than giving the demeanor of their whole life. The Bible is honest, these people are not. It is from the whole of one's life that we learn what a person really is. This is usually summed up by the way they speak of their Creator!

It is from the foundation of Christianity in our nation that the kindness of God was extended to poor people from other countries seeking refuge. This foundation has provided great wealth and prosperity, it has amassed the greatest military force known to man and food enough to feed the needy in far away places. Yet, there are those that this God loving and God fearing nation has helped that would remove this foundation that has brought them good. As Jeremiah wept over his people, as Jesus wept over Jerusalem, many Christians have wept over this erosion of God in our country.

Many of us remember our younger days in public school, when scripture was read and prayer was offered. Standards of right and wrong were founded upon accepted biblical truth. In that day, God-fearing parents had more of an input! Christ is most commonly found in the hearts of mothers, fathers, workers and poor people. These people started the schools, not those who often run them today. Spiritual wickedness in high places is bent upon the destruction of the godly foundation of America that my grandfather, my great-grandfather and their children established their lives upon. Henry Ford said, "All the sense of integrity, honor, and service I have in my heart I got from hearing the Bible read by a school teacher in the three years I was privileged to go to a little, old-fashioned grammar school. The teacher read the Bible every morning to start the day right. I got a great deal out of that influence." Surely, Christianity has historically been a part of the American public education system and it produced character and godliness. God and prayer has had a dynamic influence upon the conscience of America.

Christianity has been taken advantage of by its enemies since the first Church because Christianity will not use the sword. It will not lower itself to the hating, backbiting, repulsive methods of the world. It will not cheat nor lie about people or events. It endeavors to behave itself in a way that honors Christ and looks for their Lord to fight for them. This is our prayer.

Helpful Hints:
1. Talk about 1 Timothy 2:1,2 and how Christians should do so.
2. A great opportunity to discuss our founding fathers.
3. The religion of our country, where it came from and why.
4. What can we do?
5. A wonderful discussion to make our children wise.

"HOW LONG?"

"How long wilt thou forget me, O LORD? for ever? how long wilt thou hide thy face from me? How long shall I take counsel in my soul, having sorrow in my heart daily? how long shall mine enemy be exalted over me?"-Psalm 13:1-2

Patience is a virtue that is hard to come by, molded by the hand of tribulation, for 'tribulation worketh patience'. It is most commonly found with the hoary head. Parents might identify with "how long" in the car on a long trip. Before we get out of town we hear from the back seat, "How much longer?" It is then we recognize that tribulation and patience are making their mark upon young and old alike.

How long is the class, how long is the book, how long is the work day, how long is the wait in the doctors office, how long before vacation, how long before supper, how long is the sermon, how long before payday, how long till this job is over, how long till this day is over, this month, this year, this semester, how long till retirement, how long till this feeling is past, this trouble, this heartache.….? There is an overwhelming desire to be exactly where we want to be in life, and doing exactly what we want to be doing, and feeling exactly how we want to feel, and being with the people we want to be with. Such thoughts are a mark of impatience, a wasting of our lives. It is from this attitude that the psalmist, David, writes what is usually referred to as the "HOW LONG" psalm as he seeks the Lord's face for his petitions to be answered.......right now!

He begins his petition with an assumption, a confused feeling that we all experience in our tribulations, "How long wilt thou forget me?" And then he gives the Lord the answer, "Forever". That is why we love David so much, his thoughts are like our own. Many times, his words express what we feel in our own hearts. In our tribulation, we all feel to be forgotten by our Lord, He is wasting our time by not answering us immediately and making us suffer needlessly. Yet, if we will stop and allow our thoughts to ascend to the right hand of the Father, we will find a great King that watches over His own every moment, every day. Even David, when thinking aright, wrote in the 139th Psalm that His Lord knew when he sat down, when he got up, what he was thinking, what he was about to say and that his Lord was present with him every moment.

The character of our Lord causes us to consider why our prayers are unanswered. It may be that Lord is asking us how long: "How long before you cease from man whose breath is in his nostrils, how long before you quit trusting in horses and chariots that can not deliver, how long before you turn from your idols, how long before you give up your sin, how long before you get back in Church, how long before you get back to reading my word and how long before you remember where your prosperity comes from?" When we begin to beg, "How long", we find the truth of the matter: He has not forgotten us, we have forgotten Him. Surely, David's "How long" question should cause deep meditations of our own conscience. Perhaps our unanswered petition is God's manifestation of love, to draw us closer and to humble us. Perhaps we ask for something amiss and unreasonable or our thinking is not right and it is not His. Perhaps, we want our life to be like we want it and not what He has chosen for us. Perhaps it is to teach us patience and the answer will be in His time and in His own way. Perhaps, we have jumped in a pit of our own making and we must live out what we did not ask the Lord about in the first place. Many reasons may be found for "how long" and it does not mean that the Lord has forgotten us. Let Satan not put these words in our mind or our mouths.

Let us try to do this in the midst of our unanswered petitions: While we are anxious for the answer, for the arrival, for the event to unfold, let us not miss out on some precious moments for fellowship with the Lord and the opportunity to grow in grace. Job, in his patience said: "Who knoweth not in all these that the hand of the LORD hath wrought this?"-Job 12:9.

Helpful Hints:
1. Talk about prayers that were a long time coming.
2. Talk about unanswered prayers that we best unanswered.
3. Talk about Psalms 139.
4. What do you need to change?
5. What should we be praying for?

"HE IS ABLE"

"I know whom I have believed, and am persuaded that he is able to keep that which I have committed unto him against that day"-2 Timothy 1:12

Paul had committed much unto Christ. We might speculate about his word, "that", were we not given the rest of the sentence: "against that day". In Paul's heart, he knew there was a day coming that outweighed every other day that had ever dawned. That day was the dawning of one eternal day, the day that Jesus Christ returns.

Paul knew that on *that* particular day Christ would return with ten-thousands of His saints, raise the dead, judge the wicked, cast them into the eternal abyss of suffering and carry His people home with Him to glory. He felt to be the chief of sinners and knew if it were not for Christ, he would be banished from the presence of God and Christ forever. That is the "that" that Paul had committed unto Christ: his salvation.

That being the case, Paul saw Jesus as *full payment* for his sin. He had committed that unto Jesus. Let us commit the full price of our redemption to Jesus Christ for "all our righteousnesses are as filthy rags"-Isaiah 64:6. Certainly our Lord is well pleased with our righteous efforts to serve Him. Yet, when we hold those labors up to the Father's face to pay for or trade off our sin they are offensive to Him, they are as filthy rags. Nothing else is pleasing to the Father than the suffering of His Son. Even an apostle must confess his own weakness and commit his salvation to a faithful creator. Let us commit this unto Jesus. He is good for the debt.

Paul must have also committed his security *from falling* to Jesus. How confidently he could write, "Who shall lay anything to the charge of God's elect?" In other words, "Take it up with Jesus, He is my intercessor, my ransom, my payment and my Savior. I have committed this to Him and not my own fickle love."

Surely, Paul's sufferings were equally committed unto Christ.

With this confidence he wrote, "There hath no temptation taken you

but such as is common to man: but God *is* faithful, who will not suffer

you to be tempted above that ye are able; but will with the temptation

also make a way to escape, that ye may be able to bear *it"(1* Corinthians 10:13). Paul was suffering the pains of persecution when he wrote this letter, yet he had committed the pains and sufferings of this life to Jesus as well. We must commit each day to Jesus. Day by day, let us look to one who does not change like the world, to one who is able to keep us from sinking in the stormy waves about us. He walks on the water and in the furnace, He opens prison gates and raises the dead. He is able.

Concerning committing things to God's trust, Thomas Brooks, the great Puritan writer, declared: "The child can not better secure any precious thing it has, than by putting it into the father's hands to keep. Our mercies are always safest and surest when they are out of our hands, and in the hands of God. We trust as we love, and we trust where we love; where we love much, we trust much; much trust speaks out of much love; if we love Christ much, surely we shall trust him much." He is able!

Helpful Hints:
1. Discuss salvation committed to Christ vs. our own works.
2. Other things that Paul may have committed to His trust.
3. Things that we should commit to His trust.
4. The blessings of such commitment.

"WALKING WITH JESUS"

"And, behold, two of them went that same day to a village called Emmaus…Jesus himself drew near, and went with them
-Luke 24:13-15

Today our mind is focused on the special appearance our Lord made with two lonely travelers on their way to Emmaus. The Omnipresent one could have been anywhere He wanted to be on that occasion. He could have been in Caesar's castle, on the Caribbean or just visiting with a few angels. But He chose to be with two confused travelers on their walk. He is sovereign in His choice concerning the every day affairs of life and His choices of fellowship are not based upon money, titles and position. As we find in this event, many times His visits are unexpected!

As Jesus walked with them, He opened up the scriptures to them, "they said one to another, Did not our heart burn within us, while he talked with us by the way, and while he opened to us the scriptures?"- Luke 24:32. Surely, this is how we know we have been with Jesus. Our heart burns with us and He opens up the scriptures.

Fellowship with the Lord's people gives a kindred experience. We look back on the experience and our hearts burn to be with those people again. They, too, play their part in opening up the scriptures for us. Pastors, preachers, evangelists and brethren all have a part in this ministry. John wrote, "We know that we have passed from death unto life, because we love the brethren"- 1 John 3:14a. We love to be with those who love our Lord. We always look forward to another opportunity to be with them again. It seems to me that Satan has succeeded in dividing Christians. Many times we hide behind our manmade traditions and doctrines and separate ourselves from others who equally love our Lord Jesus Christ. Let it not be so. Let us look for Christ in others and love them for Christ's sake. If He loves them, and takes the time to walk with them, should we not as well? This is always a good rule. Those that we see walking with Jesus, we will walk with as well. Perhaps something will be opened up unto us!

Though we may not realize it, when we minister to others, we become like our Lord. Any thing that we can do for another, expecting nothing in return, is ministering. Just to walk with them, talk with them, listen to their troubles and cares is a step away from self towards another's needs. So it was on that special day with our Lord and His two travelers.

As our Lord departed from His friends at Emmaus, they knew they had been highly favored. They knew their Lord had walked with them that day. Today, I hope He walks with you!

Helpful Hints:
1. Talk about your special visits with Jesus.
2. Discuss how Jesus opened their eyes with the scriptures.
3. When has your heart burned?
4. Consider election!

"A WAY OF ESCAPE"

"There hath no temptation taken you but such as is common to man: but God is faithful, who will not suffer you to be tempted above that ye are able; but will with the temptation also make a way to escape, that ye may be able to bear it"
-I Corinthians 10:13

Life is full of temptations, trials and tests, each marked with its own individual characteristics unique to its intended purpose. Though there are more kinds of temptations and tests than man can number, they come in two basic categories: God's temptations or trials to make us better and Satan's temptations to destroy. Yet, in either case, we must remember this: God is sovereign, He either allowed it to happen or He caused it. In either case, He has the answer.

The former comes from the desk of God. A good example is the greatest temptation of Abraham. We read, "God did tempt Abraham"-Genesis 22:1. Abraham's faithfulness was tested in a request that we might think to be unreasonable: "Take now thy son, thine only son Isaac, whom thou lovest... and offer him there for a burnt offering". Though God saw the outcome, Abraham must go through it to prove his faithfulness to God, himself and the world. Our trials are the same. Though many seem to be greater than we can bear, the end is blessed. They cause us to grow as our faith in God becomes stronger. They prove to our own selves and to the world that our love for the Lord is genuine as fruit is born from the experience. Jesus said He would purge every vine. He is faithful to his promise. Many times it is difficult to comprehend the trial: "Is this a trial of God or is this just life", or, "Am I being punished for sin". We wonder, we are perplexed as Job, yet our posture must be the same regardless of the category. We are to stand resolute in our faith and with our God and He will see us through.

The other kind of temptation comes not from God, though He must allow it and can restrain the degree of it. They come from the devil, referred to in scripture as "The tempter". His methods are different as well as his purpose. He tempts with evil, with lust and pride and his purpose is to destroy. God does not tempt His own people with evil. (James 1:13).

You can be sure that the devil was present when David cast his eyes on Bathsheba and when Eve ate of the forbidden fruit. Do you see the difference? Not only has the fool said in his heart, "There is no God", he has also said, "There is no devil."

Yet, in the midst of these temptations we read of this great promise: no matter what we face, it is "Common to man". Though we might sing, "Nobody knows the trouble I've seen, Nobody knows my sorrow"......they have! Somewhere, at some other time, another weary worn pilgrim has faced the exact trial, test or temptation that you are facing today. Surely, this must be a comfort. And it tells us something of the devil. He can not come up with any thing new. He is using the same techniques: anger, jealousy, hatred, pride, lust, fear, sloth, bitterness, wrath, idolatry, adultery, fornication, drunkenness and murder(Galatians 5:19-21) to divide and destroy. Now, if one of these comes before us, we do not have to be, "a rocket scientist", to figure out who is behind it. We must seek God's strength to avoid it. This brings us to the next promise.

Paul reminds us of God's faithfulness: "God is faithful". Surely He knows about our plight and He will not suffer his children to be tempted above the strength He gives them. If they were, they would have an excuse: "The devil made me do it" or "My Father left me alone". Paul condemns this attitude in Romans 1:20, "They are without excuse". Though the devil is allowed to tempt, he is also on a chain and the Lord restrain him as He wishes.

Let us be careful as we appreciate God's greatness. The Lord will make 'a' way to escape, not *many* ways to escape. This way must be a way that will cause us to "seek His face". He alone is "the way the truth and the life". He alone has the answer. When we find it, the trial becomes sweet as we gain a victory over the tempter and draw closer to the Lord.

Lord, help us to face our trials with this knowledge and when we come to the end of life's journey let us sweetly sing, "My strongest trials now are past, my triumph is begun"-Angel Band.

Helpful Hints:
1. Consider your greatest trials.
2. Discuss the trials of the patriarchs: Abraham, Job, David or Moses.
3. Discuss the subtle methods of Satan.
4. Discuss our Lord's temptation in the wilderness.

"NO FEAR"

"There is no fear in love; but perfect love casteth out fear: because fear hath torment. He that feareth is not made perfect in love"-1 John 4:18

There is a balance in God's word, instruction which keeps the pilgrim in the middle of terrible and frightening extremes. Religion has its pitfalls, false religion that is. The straight and narrow gate through which we must pass has the pillar of Jachin on the right and the pillar of Boaz on the left. We must walk between two truths, not around them, to get into the temple. It is easy to slide off into the ditch concerning any truth, so we must compare scripture with scripture to find the old path marked out by God. We find these extremes to be so concerning the subject of fear. How can God tell us: "The fear of the LORD *is* the beginning of wisdom"(Proverbs 9:10a) and then tell us that there is no fear in perfect love? Surely, this seems like a great contradiction, yet, we know they must both be true. As with the pillars of Jachin and Boaz, we must place them side by side and walk between them. We will call one pillar *terrible fear* and the other pillar *reverential fear*. The former fear, terrible, goes thus: When your fear cometh as desolation, and your destruction cometh as a whirlwind; when distress and anguish cometh upon you." (Proverbs 1:27). The latter fear, reverential, is encouraged. It is a healthy fear described succinctly as *a fear of love*. It is displayed in passages like: "The fear of God is the beginning of wisdom"(Proverbs 9:10). Thus, we find middle ground which may only be understood and enjoyed by knowledge of our heavenly Father who will chasten his children but never destroy them.

To further illustrate these two kinds of fear we might compare the attack of September, 11th to the terrible fear. This kind of fear 'torments' the soul. When we think of our heavenly father, John would not have us think this way. Our God is loving, caring and He does not torment His children. He loves them with an everlasting love and though He may chasten them as a father would his son(Hebrews 12:5), it is always for their good. It is this kind of fear that Solomon referred to when he wrote, "The fear of God is the beginning of knowledge.(Proverbs 1:7)". Here is the balance, the harmonizing of scripture. Reverential fear is healthy. It is one of the greatest evidences of sonship: to know that we belong to our Father and that His chastening is evidence of His love for us.(Hebrews 12:9-11). With this knowledge, we can expect no more from His chastening hand than what is necessary for our correction. This reverential fear is evidence proper that we are interested in pleasing Him, evidence that we love Him and evidence that we believe that He exists.

These two fears remind me of the story of the little boy who could not sleep because he had a terrible fear. He was afraid that if he died in his sleep he would go to hell. After sobbing on his pillow for what seemed to be hours, he went into his mother's bedroom to confess his fears. Usually a happy child, the mother was shocked to see her baby in such a sad state. "What is wrong with you", was her immediate response. The tearstained reply was "I'm afraid if I die in my sleep I will go to hell." As the mother, too, began to weep, the child knew only too well his sin was known to all, even to his mother, and she way crying over his hopeless estate. "She knows it too", were his little thoughts, "she knows I deserve nothing less than hell. I have been mean to my brother, I have not obeyed my parents as I should." Though his sins were small compared to the atrocities of the world, his quickened heart had been made tender by God's grace. He had little to compare his faults with, he just knew he was a sinner. But he had to ask his mother for the final sentence, "Why are you crying mom?" To his utter surprise, the most joyful news came from her mouth......something unexpected..... "If you were not a child of God, you would not be worried about it", was the reply. Suddenly, the tormenting fear was gone as he carefully examined the evidence: "Why would I think myself to be a sinner if God had not shown me. Why would He show me if He did not love me. Why would I feel this way if I were not in God's family?" Peace was given by the Prince of Peace and the terrible fear was replaced with Godly reverence.

It is the gospel that calms the tormented heart and the fear of hell. That is why it is called the "good news" and "glad tidings of good things". Jesus has risen from the grave and conquered death. He has redeemed His people with His own blood. They now belong to Him and none can pluck them from His hands. Christian, is your hope in Christ? If it is then death has lost its sting and the future is not so fearful. "Come now, and let us reason together, saith the Lord: though your sins be as scarlet, they shall be as white as snow; though they be red like crimson, they shall be as wool"-Isaiah 1:18.

Helpful Hints:
1. Consider the two kinds of fear.
2. Consider how we should fear God.
3. How we should not fear God.
4. The peace in "knowing your election".

"REMEMBERING JESUS"

"And he took bread, and gave thanks, and brake it, and gave unto them, saying, This is my body which is given for you: this do in remembrance of me"- Luke 22:19

We have all heard stories of people who have been rescued from burning buildings or snatched from twisted and burning heaps of wreckage along the interstate by some brave and caring individual. It seems that the hearts and souls of those who were rescued were knit to their savior, as Jonathan's soul was knit to David's, when he slew Israel's giant enemy. In most cases, some sense of appreciation or gratitude for the savior seems to be born and the would-be victim longs to stay in touch with their rescuer.

In the movie, "Saving Private Ryan", the last words of Tom Hanks went something like, "Make it count". The dying rescuer gave his life to save another and solemnly charged the saved to make the life he had been given count for something good. The last scene was moving, as the rescued soldier, now aged man, was visiting the grave of the man who saved his life.

Surely, this kind of thankfulness and love is manifested among the Lord's people as they meet together to remember their Savior who saved them not from burning buildings or burning wreckage, but from a burning and eternal place of torment. Yet, they do not stand over an occupied grave. They stand before their living Savior for He is always present in the memorial service!

Many of the early disciples knew Jesus personally in the days of His earthly ministry. As the infant church gathered together to break the bread, they remembered their friend who walked with them, talked with them, taught them, healed them, and ultimately died for their transgressions. As the bread was crushed and broken in their hands, their minds and hearts were upon the body of their friend whose body was crushed and broken for their sin. Oh, that we might break the bread with such affection today!

It is difficult to tell just how frequently they observed their Lord's body in this way. At Troas, they came together to break bread upon the first day of the week (Acts 20:7). In another place we read where they, "continuing daily with one accord in the temple, and breaking bread from house to house, did eat their meat with gladness and singleness of heart"(Acts 2:46). As we read these passages, we find their fellowship so closely knit that it is difficult to tell where the Lord's supper ended and their regular meals began. Much of the time, circumstances required the early Christians to meet in their own homes to worship together and break the bread. As they brake the bread from "house to house" I can almost hear them say: "I want to observe the master's death at my house". To them, it was a blessed privilege to observe the memorial service in the confines of their personal dwellings. What a testimony it must have been to their immediate family and their neighbors as they worshiped the Lord and brake the bread and told the story of Jesus Christ and Him crucified. Every baptized believer should joyfully anticipate that special time when the saints of God gather together and remember Jesus in that sacred ordinance of "the breaking of bread".

Symbolically, the manna in the wilderness represented the Lord Jesus Christ, the Bread of Life. This "manna" in the wilderness provided sustenance and strength for the Lord's people. As we journey through the wilderness of this world, the doctrine of Christ crucified is now as strengthening and comforting to a believer as ever it was. As the manna was sweet in taste and sustaining to the natural body so is this "living bread" to the hungry soul. We enjoy the sweetness of his fruits, His word, His doctrine and ordinances; those meats which include in them all happiness. They looked for this manna daily and so should we for He strengthens our soul and causes us to rejoice!

Helpful Hints:
1. Consider the importance of communion time.
2. Why many avoid it.
3. Why we should remember Him.
4. How great was His sacrifice.

"ADDICTED"

"I beseech you, brethren, (ye know the house of Stephanas, that it is the firstfruits of Achaia, and that they have addicted themselves to the ministry of the saints,)"-1 Corinthians 16:15

Addiction goes like this: Whatever thing or substance one becomes addicted to, they have surrendered to it and it has become their greatest source of pleasure. It is common to hear of those addicted to drugs, to alcohol, to tobacco, to television, to gambling and to certain kinds of music. A beautiful thought we have before us today concerning the house of Stephanas, who were "addicted" to the ministry of the saints". It seems that they had surrendered themselves to the Lord and His followers. Ministering to them was their greatest source of pleasure.

Simply put, ministering is doing something for someone else, expecting nothing in return. We must become smaller in our own eyes to become thus addicted. It must involve self emptying, just as Paul described Jesus, "Let nothing be done through strife or vainglory; but in lowliness of mind let each esteem other better than themselves"-Philippians 2:3. This is diametrically opposed to the thinking of the world, to the flesh and to our natural instinct, yet, the joy of this posture is beyond description. We find Jesus in a ministering posture as He washed the disciple's feet. He told His disciples, "If ye know these things, happy are ye if ye do them." The happiest people are those who find a constant joy in waiting on others and ministering to their needs. Joy is found in this addiction.

There is much written between the lines in this scripture, for we are made to wonder how many were involved in this house.....wife, children, servants? Yet, they were all of one mind and one heart. Stephanas must have been a good example to all his house!

We should also wonder how they ministered. Was it of their substance, their carnal things, food, clothing, encouragement? Surely, all that was left unsaid is as profitable for us to consider as what is said for it allows us to consider the many ways of ministering to others. Equally, it allows us to examine our own ministering.

Apparently, the Lord was well pleased with this addiction. They have found their place in His book of remembrance. May their tribe increase!!

Helpful Hints:
1. Is your house addicted to ministry?
2. Examples of ministering to others.
3. How may we become so addicted?
4. The purpose for and the byproducts of.

"IS DOCTRINE IMPORTANT?"

"And the scribes and chief priests heard it, and sought how they might destroy him: for they feared him, because all the people was astonished at his doctrine"-Mark 11:18

Just how important is doctrine to the Christian Church? What role should it play in the worship service? Without question, doctrine was of paramount importance to Jesus. He taught doctrine. His whole life and ministry was dedicated to doctrine and it was from Him, that the apostles learned doctrine and taught it to the infant Church.

When Jesus came, the doctrine of God's people had become so shifted and vague, that those professing godliness were "astonished at His doctrine". They were so astonished, that He was an offense to them and they were willing to kill Jesus to keep *their* doctrine. Doctrine is important because it teaches us everything we need to know concerning life and godliness: "According as his divine power hath given unto us all things that *pertain* unto life and godliness, through the knowledge of him that hath called us to glory and virtue:"- 2 Peter 1:3.

I have always loved the illustration that Charles H. Spurgeon gave as an encouragement for people to attend a church for truth taught. His story went something like this: "I asked a man what he believed and he said, 'I believe what the church believes'. I then asked him what his church believed and he said, 'They believe what I believe'. I then asked him what he and his church believed and he said, 'We both believe the same thing'." His point was obvious. The man's faith was void of doctrinal truths because his church did not teach them.

Fuzzy ideas, found somewhere in the bible, given from a mouth but unfound by scripture will never comfort a troubled soul. Is this something we should be concerned about? Is doctrine that important? Are we expected as Christians to be able to explain what we believe?

The first disciples turned the world upside down with doctrine. They must have been dogmatic. People are dogmatic and passionate about many things that contradict scripture. Surely, Christians today should be dogmatic about things that we can prove to be basic bible doctrines and point our finger to the verse where it can be found. Paul was dogmatic. I know that it is said that we should not talk about politics and religion. Jesus talked about both and I am glad He did!

It is true, we are living in a day in which people are less concerned about doctrine than in a former time. People will choose a church by the entertainment it provides, by the size of the church, by the physical appearance, by the musical attractions, by what is provided for children or by what the church can do for them rather than what is taught and believed. Truth is often somewhere far below all of this. Bells and whistles are sought above truth reverence. Historically speaking, and even biblically speaking, doctrine has always been the most important facet of the church. It is the superstructure upon which any real Christian Church is built, for the church is described as "the pillar and ground of the truth". Thus, a desire for accurate doctrine has always been the hallmark of the true Church. Ministers should be identified and ordained because of the gift that God has given them to understand and proclaim the great doctrines of scripture...to rightly divide the word of truth. To often, men graduate from seminaries who openly deny the deity of Jesus Christ. As long as some people have the programs it seems to be of little concern to them.

A desire for clarity and accuracy of doctrine has caused some of the greatest uproars in the church since Christ. The first great controversy in the church is found in Acts 15 and it was over doctrine. In an environment in which peace was necessary for prosperity, the men of that day considered their differences in a spiritual way. They did not ostracize men or churches; they did not poison the waters of fellowship; they did not mark a man for destruction; nor did they destroy a man before the eyes of his own congregation. They came together, considered the matter scripturally and returned to their own labors. Many of these men were apostles who had the care of all the churches. No man has this authority today. The particular flock that the Holy Ghost has made them the overseer is the only authority any man has today.

These men knew that Godly doctrine separated the church from the world and the wrong doctrine would make the church *like* the world. It is doctrine that allows our beliefs to become bonded to something that God has said. It is doctrine that transforms vague ideas found somewhere in the bible into firm facts. When doctrine is respected, it should produce holiness, it should promote a change in the lives of the people that hear it. Doctrine gives the proper outlook of life in general. It is doctrine that gives a face to the church, the face of Jesus Christ.

How about you? Are you astonished when you hear the doctrines that Christ and the apostles taught? Doctrines like the sovereignty of God, original sin, imputed righteousness, depravity, unconditional election, particular redemption, grace, perseverance, preservation, predestination and of course the resurrection of the dead? Do you understand faith, justification, the reason of the hope that lies within us, the purpose for trials and tribulations and the eternal love of God our Father? If Jesus came today and preached would you believe Him?

Helpful Hints:
1. Discuss the importance of doctrine.
2. Talk about some of the doctrines mentioned.
3. Some of the reasons that people choose other things.
4. How doctrine affects us.

"THOU COMPASSEST MY PATH"

"Thou compassest my path and my lying down, and art acquainted with all my ways. For there is not a word in my tongue, but, lo, O Lord, thou knowest it altogether. Thou has beset me behind and before, and laid thine hand upon me."
-Psalm 139:3-5

There is a song in our book which begins with these words:

"Thus far the Lord has led me on;
thus far his power prolongs my day."

I find these words to be of great comfort. If our eyes are open, we know it is by the Lord's mercy and grace that we are here today and that we have made it *thus far.* David gives the reason for our survival. It is because the Lord compasses our path. It is good to reflect upon this truth because from it we may come to this conclusion: if our Lord has been with us in the past, he will not desert us today, tomorrow or in the years to come.

Compassing the path speaks of the Lord's abiding *presence.* When David wrote, "Thou hast beset me behind and before, and laid thine hand upon me", he was revealing God's presence in three dimensions: past, present and future. When David used the word, "Behind", he saw the Lord's hand of providence in his past life leading him, blessing him and guiding him. As they say, hindsight is 20/20. Many times, God's hand is made plainer as we look back. His sovereignty in our afflictions are better understood. His purposes enable us to see that He was there all along.

As David uses the word "before" I find comfort and hope for the future. David EXPECTS the Lord to be in his future life. The future is something that is greatly feared and we have the ability to imagine great evils which may never occur. As our Lord said, "Sufficient unto the day is the evil thereof ...take therefore no thought for the tomorrow." We are thus taught to live day by day, in day-tight compartments. When the submarine hits a mine, each compartment is sealed off, securing the air and precious cargo. When we hit a land mine in our life, let us seal off the day, day by day, for the Lord, taking one day's trouble at a time. We can all get down and depressed if we do not live for the present blessings. Surely, we should look for them and be thankful for the good we have in hand. Many blue tomorrows are the offspring of a red hot today. Let us stop and meditate upon the fact that our Lord not only knows tomorrow, He also holds it in His hand.

But what about today? Did David's Lord, know his present plight? Does He know, or even care, about ours? To describe our Lord's present presence David uses the word, "thine hand upon me". Here is a hand that can not be moved. Our Lord's abiding presence in our lives is strong. He is a friend that "sticketh closer than a brother." Jesus is a faithful high priest who is touched by the feelings of our infirmity. He, too, walked the shores of time. He saw troubles, He saw conflicts and disappointments. People misused Him, even people He loved. Yet, He did no sin. I love what one preacher said to his member when they informed him that they did not feel as close to the Lord as they once did. He asked them this question: "Who moved?" No, we are not promised that we will not see troubles and conflicts. In fact, we are guaranteed that we will. But we are promised that He will walk with us through them as He did with Daniel in the den of lions and the Hebrew children in the fiery furnace. His hand was upon them as well. Though He may not change the present difficulty, it is a great blessing to know that He walks with us through them. Thus far!

Helpful Hints:
1. Consider God's hand in David's life.
2. In your own.
3. The rod of chastisement and its purpose.
4. Looking back, what do you see?

"WHO AM I?"

"Then went king David in, and sat before the Lord, and he said, Who am I, O Lord God? And what is my house, that thou hast brought me hitherto?"(II Samuel 7:18)

Today, our thoughts are centered around a prayer of David as he expresses his gratitude for the Lord's mercy and kindness towards his house. As David spake thus to his Lord, he was not asking who he was in regard to his person, but rather, who he was that the God of glory would take notice of him and bless him thus. His speech concerned the lowliness of his character. God's grace was so amazing to David that he could not find words to express his feelings and vent his soul properly. He is amazed, dumbfounded by God's grace.

When we see God's wonderful grace many questions come before us because grace first appears a mystery to us. Why so free? It sometimes seems offensive to us because we are such graceless creatures ourselves, that when someone first makes the proposition of grace to us, we are offended, we demand that we must merit every jot and tittle of God's blessings. We are accustomed to asking why when adversity strikes, for our pride tells us we did not deserve the unkindness. Yet, when God is so kind, we ask the same question as if a sovereign God can not give and take as He pleases.

Grace is that way. It goes against the common thinking of mankind. That is why David wrote a few verses later, "And is this the manner of man, O Lord God?" David knew that it wasn't. It was not Saul' manner toward him nor was it his own manner toward Nabal the Carmelite.

If we are honest, if we survey our own life, we will be as David in another category. We will not be able to find enough merits to match the blessings we have received. Surely, if we went tit for tat with the Lord we would find his graces far outweighing our merits. David didn't say, "Because I am king", because his kingship was by given by grace. He didn't say, "Because I slew the Philistine giant", because he knew his stone was guided by Jehovah's hand. What could he say? So he said, "What can David say more unto thee?"

God's grace *humbles* us. David uses the phrase "thy servant" eight times in this one prayer which shows us how grace, and not law, brings loving obedience. I feel that David wanted to do more for his Lord at this moment of his life than every other moment put together. This is the byproduct of genuine grace experienced! Many serve God by fear because *thou shalt nots* ring in their ears. But the Lord is most delighted when obedience is spawned by a thankful heart! When a hateful Saul of Tarsus first experienced grace he said, "Lord, what wilt thou have me to do?" When hearts were pricked at Pentecost, the response was "Men and brethren, what shall we do?" The cross, not a whip, was the place where matchless grace was displayed. Followers of Christ do so out of love, not the fear of Sinai's thunder. Jesus is the mediator of a better covenant which is established upon better promises. So we ask, "Who am I that God would love me with an everlasting love? Who am I that I would be chosen in Christ before the foundation of the world? Who am I that God would send His beloved Son to die for my sins? Who am I that God would number the hairs of my head and watch my every step? Who am I to receive an inheritance, incorruptible, undefiled that fadeth not away? Who am I to enjoy the earnest of my inheritance, knowing my redeemer and exploring the merits of His sufferings? Who am I"? The best answer I have found goes thus: A worm in the dust, yet an object of God's amazing grace!!!

Helpful Hints:
1. Consider God's grace.
2. Why grace is offensive to some.
3. Legalism vs. grace.
4. The blessings of grace.

"ONLY TRUST HIM"

"They that trust in the Lord shall be as mount Zion, which cannot be removed, but abideth for ever"-Psalm 125:1

It is difficult for us to trust in the Lord, to put our lives, our hopes, our fears and our labors in the hands of another. Yet, there is a great peace given to those who do so: they "cannot be removed".

This trusting does not mean that we should not pray for a desired end, nor does it mean that we should sit on the stool of do nothing. David fought the Philistines, but he prayed. The apostles trusted in the Lord, yet they were busy in their righteous endeavors to serve the Lord and promote His kingdom. It also does not mean that we should go about life, ignoring God and forgetting to pray for our daily bread. Trusting God means that we leave the god's of the Canaanites alone and look to the true God for our comfort and protection. It means that we labor with sword in one hand and a trowel in the other, trusting God for strength and success. If our trust is in horses and chariots, in the stock market or in the economy, in our national defense or our own wits, we have much to fear. Our peace is as volatile as they. Trust in the Lord of hosts,

He is solid and unmovable. Our eyes are upon the Creator, not creation. And that is the thought. When we learn to trust in something unmovable and eternal we become so attached to Him that we can not be removed either.

Surely, the creature puts too much trust in self. His victories are attributed to his intellect and his will rather than the giver of every good and perfect gift. We can become so bent upon personal pursuits and desires that we can forget the Lord's will for our own personal lives. We can be as Saul of Tarsus, who kicked against the pricks to his own hurt. Surely, trusting in the Lord is a difficult task. If it came natural to us there would be no reason for the psalmist's words. We must place the future in the hands of one who unfolds history like a flag and waves it before the unbelievers. Are you trusting Him today? Lord, help us to do so today and find the peace which passeth understanding! Amen.

Helpful Hints:
1. Talk about Israel's lack of trust and their turning to horses and chariots.
2. The end result of it.
3. How we should trust.
4. What we should trust Him with.

"THE SECRET PLACE"

"He that dwelleth in the secret place of the most High shall abide under the shadow of the Almighty"- Psalms 91:1,2

There is a place where the believer may go to find comfort and protection, a place to renew strength; it is the secret place of the most High. As the psalmist describes this secret place, he alludes to the Most Holy place, that sacred cubicle to which the High priest alone had access. The most prominent figures therein were the golden Cherubims, perched above the mercy seat, with glittering wings outstretched from wall to wall. The reason for our observation is found in verse four where we read: "He shall cover thee with his feathers, and under his wings shalt thou trust."

In the inner court of the tabernacle, God's presence was manifested by the Shekinah of light, piercing upon the golden mercy seat, radiating reflections of resplendent light, causing a shadow to fall beneath the wings of the golden Cherubs. The psalmist's figurative language places us beneath the shadow of these wings, away from the noise, away from the crowd, away from the heat of the day, a place of prayer and solitude, alone with God....the secret place.

This psalm is attributed to the pen of Moses. If we can view it through his experience we can learn much about his suggestive metaphors. He certainly knew about the tabernacle, for God gave him the blueprints for it on the mount. Perhaps during the building of it, this was his special "bower of prayer", his closet place alone with God, under the wings of the Cherub.

We do not find Moses "dwelling" in this place when God called him. This kind of trust is usually developed by experience. When God called him to deliver his people, many excuses were given for his fears. He even asked God to send another. His faith and trust were strengthened beneath the wings of the Cherubims. Therefore, to dwell in the secret place must be a symbol of closeness, of one being well acquainted with the object of their trust. Many times, we peer through the torn curtain into the inner sanctuary when troubles arise. Yet, few of us can say that we have lingered therein with God.

To describe the secret place, Moses uses the words "refuge" and "fortress". A refuge is a place the hunted animal seeks out for protection and rest. A fortress is a stronghold, a safe place where one runs to keep the enemy out. These are not places of duty. It is a place where we trust our problems to another. Who can labor when hunted and who can step out on promises when they are weary. Many of life's battles are that way. There is nothing we can do about them. We can lose our sleep and even our sanity until we find this secret place and abide therein. Are there sins of the past, take them to the secret place and rest for a while under the shadow.

It is a comfort to know that such a place exists. Since the curtain was rent in twain at the death of Jesus, every heir of grace has access to this secret place, for every believer has been made a king and a priest with God. Lord, help us to find the secret place and dwell therein!

Helpful Hints:
1. Discuss the tabernacle and the many types and shadows.
2. Private prayer!
3. The Cherubim.
4. The peace found.

"WHO HATH SAVED US"

"…God; Who hath saved us with an holy calling, not according to our works, but according to his own purpose and grace, which was given us in Christ Jesus before the world began"
-II Timothy 1:9

In this affectionate letter to Timothy, Paul did not attribute his own salvation to creature works, nor did he claim to have saved Timothy. He gave the honor and glory to the only savior of sinners: "God, who hath saved us".

The word "us" is very suggestive. It goes beyond Paul and Timothy and includes a multitude of people, more numerous than the sand of the seashore and the stars of the sky. It is indicative of all of God's family, chosen in Christ before the foundation of the world!

Many say, "Yes, it is God who saves the sinner, but he uses means." When we hear the word *means* we know what it MEANS: it means that man and his works are going to be placed before Jesus the only Savior of sinners. These "means" usually vary. Some use a lot of *means* and some use very little, but it always *means* that God needed a little help in the redemption process; it *means* that Jesus paid most of the price and a small balance yet remains for the sinner; it *means* that Christ's work upon the cross is not 'finished'; it *means* the final occupants of glory are unknown and yet unsettled; it *means* that Jesus did not save His people...just yet. So, Paul continues to write to Timothy so that Timothy will never think that he is the Savior.

In his fatherly wisdom, Paul rightly divides the word of truth and in this letter marks the difference between the *gospel* call for *conversion* and God's holy call to *regeneration*. The holy call is from the mouth of God, not the mouth of man. Comparing the Holy call to the gospel call is like comparing sight to eyeglasses. The Holy call creates sight in the blind. The gospel allows those with sight to see what is. The Holy call is sure to all of the elect, none are left out: "My sheep hear my vice, and I know them, and they follow me: And I give unto them eternal life; and they shall never perish, neither shall any man pluck them out of my hand." The means of man always depends upon man. It depends upon money, upon success, upon availability, upon resources. There are too many *ifs*. What *if* the ship sinks on the way to the meeting and it has; what *if* the preacher is sick and he has been; what *if* the money is not available and it has not been; what *if* the preachers are thrown in jail and they have been; what *if* the bibles are burned and they have been...to many *ifs* when we think men must save. The power is lacking as well. If man could get to every sinner, his voice can not give life. Only the life giving voice of the Son of God can do this.

Some seem to glory with their means, yet others, who take it seriously, realize that it is a weight that they can not bear. It is then that grace becomes so precious. When means are seen for what they are they become filthy rags held up to a Holy God in payment for sin. This was Paul's experience as a self-righteous Pharisee. But when he met Jesus, his eyes were opened and *his means* became dung. Now he can write: "Not according to our works, but according to his own purpose and grace, which was given in Christ before the world began." This is what makes grace so amazing, it is void of means, of creature works.

If all of this is so, the rest of Paul's thoughts make sense. The purpose of the gospel, of man's call, is not to impart life, but to shed the light upon the life that has been given by God's Holy call. The gospel gives light not life: "who hath abolished death, and hath brought life and immortality to light through the gospel". The light of the gospel will not place Christ in the heart, but it does reveal. It reveals life, spiritual life. It brings immortality to light.

Helpful Hints:
1. Discuss the purpose of the gospel.
2. Discuss the difference between conversion and regeneration.
3. Talk about the power of the gospel.
4. Talk about the power of God's holy call.
5. Discuss the man made means.
6. Discuss how this holy call was as effective for the Old testament Saints as it is for us today.

"ELECT ACCORDING TO THE FOREKNOWLEDGE OF GOD"

"Elect according to the foreknowledge of God the Father...."
-I Peter 1:2

Today, we hope to encourage God's people in the same way that Peter encouraged and strengthened the scattered strangers of his day. Though they were persecuted and could have thought that God had forgotten them, Peter reminds them they are God's elect. Peter had found great comfort in this glorious doctrine, so he comforts his brethren with the same comfort he had enjoyed in being a member of a chosen and redeemed family. He could find no words more fitted for their comfort than "Elect according to the foreknowledge of God the Father".

Spurgeon said, "There is a prejudice in the human mind against this doctrine." Though it is well documented in scripture, we find much the same attitude today. Election is not only logical, it is also biblical. Peter obviously preached it, Paul preached it and Jesus' sermons abounded with the fundamental doctrines of election and the sovereignty of God. We find election stated in obvious terms like, chosen, choice, elect, elected, my sheep and foreknown.

Every miracle that Jesus performed for a particular person declared election in its most sublime terms. He healed those who could not heal themselves....He passed over some and healed others. To the human mind, it seems unfair, that God would pass over some and choose others, yet, Jesus did not heal everyone. Spiritually speaking, the Lord would have been just in leaving all of mankind in his fallen condition.

Some will say that they believe that God looked down through time and saw those who would do good and chose them for the good He saw in them. Yet, we can not forget what is said of man, "There is none good, no not one". Left to himself, man is not good.

To keep the church from assuming the argument that God looked down through time to see who would do good, Paul wrote, "For the children being not yet born, neither having done any good or evil, that the purpose of God according to election might stand, not of works, but of him that calleth." Before they were born, before they could do any good work, God chose Jacob....NOT OF WORKS.

Election does not limit, rather, it makes the impossible possible. It includes masses who may never hear of the grace of God. Others mock election by saying, "If I believed that, I would live any way I wanted to because I was chosen to go to heaven." Yet, God's love says that those who truly love me will honor me. Those who would take election and use it for an occasion to sin give no evidence of life. Unless a drastic change occurs at some point in their life, they were never elected in the first place. Well did Jesus say, "By their fruits shall ye know them." If we find those who love Jesus Christ we can say they are of the elect. If they love the Church, the Lord's people, the solemn assembly, the truths of God's words they are of the elect.

Historically speaking, the doctrine of election has always been believed and taught by the church in all ages. You will find it recorded in the confessions of faith among the ancient Waldenses who were persecuted for their faith just a few centuries after Christ's death. It was owned by the Puritans, by the great voices and martyrs of the reformation, by the first Methodists, the early Presbyterians, and by Baptists in all ages. A mere perusal of their original creeds will testify to this fact. What a great comfort we find in the knowledge of God's eternal choice and love which was made "before the foundation of the world!

Helpful Hints:
1. Note and discuss the many places the word elect is used in scripture.
2. Consider the sermons of Jesus where this is taught.
3. Consider the many passages in the Old testament where election is taught.
4. Discuss why this doctrine is avoided by many.

"COMFORTERS"

"…that we may be able to comfort them which are in any trouble, by the comfort wherewith we ourselves are comforted of God"-2 Corinthians 1:4

Today, we find the apostle comforting the Church at Corinth with the same comfort he had received of God. To reach out and comfort a brother or sister in Christ is one of the greatest marks of Christianity.

To comfort another, we must have empathy, even pity for those who are distressed and love them as a member of our redeemed family.

Every born again believer has the ability to comfort others. In his listing of spiritual fruit, Paul mentions love, gentleness and goodness to be among the spiritual graces of the believer(Galatians 5:22). These graces are like muscles in our body. They lie dormant until used. When used, they grow into a tree, springing forth bearing fruit unto others around us!

Paul mentions the fact that he would comfort others by the same comfort he had received of God. The best comforters are those who have trodden the low valleys themselves, those who have recovered from a deep dark pit in their own lives. They have been down themselves and well know the terrors of Hopeless Canyon, Failure City and the pit called Discouragement. When we are uncomfortable in our lives we have a tendency to look upon other people's problems with a little more sympathy, rather than a haughty, self righteous spirit. I remember a cold winter morning at the bus stop, a little girl falling on the ice as we waited for the school bus. She came from a very poor family and was sadly dressed for the winter temperatures. When she fell, some of the children around her laughed and pointed at the fallen victim. I felt sorry for her and watched as many of the children snickered at their entertainment. I wanted to help her up but my pride kept me from it. She needed some comfort.

To get others out we must condescend as Jesus did. We must get in there with them and remind them of the God of all comfort and the value of Christian friendship. Many times, our pride will not allow us to admit that we have been down. Yet, the prophet has marked the Lord's people being "an afflicted and poor people" whose trust is in the Lord. The greatest comfort one may receive would be a visit from someone who has been through the same struggle and survived! What have you been through? Seek others who have been through the same and comfort them with the same comfort that got you through. Bring to them the comforts of God, His promises, His forgiveness, His faithfulness and His everlasting love for His people........ even when they fall! When we are busy getting others out, I am sure we are less likely to fall back in ourselves.

Helpful Hints:
1. Who do you know that needs some comfort?
2. Consider some of the comforting words of Christ.
3. Who are the comforters of your church?
4. How to they comfort?

"MAKE HASTE, O GOD, TO DELIVER ME"

"To the chief Musician, A Psalm of David, to bring to remembrance.Make haste, O God, to deliver me; make haste to help me, O Lord"-Psalms 70:1

Many were the persecutors of David. They lurked in secret places, constantly looking for a slip of the tongue, an improper gesture, a wrong move or any thing that might bring a reproach upon his stewardship. We, as David, are not exempt from those who would seek our hurt. As Christians, we should know that Satan can not stand those who honor our Lord Jesus Christ, his sworn enemy. So, he constantly hunts for the precious soul, to defame and cast down. Let our language be as David's, "Make haste, O God, to deliver me; make haste to help me, O Lord. Let them be ashamed and confounded that seek after my soul: let them be turned backward, and put to confusion, that desire my hurt, Let them be turned back for a reward of their shame that say, Aha, aha."

Notice David's weapon. It is *humility*. He did not take matters into his own hands. He did not take an eye for an eye. How well David demonstrates the great maxim of the kingdom, "Vengeance is mine; I will repay, saith the Lord." Prayerfully, David turns the whole matter over to the great Judge of all. As a man would sic a dog on his attackers, David turns the Lord on his accusers and stands back to see the end.

David further demonstrates his humility with his request, "But I am poor and needy....". Those who are poor and needy have nothing to avenge themselves with but the sacred arm of God. That's enough! It will be God's salvation in the matter or none at all.

Great peace is found in our ability to turn hateful matters over to the Lord. And though David was not beyond reproach, he was beyond destruction, because the Lord loved David.

Helpful Hints:
1. Consider the many enemies of David.
2. Consider David's character with them.
3. Consider Christ and His enemies.
4. The final beatitude.

"THE FAITHFULNESS OF GOD"

*"Let your conversation be without covetousness; and be
content with such things as ye have: for he hath said, I will
never leave thee, nor forsake thee"- Hebrews 13:5*

One of the greatest comforts to God's children is the
knowledge of their Lord's faithfulness. When it seems
that the Lord has forgotten us and that our prayers go
no higher than our heads, it is of great consolation to
remember the words that Paul gave as encouragement to
his Hebrew brethren, words that God had spoken long
ago to Jacob: "I will not leave thee." (Genesis 28:15).

Faithfulness is the *backbone* of anything good: a
marriage, being a parent, an employee, a church member,
even being an American citizen. Without faithfulness,
things, good things, are broken down and are always *less*
than what they should be. We would love to tell you just
how faithful man has been to his Creator; how faithful
Adam and Eve were in the morning of time, when
everything was "good and very good"; how that David
was faithful in his kingdom when all of his enemies were
subdued around him; how all the kings of Israel ruled with

love and integrity for Jehovah; and how faithfully they followed Jesus when He made His advent into the world. Yet, amidst the black backdrop of man's unfaithfulness, we find a glittering jewel in the breastplate of God's character: His faithfulness to His people!

Love is the *strength* of faithfulness. Great love produces unending and abiding faithfulness. Thankfully, the Lord's faithfulness to His elect is not based upon their love for Him, for our love can be fickle, it can wane as the moon and go in and out as the tide: "but because the Lord loved you, and because he would keep the oath which he had sworn unto your fathers", are the grounds of a faithful Creator. Our faithfulness to God and His house is a direct reflection of our love for Christ as prescribed by these words: "If ye love me, keep my commandments". Though we may please the Lord by our faithfulness to Him, we can not make the Lord love us any more than He already does. His faithfulness remains as everlasting as His love. Moses said it endured to "a thousand generations" and David said "thy faithfulness reacheth unto the clouds." Great men of God have always searched for words to aptly portray the unending faithfulness of God to His people!

It was the Lord's faithfulness that gave, Jeremiah, the weeping prophet, hope in a dismal day, "This I recall to my mind, therefore have I hope… his compassions fail not. They are new every morning: great is thy faithfulness." Every day, in all of our challenges and temptations, "God is faithful, who will not suffer you to be tempted above that ye are able." This is where we get the promise that the Lord will not lay more upon us than we can bear. We may lay more upon ourselves than we can bear and our sin can bring great weights upon us, but God is faithful who will not forsake us.

One of our greatest mistakes is to misjudge God when He chastens us. Like a loving Father, our Lord is faithful to chasten His children when they stray. He does not throw His children away or disown the people of His covenant. "If they break my statutes, and keep not my commandments; Then will I visit their transgression with the rod... I will not utterly take from him, nor suffer my faithfulness to fail." Surely, children have become angry and made this mistake with their parents when chastened by them, not realizing it was for their own good.

He is equally willing to listen to us when we sin, "If we confess our sins, he is faithful and just to forgive us our sins". Though Satan will tell us to give up and surrender to a sin that has us bound, we are encouraged to continue to take it to the Lord. His forgiveness is as faithful as His love! Come, today, to the throne of God's unending faithfulness and place your cares in the hands of a faithful Creator!

Helpful Hints:
1. Note God's faithfulness in your own life.
2. See it at the cross!
3. Consider it at the return of Christ.
4. How have we been unfaithful.

"THE LOVE OF CHRIST, WHICH PASSETH KNOWLEDGE"

"And to know the love of Christ, which passeth knowledge,
that ye might be filled with all the fulness of God"
- Ephesians 3:19

Surely, the love of our Lord passes the comprehension of mortals. As the old song goes:

"The love of God is greater far,
than tongue or pen can ever tell;
it goes beyond the highest star,
and reaches to the lowest hell.
When years of time shall pass away,
and earthly thrones and kingdoms fall,
when men, who here refuse to pray,
on rocks and hills and mountains call,
God's love so sure, shall still endure,
all measureless and strong."

We forget that we are fallen creatures who yet see through a glass darkly. Many times we judge the love of God through human emotions and feelings rather than through the looking-glass of God's word. Thus, God's love not only passes our knowledge, we are also prone to *misjudge* the love of God.

Without controversy, Calvary is the greatest love scene in history. How can we fully understand that God became man, laid aside His glory, became a tiny babe, walked the shores of time and allowed the hands of cruel men to slay Him upon a cross? As our apostle of love writes: "Greater love hath no man than this, that a man lay down his life for his friends"(John 15:13). It passes knowledge!

The apostle reminds us of another facet of this love that is greatly misunderstood, even by Christians: "We love him, because he first loved us"(1 John 4:19). God's love must come first and change the sinner before he will, or can, love Him, because man, by nature, is an enemy to God and His Son. This is one of John's evidences for his little children. To know they belong to God: If we love the Lord, it must be because He first loved us. Is not this love greatly misunderstood?

Who God loves passes our knowledge and many times God is accused of being unjust by His particular redemption. Many will have God loving Judas as much as Peter and sentimentality place God's love upon the fallen angels and Satan himself. God's love is particular, specific and sure. He does not change His mind each day toward the jewels in His breastplate. They are fastened securely next to His heart. Surely, God will not allow any object of His love to suffer eternal torments in the lake of fire. If we believed this, we would have to believe that Satan was stronger than the Father. Universalism says that God loves everyone and died for all of mankind yet they can not tell us how some will spend eternity in hell.

I would rather believe scripture, that Christ's love and death was effectual for everyone He represented than to believe it was sure for no one in particular. Surely, surely, when Christ returns, He will never stand before anyone that He loved and say, "Depart from me, ye cursed, into everlasting fire, prepared for the devil and his angels". His love is distinguishing, particular, specific and effectual. It reaches to the lowest hell and snatches rebellious sinners from the clutches of Satan. It lifts the beggar from the dunghill, not by their free will, but by His amazing grace and sets them among princes to inherit thrones of glory.

Surely, the *security* of God's love passes our knowledge. No wonder many ascribe to the "in today and out tomorrow" doctrine of God's love. They erroneously compare God's eternal, abiding love with their own fickle, shallow feelings. The eternal security that Paul enjoyed in God love was not founded in his own works, but in God's eternal love: "Who shall separate us from the love of Christ? Shall tribulation, or distress, or persecution, or famine, or nakedness, or peril, or sword? As it is written, For thy sake we are killed all the day long; we are accounted as sheep for the slaughter. Nay, in all these things we are more than conquerors through him that love us. For I am persuaded, that neither death, nor life, nor angels, nor principalities, nor powers, nor things present, not things to come, Nor height, nor depth, nor any other creature, shall be able to separate us from the love of God, which is in Christ Jesus our Lord." Consider each category and we must be convinced ourselves. Consider every angle, every possibility, every nuance, every false doctrine preached, every false apostle's efforts, every new imagination of man and a world of worldly wisdom and you will find God's love for His people unsevered. This is God's word, this is God's love!

Helpful Hints:
1. Consider the objects of God's love.
2. Talk about *why* God loves His people.
3. Talk about the security of God's love.
4. Talk about why we love God.

"AS DEAR CHILDREN"

"Be ye therefore followers of God, as dear children"
-Ephesians 5:1

In his letter to the Ephesian Church, we find some of the apostles most endearing pleas for Christian living. The order of the epistle is *significant*. The first three chapters are primarily *doctrinal*. Concerning these chapters, one scholar called them "The profoundest thing ever written. He sounds the heights and depths of truth." The last three chapters are practical, dealing with the Christian walk. The significance of this order is noteworthy. First, Paul reminds them of their calling and election, blessings they had received by God's grace. After he had shown them all that their heavenly Father had done for them through His Son, he pleads with them to become "followers of God, as dear children" and live up to their calling. Being a Christian is two dimensional: knowing and doing.

This has always been the basis of true Christian *unity:* Doctrine first, fellowship second. It is sad to see the pragmatic methods adopted by many. today that send out letters to find what the world wants in a church and then set out to build a pseudo church on the world's desires. Fun and entertainment with a little Jesus mixed in is the result of these methods. This has greatly *harmed* the Christian Church. We find the pattern in the New Testament to be quite different. Christ and His doctrine was first preached and the fellowship of the saints was the byproduct of like precious faith, not worldly entertainment. The apostles were not there to count heads but rather to count disciples of Christ; they did not assemble for the entertainment and fun, but for the preaching of sound truths. That is the method of Jesus, of John the Baptist, of Peter, Paul and every other person we find recorded in scripture. Since nothing has changed in regard to man's condition, he is still a bankrupt, guilty, sinner, the remedy for his condition is the sound of the gospel trumpet. True Christian *fellowship* and *unity* are the byproducts of shared doctrinal sentiments.

We find another valuable lesson in this order of teaching: the Christian's *obedience* is the byproduct of their doctrinal sentiments. Peter preached Christ crucified by wicked hands. The audience heard, obeyed and were baptized. Doctrine first....walk followed. Peter's method was not to attract a crowd by methods, games and entertainment and then try to teach a doctrine. It was a total reversal of what we see in many places today. Paul and Peter both preached Christ and Him crucified for sins. That was the *beginning* of their fellowship, not something that they would bring up at a later and more convenient time! John the Baptist was not working on programs and drives, nor did he baptize all that came to him. He declared the coming Messiah and genuine repentance for sin. He placed truth above numbers! These great men were not in competition with the church down the street, trying to outdo and outgrow. They preached the truth and allowed the Sheep to find a convenient pasture where the same message was preached.

Helpful Hints:

1. Talk about he methods man has invented to grow churches.

2. Talk about the God ordained methods.

3. The examples of this method in scripture.

4. Its success.

5. Why we should go to church.

"WHO KNOWETH?"

"Who knoweth whether thou art come to the kingdom for such a time as this?"-Esther 4:14

Our thoughts today are centered around the soul searching question of Mordecai, which question all believers should consider in their own hearts. The question is one of speculation, as to whether or not God had orchestrated the events surrounding their present plight for Esther to go before the king and deliver her people. It concerns the beautiful thought of God's *providence,* of Esther being in the right place at the right time to be used of God in a mighty way.

The word providence abounds with thought and imagination. Not only does it mean that God is actively involved in the most minute events of our lives, it also means that the Lord *provides* His people with the things they need. When Abraham took his only son, Isaac, to the top of the mountain to offer him as a burnt sacrifice, God provided a ram caught in the thicket to be offered in his place. It was there that Abraham called God, Jehova-jireh, which means the Lord will *provide.* Like faithful Abraham, it is by faith that we see our heavenly Father this way and every detail of our lives are marked with this question, "Who knoweth".

But let our answer *always* be in the *affirmative*. The beautiful book of Esther has taught us to say so. There is nothing that happens in the universe that God does not cause or allow. As one preacher said, "History hinges on minute events". The *broadness* of His providence was illustrated by Jesus when He said that a sparrow can not fall to the ground without the Father. In every nook and cranny of the universe, not one sparrow may fall without the Father's permission. His providence is equally *specific*. The very hairs of our heads are numbered by the Father, He telleth the number of the stars and counts the ticking seconds till His return.

Esther did not take providence for granted. She asked for her people to *pray* for her as she approached the king. Though they thought the Lord might be in it, they did all that was humanly possible in seeking the favor of the Lord. Yes, the Lord comforts us with the knowledge of His providence, yet He is honored by our holy petitions.

As we view the chain of events that brought Esther to her position, we must acknowledge that God *is* a God of providence. Why did the king call for a feast? Why did he request the presence of Vashti? Why did she refuse to come? Why was Esther brought with the virgins to the kings palace? Why was she chosen? All of this was orchestrated by God. If one event in the chain had failed, the outcome would have been much different for God's people. Surely, the Lord provided.

Providence is very *punctual*. The Lord was right on time with the best provision. Haman was hanged on the very gallows he had provided for Mordedcai. Esther was heard at the most convenient time and even placed in charge of their circumstances. What a great comfort is given to the sheep of His pasture in knowing that the Good Shepherd watches over his sheep in just this way. He leads them to pasture, beside the still waters and counts them daily as they go in and out. He even guides and protects them with the rod and staff. He clothes the lilies of the field and feeds the ravens by His bountiful hand of providence. Lord, today, we acknowledge thy kindness to us and we acknowledge thy hand of providence in our lives as we count our many blessings.

Helpful Hints:
1. Talk about God's providence.
2. In the scriptures.
3. In your own life.
4. Talk about the invisible God in this beautiful story.

"SHADOWS"

"And thou shalt make holy garments for Aaron thy brother for glory and for beauty.... And they shall take gold, and blue, and purple, and scarlet, and fine linen."-Exodus 28:2,5.

The Old Testament abounds with types, shadows and figures of the coming King. In his letter to the Hebrews, Paul referred to them as "patterns of things in the heavens"(9:23), "figures of the true"(9:24), and "the example and shadow of heavenly things"(8:5). The person of Christ and the story of redemption were meticulously played out by the Hebrews as they worshipped under the law. This is important to us today. It reminds us that that the plan of redemption was thought out and planned before creation; the full story is found in the innocent victims that were offered, in the furniture and vessels in the Tabernacle, and in the priests themselves performing the office. Furthermore, it reminds us that the Old Testament is more than an outdated history book as our enemies would have us believe. God was preaching salvation through the Messiah by His types and shadows long before the New Testament Church!

How beautifully we see our Lord depicted in the person of the High Priest! He alone could enter into the most Holy place and offer the yearly atonement for the chose tribes. We see Jesus in the beautiful garments the high priest wore. These were beautifully designed according to the pattern given to Moses on the mount.

The golden thread running through the garment depicted the value of His *suffering* to His Father and His people. It was beaten from fine gold. Its task was to hold the whole garment together, a figure of His redeemed family. Gold is a precious metal that will not perish. Thus we see the eternal value of His suffering, it was once, forever. He would continue a priest forever, victorious, triumphant.

The blue represents His *origin*, heaven itself. From His own mouth He declared, "I came down from heaven not to do my own will". His own people rejected His testimony and many today say He was just a good man with some good ideas. Should they not look back and see the figure written thousands of years ago that declared His Godliness?

The purple is indicative of His *royalty*. He has always been King of Kings and Lord of Lords. Even as a babe the angelic host worshipped Him and declared "glory to God in the highest". His kingdom is not of this world, He reigns in the minds and hearts of every believer and one day He shall return to claim what is rightfully His. On that day every knee shall bow and every tongue shall confess that Jesus Christ is Lord!

The scarlet depicts the *price* of redemption: His blood. We are not redeemed with corruptible things, traditions and ordinances, "But with the precious blood of Christ". The thousands of gallons of blood, offered by the priests from their slain beasts, could never take away a single sin. It could not even roll sin back. It was a perpetual reminder of their need for a perfect victim whose blood was incorruptible and would pay the dept, once for all. He was offered once forever for the sins of His people, "By the which will we are sanctified through the offering of the body of Jesus Christ once *for all*"(Hebrews 10:10). No one, neither angel or man, may require further payment for sin.

Finally, the fine linen represents His *purity*. He is and was, "holy, harmless and undefiled". An eternal Lamb without blemish was the necessary price of atonement. How well Satan knew this as he tempted our Lord. Yet, all that Jesus did was without guile, malice and sin. What a wonder Savior we have! We see His beauty so wonderfully displayed in the shadows of our Lord!

Helpful Hints:
1. Discuss the beautiful types and shadows found in the tabernacle: the furniture, the priests, the animal sacrifices and the different types of offerings.
2. Discover the full redemption story.
3. Find Christ.
4. Find yourself.

"THE FATHERHOOD OF GOD"

*"After this manner therefore pray ye: Our
Father which art in heaven..."*
-Matthew 6:9

What a blessed invitation we have before us today.
The Creator of heaven and earth encourages His children
to talk to Him and to *ask* for their needs. This invitation to
come before our heavenly Father is well noted in William
Bradbury's song, "Sweet Hour of Prayer" with these
words:

*"And since He bids me seek His face,
Believe His word, and trust His grace,
I'll cast on Him my every care
And wait for thee, sweet hour of prayer!"*

The language of our Master in this model prayer
is given as a *blueprint* for us to build many houses of
prayer upon. Though we may recite it verbatim, its
purpose is to encourage prayer and demonstrate the most
important things to pray for. Each child is to fill in the

individual categories with their own particular needs and circumstances.

The invitation in itself, displays the lovingkindness of our Holy Father. The smallest child and the weakest faith may approach Him at any moment. We do not need a press conference or a Camp David to visit with Him. His ears are always open to the cries of His elect. He is unlike Allah, who they say will only speak to his followers though prophets and angels. His small still voice is heard daily. Unlike the Greeks and Romans, who invented a pantheon of gods to fulfill their needs, He is the Father of all mercies and comforts. He is not capricious, as the heathen gods, given to sudden change and emotions, ready to judge and destroy. His love and compassion is unending. He is truly a Father to all who call upon Him.

"Our Father" also displays *love* because we are encouraged to call Him *Father*. When we consider this thought we must exclaim with John, "Behold, what manner of love the Father hath bestowed upon us, that we should be called the sons of God". What manner of love is this, that He who is everything, invites worms of the dust to call upon Him and ask as they will? What manner of love is this that sinners are invited into the presence of perfect righteousness? If our lives were displayed before the world we might be called many things, yet, by His grace He calls us sons and daughters!

The language also implies *adoption*! Some will say that we are His children by reason of creation. To this we must disagree. Are the stars and the heavens, the tokens of His handiwork, called His children? Though the Cherubim and the Seraphim are His own peculiar creation, they are never referred to as His children. Surely, we have become His children by the spirit of *adoption* and the new birth. We have been *elected* from a fallen and sinful family, the family of Adam and sovereignly placed in His spiritual family. In adoption, the adopter always makes the choice, not the adopted. What a privileged position! Each child has been given a new name that He alone knows. They have been given a new heart and an inheritance among the saints of glory. Thus, we have received the "Spirit of adoption, whereby we cry, Abba, Father."

We must also see brotherhood in our invitation. We are not to say, "My Father", but rather "Our Father". Though doctrines may differ, He is the Father of a great multitude who call upon Him. Father, help us to think upon thee in this way and to remember that our smallest petitions are important to thee!

Helpful Hints:
1. Discuss this relationship we have with God.
2. Areas of discipline.
3. Our responsibilities towards our Father.
4. His promises to His children.

"PRECIOUS DEATH"

"Precious in the sight of the Lord is the death of his saints"
- Psalms 116:15

There are many precious things in the world. Their being precious is owing to their *rarity*. If we were to dig diamonds in our back yards, who would wear them on their fingers or give them as tokens of love? And if gold grew on trees it would be worth little for exchange. So, things being *scarce*, become *precious* in our sight.

The Bible sets things aright concerning what is *truly* precious. David, in his 139th psalm, declared the Lord's *thoughts* to be "precious" and in the book of Proverbs, Solomon raises *wisdom* to the platform of "precious" things. Peter tells us that the trial of our faith is more "precious" than gold and he found the promises of God to be exceeding great and "precious". Though we have heard of people paying millions of dollars for a trinket that belonged to a movie star, how can that compare to the "precious blood of Christ" that paid for the sins of a multitude? These, and many others, we might easily understand to be precious, but how does death fit into this category of "precious" things?

I have heard some say that this speaks of the death of God's people, when they depart from this life to be with the Lord. Yet, I find Jesus weeping at the tomb of Lazarus and He who knew the end of the story did not say this was a precious sight. He did not call for a party. The grief of His friends became His own. This death of the saints must be something else.

If you will notice, the psalm from which out text comes begins with prayer as it speaks of sorrow, trouble and anguish of soul. The psalmist wrestles with himself, seeking the righteous arm of the Lord in the midst of troubled waters. The psalmist found a death, a death that was precious in the sight of the Lord, a death that gave him peace: he died to himself!

This dying to self is painful, it is the dross consumed and the gold refined. This dross, which diminishes the luster and value of gold, is burned off by the trials and tribulations of life. When we die to our own selves we have died to our own ambitions and desires.…..in short, having our own way. We are no longer angry with the world and God because they did not live up to our expectations. It also means that we have bruised the serpent's head concerning a particular temptation or sin. A death to self and to sin, is most precious in the sight of the Lord. It does not happen all at once, though some fires are hotter than others. As Paul said, "I die daily", we all do the same. Little by little the sculptor chips upon the object of his affections molding it to His own desired appearance.

It also means that we have died to anger, to bitterness, to a backbiting tongue, to a lustful thought, to hatred and even to fears. It can even mean that we have died to our own mistakes, failures and sins of the past, that we have taken them to Jesus and crucified them on His cross. Surely, these things are rare in a world focused on self gratification. Yet, I believe the psalmist to be wise. His peace was found in the precious things of the Lord. Father, let this precious truth sink deep in our souls. Help us to die, that we may live for thee and let our death become precious in thy sight!

Helpful Hints:
1. Consider the things you have died to.
2. A great opportunity to talk about the providential hand of God in our lives leading us in a way that we knew not.
3. Our ambitions vs. God's use for us.
4. David's scheme vs. God's for his life.

"A FAITHFUL SAYING"

"This is a faithful saying, and worthy of all acceptation, that Christ Jesus came into the world to save sinners; of whom I am chief"-1 Timothy 1:15

Paul felt himself to be the *chief* of sinners. He did not feel himself to be just one of the *many* sinners, he felt to be the *worst* of the *worst*. This was not a *one time* experience that he felt prior to his conversion and baptism, this was the way he felt *all* the time. If one were to tell their doctor, "Sir, I feel to be the chief of sinners and I am prone to experience depressed spirits from time to time", the doctor might prescribe a pill, attach a big word to the circumstance, suggest worldly counsel or all of the above. Yet, Jesus pronounced a blessing upon those who feel this way, "Blessed are the poor in spirit: for theirs is the kingdom of heaven." Surely, this faithful saying describes emotions and feelings that the world does not know. The true Christian identifies well with the apostle for they, too, have felt to be the *chief* of sinners.

One of the most striking features about this feeling is that it is not confined to any one class or race of people. It has no *boundaries.* Paul was a rich and influential man.

Yet, this feeling that the world would call a sickness, came upon him in the midst of his prosperity. It was so powerful that he saw his wealth, his position, his birthright and everything that the world would envy, as dung. Modern expositors have toned down this word, dung, but in reality it is what we shovel from the stalls in the animal kingdom. Rich people, poor people, adults and children, people from all races and backgrounds meet together in this place when the Lord touches them with His powerful and influential Spirit.

The knowledge or our risen Savior brings His children to know their condition as sinners in need of Him. It was when Christ revealed Himself to Paul that He came face to face with his sin. Man can take no credit for this. It is under the sound of the gospel that we discover why we feel this way and we learn the cure for our malady. It is Christ Jesus and Jesus alone that fills this aching void. To our souls He becomes the lily of the valley; the pearl of great price; the chiefiest among ten-thousand; and a friend that sticketh closer than a brother.

So, we come to our final point and then we shall leave you for the day. What kind of sinner did Jesus come to save? Paul's words are unqualified. He came to save all kinds of sinners. And what about you? Are you a sinner? If we can answer in the affirmative, we have great evidence that Christ is ours and we are His, and we have great hope, because "this is a faithful saying".

Helpful Hints:
1. Consider the degree of the apostle's sin.
2. How do we come to know we are sinners?
3. The good news of the gospel.
4. Our peace?

"A MATTER OF PRIORITY"

"But seek ye first the kingdom of God, and his righteousness; and all these things shall be added unto you"- Matthew 6:33

Among the many things that Jesus taught in His sermon on the mount, He taught His disciples that His kingdom must have priority in their lives. From our earliest existence, many of us have heard similar words from parents and peers, "you need to go to church". Until we understand these words of Christ, the reason for such counsel seems vague and obscure. Many of us first began to attend church out of a sense of duty, because we *should*, rather than for the blessings that are found therein. Allow me a few sentences to expand upon our Lord's counsel and encourage you to His house.

First, let me say that the Lord and His Church *should* have priority in our lives above all other things. "All these things", food, clothing and whatever trappings the paycheck may bring, should come somewhere in the back of the throng. Yet, where do we find "these things" in the minds of most people. "Things" come first and the Lord and His house come last. People want things, they pray for things, they hope for things and as we see from these actions, it is the things they are really worshiping.

Did you notice who Jesus was talking to? He was not talking to people who were ignorant of Christ or His house. This speaks volumes about what can happen to disciples of Christ. They can become sidetracked and distracted seeking after "things". How subtle are Satan's devices in these areas. Consider Solomon. He was a man who loved God, a zealous man who built a beautiful temple to worship in. The Lord blessed him with wisdom and riches beyond comparison. It was the "things" that got the best of him. Too many things, to many wives, too many opportunities to be away from worship, too many toys and beautiful people. In the end, this man with wealth and many things, finds depression and everything under the sun become "vanity and vexation of the spirit". "Seek ye first" is more than a commandment, it is more than good advice, it is spiritual counsel with a promise couched within. The Lord who does not lie will faithfully keep this promise just as He is faithful to all of His promises.

The reasons for our Lord's promise are numerous. First, our Lord is "a rewarder of them that diligently seek him"(Hebrews 11:6). This does not agree with the "name it, claim it" idea we hear from the false prophet. The reward, or blessing, is based upon our needs, not our wants. Would you rather be seeking "things" on your own or be looking to the faithful provider of the sheep? He knows best what our needs are before we ask or seek them. He knows what will destroy us and what will bless us. We are to seek, He will add.

The next reason is that God's counsel, good counsel for living is found in His kingdom. Martyn Loyd Jones, one of the great preachers of the last century was first a medical doctor. He found that many of the problems that his patients encountered were really the result of spiritual problems. As a medical doctor, he had that people who attended a church where the bible was preached needed less counsel than those who did not attend because they were receiving Godly counsel and advice in the sermons they listened to. They learned about marriage, raising children, faithfulness responsibilities at work and etc. It is all in the book of books. As the psalmist hath said, "Thy testimonies also are my delight and my counsellors."

This brings us to the next reason for seeking the Lord's kingdom first: *knowledge*. Knowledge of God, His view of the world, of sin, of Satan and his devices are found here. The "ground and pillar of the truth" will always stand in opposition to worldly advice.

Finally, great fellowship is found therein, fellowship with the right kind of people who set godly examples before us on a daily basis. Christians are not perfect, yet, look the world over and you will not find a kinder and gentler people. As Jesus said, you will "sit down with Abraham and Isaac and Jacob in the kingdom of heaven".

Some have made some very appealing reasons for negating this promise and using the Sabbath day for recreation. Some say they are strengthening their family and marriage. They have become wiser than the wisest who gave this information. We see more broken homes and marriages today from all of this activity than a former day when families went to church together. What can strengthen a family or a marriage more than the Lord and His house? Surely, there is nothing wrong with seeking other things and enjoying all of the above with family and friends. It is a matter of priority: "But seek ye first the kingdom of God, and his righteousness; and all these things shall be added unto you."

Helpful Hints:
1. The blessings found within the kingdom.
2. How they have helped us.
3. The excuses we have used.
4. The world's distractions.

"THE DEAD SPEAKING"

"By faith Abel offered unto God a more excellent sacrifice than Cain, by which he obtained witness that he was righteous, God testifying of his gifts: and by it he being dead yet speaketh"
- Hebrews 11:4

Christian, what will be said of you after you are gone? Will your friends and neighbors say: "That man was a great sportsman; that woman could tell a good joke; they were the life of the party?" By this thought, we come to the sober conclusion that the dead do speak long after they have departed this life. What is said after our decease should be the concern of every real Christian.

It is a great advantage to have family members who speak good things to our souls after they have departed this life. Even our peers, teachers and those we looked up to as children, speak long after their decease. Young men will ask the question, "Would my father do that?" Young women will search their hearts and ask, "Would my mother do that?" Many, who did not have this example at home will ask: "Would my grandfather, my teacher, my coach do that?" So, we learn that our lives speak volumes, not only while we live, but long after we are gone. They have an impact upon our posterity. The Christian lives not for this life alone, but with an eye to a future generation that will honor Christ!

Certainly, the lives of the righteous speak longer and louder than the unrighteous. People do not search out their family tree to find a horse thief. They search to find Abels. Though Cain is recorded along side Abel, his name is recorded for the evil. Ask him today and he might say, "Erase my name and my actions. My life is not an example, it is a warning." A worthless life is not worth recording, much less, remembering. Consider this, Christian.

The *way* the righteous dead continue to speak, long after they are gone, is by the righteous sacrifices they made for God and others during their life. This is faithful walking with God. Cast your bread upon the waters, you have more than you need. It will return after many days, perhaps long after you are gone to the encouragement of others.

The *object* of this speaking is the hearts of other believers. A quickened heart is genuinely touched by sacrificial acts of others. This is how the death of Christ speaks to believers. How powerful is this argument! We have all been touched by similar arguments: a father's sacrifices to bring in the bread for his family; a mother's lost sleep and caring hand; or a friend who came to us in time of need. This language of the heart is never forgotten.

The *effect* it has is to produce a sense of urgency in the consciences of other believers to "Go and do likewise". As we have noted, it has an impact upon our posterity. Good mothers are made from good mothers and faithful fathers are the offspring of the same. Great Christians are, likewise, the offspring of other faithful Christians who being dead, yet speak to our souls. Abel, faithful Abraham, meek Moses, conquering David, fearless Joshua, attentive

Lydia are among the many who continually speak to our souls with this urgency: "how can I be like them?"

The *purpose* of it all is to give God glory in our earthly pilgrimage. Not only do the dead yet speak to flesh, they continually speak to their Creator who gave them their faith to use for His glory. They perpetually stand in the flesh as living proof of the existence of the eternal, invisible God. Their lives speak of His indwelling within the souls of the redeemed. The righteous endeavors of the Saints is not without purpose.

Though there may be those who will pick and point out our faults, do not give up Christian. We ever stand before the great King, who forgives and restores and He alone writes our record. Let us live in such a way that when we are gone our lives will yet speak for our Lord!

Helpful Hints:
1. Consider the two sacrifices.
2. Who speaks to you today?
3. Consider the encouragement.
4. Make a promise with your family to go and do likewise.
5. Consider God's love for you and the difference it has made in your life.
6. How have you shown your love for God?

"PAUL'S SPECIAL REQUEST"

"Grace be to you, and peace, from God our Father, and from the Lord Jesus Christ"-Ephesians 1:2

Of the many petitions Paul could have placed before the throne of grace for the believing Ephesians, this prayer adorns the opening comments in each of his letters to the Churches. At first glance, we might read these words as glibly as the salutation of a letter. Yet, if we consider the request, we find these words to be fraught with wisdom, much more than words to fill up the page. Of all the treasures in the Father's hand, Paul asked for *grace* and *peace*.

Grace simply means *unmerited* favor. It means that God gives something to someone who doesn't deserve it. Though the Church is the bride of Christ, it continually stands in need of God's grace to function, thrive and grow. Grace also means that blessings received are blessings unasked for. The Church never has or never will know everything they need. As one Christian woman prayed, "Give me the grace to know my need of thy grace". Do we really know what we need from day to day to conquer our enemy and live acceptably before our Lord and our neighbor? How many traps have been thwarted by the invisible God? As we survey Calvary we see our ignorance as to what we needed and how to carry it out. Who, but God, would have imagined that redemption would take place by God becoming flesh and suffering in the most despicable manner? What mortal could have known of their need for Calvary and contrived the scheme to rescue fallen man? Our need of grace reminds us that we yet see through a glass darkly and our real needs are unknown. We need God's *restraining* grace to keep us from temptation and sin. We need his *distinguishing* grace to embellish our churches with the various gifts necessary for the ministration of His people. We need His *"amazing grace"* to forgive us when we err. We need His *sufficient grace* to face our enemies and our thorn in the flesh. We need *seeing* grace to understand the scriptures. We need *speaking* grace to preach with power. We need *hearing* grace to understand the messenger and we need *anointing* grace to apply the message to our lives. There is not end to the amount of grace we need every day, every moment every second. Without God's grace we could not take another breath. We are utterly dependent upon His sovereignty and majesty. Is there any wonder that this great apostle places grace at the top of his prayer list for the Churches?

Alongside grace, Paul placed *peace* in most every request for the churches. Grace and peace go together like a nut and a bolt. You must have both to hold something together. Grace without peace is a wasted gift because disharmony destroys all the good that grace lays at our feet. It is hard to imagine that the gift of grace, as precious as it is, can be wasted, yet, this is the case many times. Paul said it like this to the church at Corinth: "We then, *as* workers together *with him*, beseech *you* also that ye receive not the grace of God in vain."(2Corinthians 6:1.)

God can give a church all of the graces mentioned above, yet, without peace it is wasted, nothing comes of it but vanity, a puff of smoke, a passing vapor. We have all witnessed this. Just one person in a congregation who is given to a temper, a hateful tongue or a controlling spirit can destroy an entire fellowship of believers. Peace is the only atmosphere conducive to church prosperity.

Peace defined means *prosperity*. As David encouraged much the same prayer for the Old Testament Saints we find prosperity couched within his prayer of *peace*: "Pray for the peace of Jerusalem: they shall prosper that love thee"(Psalm 122:6). Do you see his methodology: peace...... then prosperity. We do read of some Pentecost days in the Bible where there is prosperity and growth almost instantaneously. But most of the time, Churches being established as they are, you will never see prosperity come before peace in a Church.

We must never forget that above all things, we must have Christ. We must have fellowship with Him. He is the key to our grace and peace because He is the Prince of peace. When we lose our peace, or the peace of our church or churches, it must be because we have lost Him! This peace fragments into every facet of our lives. Not only should we strive for peace in our Church, but also in our own hearts. This peace should extend outside the bounds of our church to our families and our neighbors. My, how valuable this peace is to our souls. No wonder some have called it *soul prosperity*. This is when we can look in the mirror and feel to a great degree that we have things in order with our Lord and the world around us. Soul prosperity outstrips the vain treasures of this world. We have seen many who possess a ton of this world's goods and can not enjoy a bit of it because they have lost their peace. Yet, we have seen those who are poor and cast down, whose lives are filled with joy in the

Holy Ghost because they have this peace which passeth understanding. Let us pray for this grace and peace in our lives and in the midst of our churches today!

Helpful Hints:
1. Notice this prayer in all of Paul's epistles.
2. Consider the need and why.
3. Keep this prayer daily in your heart.
4. How may we labor for peace?
5. What do we need grace for?

"SPIRITUAL BLESSINGS"

"Blessed be the God and Father of our Lord Jesus Christ, who hath blessed us with all spiritual blessings in heavenly places in Christ: According as he hath chosen us in him before the foundation of the world, that we should be holy and without blame before him in love"-Ephesians 1:3,4

The Christian has great reason to be thankful. He is the recipient of "all spiritual blessings". There is a purpose for Paul's categorical listing of our spiritual blessings. He wants the church to understand the *mechanics* of their salvation. While many understand redemption at the cross, they fail to see all that went on behind the scenes: the events that brought Christ to the cross and the full result of all that He accomplished. This is His work alone. We will not find the name of a preacher, a church, a denomination, a creed or an ordinance in this list of spiritual blessings. As the Holy Ghost has said: He trod the winepress alone!

This list of blessings is not only spiritually, it is equally *logical* and *progressive*. It begins before the foundation of the world, climaxes at the cross of Christ and continues throughout eternity.

The first of the spiritual blessings that the apostle brings before the church at Ephesus concerns the wonderful doctrine of *election*: "he hath chosen us". While many hold their free will before the Father, Paul raises the head of his Savior, Jesus Christ. This choice was made in and through the person of our Lord Jesus Christ. As the whole human race was in Adam when he fell, these chosen were in Christ when He was raised. This is the platform for all spiritual blessings, the foundation from which the others must rest.

This word election scares many Christians. They feel it might exclude persons who want to be included in God's redemptive process but can't get in. When we understand it correctly, we will find that it does just the opposite. It is a word that goes beyond man and his religion to include a people who lived millenniums before the cross, people who lived behind iron curtains and those whose mental faculties excluded them from the knowledge of the gospel of Christ. For any who might fear that their names are left out, the fact they want to be included in the cross of Christ is evidence that they already are. Why would they be worried about sin and a saviour if Christ did not already dwell in their hearts? Why does the name of Jesus sound sweet in their ears? The word elect is larger than the militant church and includes a people out of every kindred, tongue and tribe. Paul wrote about it most because he rejoiced in the fact that election was not predicated upon his works, seeing himself as the chief of sinners. Surely, this is a reason to bless God!

God's purpose in election is no secret. Paul explains it thus: "that we should be holy and without blame before him in love." This was God's mind and heart from the beginning of His salvation process: To save His people from their sins, to make them holy and without blame before the bar of divine justice. No wonder the apostle would write, "Blessed be the God and Father of our Lord Jesus Christ, who hath blessed us with all spiritual blessings in heavenly places in Christ ".

Helpful Hints:
1. Notice the progressive doctrine of our salvation that Paul sets forth.
2. Consider the doctrine of election, predestination and adoption.
3. How does this affect the saints of the old testament?
4. When did all of this begin?
5. Who did it begin with?

"BAPTISM, THE ANSWER OF A GOOD CONSCIENCE"

"The like figure whereunto even baptism doth also now save us (not the putting away of the filth of the flesh, but the answer of a good conscience toward God,) by the resurrection of Jesus Christ" 1 Peter 3:21

Through the centuries, the ordinance of Baptism has been misrepresented as to its purpose and benefit in the New Testament Church. It was during the 1800's, that Spurgeon preached his great sermon against "Baptismal Regeneration", which sermon is still available today in the reprinted sermons of this great preacher. Simply, and we must add, biblically put, baptism is "the answer of a good conscience".

What does this mean? It means that baptism is the answer back to God from a conscience that has been relieved of guilt by the revelation of who Jesus Christ is and what He has done for that person. The eye of faith has seen Christ and placed all hope of redemption upon the Jesus, the sin bearer. This is the best way to describe a conscience that has been made good: it has been comforted and relieved from fear of hell: "Then he is gracious unto him, and saith, Deliver him from going down to the pit: I have found a ransom." (Job 33:24).

Before we are baptized, the conscience should be made good towards *God* and *self*: towards *God* because the wrath to come has no more power over the conscience for it has found its ransom, its resting place, its scapegoat, its hiding place, its atonement in the person of Jesus Christ.

The conscience is made good towards *self* because the sinner has come to the end of self. There is a good and peaceful feeling towards God. Our Holy Father is no longer seen as Mt. Sinai which thundered and smoked. Now we know Him as a loving Father who loves us, watches over us and has provide what we needed to dwell with Him in glory.

We must equally understand what this does not say. It does not say that the ordinance of *baptism* itself makes the conscience good. If this were the case John the Baptist would have baptized all who came to him and given them a good conscience. The act of immersion can not make a sinner who has not found their Savior feel good. If the conscience has not first been made good by the revelation of Jesus Christ, the immersed candidate will come up out of the water with a conscience just as condemned as when they went in. But once a person has found Christ and has seen their sin debt paid in full by His precious blood upon Calvary's cross, they can then, and only then, give an answer back to their Holy Father in the only way the He has ordained: by water baptism.

There have also been various arguments as to whether baptism should be in running water or a standing pool. I remember attending a baptism as a child at a river in our area. When the young man was immersed, his mother said that his sins were floating down the river. I looked, and I did not see anything floating down the river. I suppose if our sins were as earthy as the water it could be so. Yet, sins are spiritual and nothing can wash them away except the blood of Christ. As the song goes, "What can wash away my sins, Nothing but the blood of Jesus."

The purpose and intent of complete immersion is to represent something. As Peter said, it is a "figure": It is a figure of the death, burial and resurrection of Jesus Christ. One who desires to give an answer to the relieved conscience should have a desire to be identified with the One who was crucified, buried and raised for their redemption. I suppose we could shout, "I love Jesus" at the top of our lungs to make this public confession. Or, we could just walk up to the front of the Church on Sunday morning and say, "I Do", as is common in the weeding ceremony when we marry. But this is the way that Jesus has ordained that we confess our love and devotion for Him: by baptism. It speaks publicly, loudly and clearly of one person, the only person who has risen from the grave.

Baptism will not make a person walk aright the rest of their life nor will it cause a person to be faithful. This is witnessed by the believing Church as some who have been baptized have departed and brought reproach upon the house of God. If this ordinance gave life, spiritual life, we must say that it has failed in many instances and God must be charged with folly. Yet, it should be the mindset of every person who has confessed Christ: that we should rise from the watery grave to walk in newness of life (Romans 6:4).

There are spiritual benefits to be enjoyed by those who *obey* their conscience. In these we witness an extra measure of the Holy Ghost poured out upon their souls, which adds force and strength to their confession and character. As Peter so beautifully said, "And we are his witnesses of these things; and *so is* also the Holy Ghost, whom God hath given to them that obey him"(Acts 5:32).

The Holy Ghost is give to those who obey and it is taken from those who disobey. In any act of obedience, the Holy Ghost is given in an extra measure providing peace, comfort, strength, light, wisdom and all of His endued powers.

Baptism has always been a *believer's* response. Only those who believed in Jesus Christ, who He was and why He came, were allowed to be baptized in the New Testament Church. John the Baptist forbade many who came to his baptism demanding that they bring forth fruits of repentance before he would administer the ordinance. As we have already noted, if the liquid ordinance would have had any redemptive or changing influence on the person, John would have baptized all who came to him.

Jesus fulfilled all righteousness by being baptized at the hands of the Baptist. Thus, baptism is a righteous act and the fulfillment of our earthly pilgrimage as Christians. Jesus was certainly not born again at that moment, nor was anything added to His spotless purity. It did for Jesus as it will do for us today. It identified who He was. The Father and the Spirit were present to identify the Messiah and this witness becomes our own when we, too, fulfill all righteousness.

As we have already noted, this is the 'Only" answer that God has given for the conscience of the believer to truly answer with. It is the ordinance that God the Father ordained for the Saints in light to display to the world that they love and belong to Jesus. It is humbling and distinguishing. It is more difficult to the flesh than giving money, than going to church, than reading the bible and being seen with other Christians. It is the Cum Laude of our experience because before we are baptized we must come to some conclusions. We must decide what we believe, who we believe, who we are and where we are going. Then the conscience is made good. If the Father has spoken to our hearts, surely we should answer Him back!!

Helpful Hints:
1. Have you been baptized?
2. If not, why not?
3. Who would John not baptize and why?
4. What are the blessings and benefits of believer's baptism?

"THREE THAT BEAR RECORD"
"For there are three that bear record in heaven, the Father, the Word, and the Holy Ghost: and these three are one"-1 John 5:7

The doctrine of the trinity has always been a cardinal doctrine of the Christian Church as we can tell by the writing of our beloved John. The oldest confessions of the Christian faith emphatically declare a belief in the trinity, and most importantly, we find it declared from Genesis to Revelation. It sheds light not only on our personal experience with God, but also reveals the roles that the Father, the Son and the Holy Spirit play in our salvation.

This orthodox Christian doctrine is referred to as *Trinitarianism*. Trinitarianism differs from *Tritheism*. While the former affirms the Three-Oneness of God, the second declares that there are three distinct gods, acting separately and independently of one another, becoming a plurality of gods. Trinitarianism also differs from *Unitarianism*, which make the Father, Son and Holy Ghost of temporary essence, fulfilling their mission and returning to the original Monad. Various forms of this idea have resurfaced through the centuries denying the divine essence of the Holy Trinity.

The first verse in the Bible declares the trinity. The word "GOD" comes from the word, Elohim, with literally means "The Mighty Ones". Alone, El, means The Mighty One, and is used to express a single characteristic of Elohim as we find in El-Shaddai. Thirty times in the first chapter of Genesis, twenty-two hundred times in the Old Testament, we read of Elohim, The Mighty Ones. Without academics, one must come face to face with the language of Genesis 1:26, "And God said, Let us make man in our image, after our likeness…..". *Us* and *Our* are plural! In the New Testament, we find all three present at the Baptism of Jesus and we hear the Father speak to the Son on numerous occasions as on the Mount of Transfiguration. If language means anything, there must be a Holy Trinity.

Concerning doctrine, this is of utmost importance if we are to rightly divide the word of truth. According to Ephesians, chapter one, we are chosen by the Father, redeemed by the Son and quickened by the Holy Spirit. They agree in one, for all that the Father Chose, the Son redeemed and all that the Son redeemed will be regenerated by the Spirit(Romans 8:30). None will be lost or else, Christ is a failure.

Our spiritual experience will agree with these truths. We are taught by our Lord to pray to the Father, "Our Father which art in heaven"; since we see through a glass darkly and many times know not what to pray for as we ought, the "Spirit itself maketh intercession for us with groanings which cannot be uttered" (Romans 8:26); and even today, Jesus intercedes for undeserving sinners who approach the throne of grace and "searcheth the hearts", making "intercession for the saints according to the will of God"(Romans 8:27). Thus, even in our prayers we come into contact with three. Though man may say that he will not believe in a God that he can not completely understand, we would suggest that the God that man can completely understand is no God at all!!

Helpful Hints:
1. What part does each person of the Godhead play in our salvation?
2. In our prayers?
3. Where do we find all three present in scripture?

"BAPTISM: A BELIEVER'S CONFESSION"

"And Philip said, If thou believest with all thine heart, thou mayest. And he answered and said, I believe that Jesus Christ is the Son of God."-Acts 8:37

Though the evangelist, Philip, desired to baptize, there was a solemn "if" in his interrogation of the Eunuch's heart. It was what he looked for in the man, or, to say it another way, it was his answer from God that he was to administer the ordinance. A firm belief in the person of Jesus Christ was the divine prerequisite for every New Testament baptism. We find it at Pentecost when their hearts were pricked; we find it in Lydia's heart; we read it in Cornelius' confession; and we understand it in the countenance of the Philippian jailer. If baptism was the portal to heaven, the thief on the cross would have had no hope, and our Lord could not have said: "This day shalt thou be with me in paradise".

There is a simple reason for the evangelist's question: Belief is the greatest evidence of spiritual life! Ordinances can never give life. Life, whether natural or spiritual, comes from one source: God! As Paul wrote to the Galatian churches which were being led into legalism, thinking that spiritual life came though laws and ordinances, "…... for if there had been a law given which could have given life, verily righteousness should have been by the law". –Galatians 3:21. Could baptism add anything to the devil or the fallen angels? Surely, baptism is a public confession of what one has come to love and believe about the person of the Lord Jesus Christ.

The evidence is certain: the believing Eunuch was alive spiritually before the ordinance was administered. We see his spiritual life displayed by his seeking. His travels were of some disadvantage to his person as he traveled through the desert. He could have gone to a ball game or to the idol's temple. Yet, we find him engaging in a search for his spiritual need. He was hungering and thirsting for righteousness as he attended the meeting at Jerusalem. On his return trip we find him seeking the One the prophet wrote of in Isaiah 53.

In his book of evidences, the Apostle John wrote, "Whosoever believeth that Jesus is the Christ is born of God" -1 John 5:1. When Philip asked the Eunuch "If thou believest with all thine heart, thou mayest", the answer could only be that of a born again soul: "I believe that Jesus Christ is the Son of God." Then the evangelist gladly administered the ordinance.

Helpful Hints:
1. Why are believers only to be baptized?
2. What did the Eunuch believe?
3. How can a person believe this?
4. What should every believer do?

"THE NEW BIRTH"

"The wind bloweth where it listeth, and thou hearest the sound thereof, but canst not tell whence it cometh, and whither it goeth: so is every one that is born of the Spirit."- John 3:8

Nicodemus, a ruler of the Jews, has come to Jesus by night that he might learn something of the Man. He came by night for fear of his good brethren who might expel him from the synagogue for seeking the Nazarene. Surely, many today would follow Him if they could leave their upper seats. Here, as we find in every instance, our Lord's conversation was immediately upon spiritual matters. Nicodemus wanted to prove Jesus with questions as to who He was. Jesus, in turn, proves Nicodemus with hard questions as to who *he* was. Our Lord spoke of "the new birth".

Nicodemus, like the rest of his Jewish brethren, thought that becoming a child of God was merely by birthright. If you could prove you were of the seed of Abraham you had the necessary evidence to admit you into the inner court and eventually into Abraham's bosom. The fruits born in the life were secondary to the pedigree. Yet, Jesus tells him, "you must be born again and this is how it happens".

There are many ideas advanced as to how a person is born again. Man, in his attempt to exalt himself, always places himself somewhere in the picture. He must always have some tradition, some performance, some free will, some special words to say, some outward shew in the flesh connected with this spiritual matter. Yet, the words of our Lord are simple: Jesus compares it to the wind!

Now, everyone knows about the wind, even the smallest child. We look out our window and there goes a leaf. The branches move according to the commands of this invisible power. How mighty is this force! The recent hurricanes have once again proven the helplessness of man and his inability to harness the wind. Our Lord's word, "listeth", decries this power: it means 'pleases'. Thus, the wind blows where *it* pleases, and I, the Sovereign of the universe, regenerate where, when and to whom I please. Man can not control or harness the wind, how can he command the Spirit of God. He can not command it by observing God honoring traditions, by speaking holy words, by going through biblical ordinances or reciting scriptural terms. God's sovereignty and the giving of His Spirit can not be reduced to mere witchcraft and enchantments. For man to think that he can perform an ordinance, say some words, or observe some tradition, and by thus doing, command the Spirit to come down immediately and blow upon a person is to place God at the command of puny man. God is sovereign in creation and He is equally sovereign in His work of regeneration. Every born again person is a new creation, created in Christ Jesus by the sovereign operation of the Holy Spirit. Man is passive in this Holy transformation. There is no other way in which this may happen. Our Lord sums it up this way: "So is every one that is born of the Spirit".

Helpful Hints:
1. Discuss regeneration and how it occurs.
2. Discuss the fruits of regeneration.
3. Discuss the evidences of regeneration.
4. Why was Nicodemus confused?

"MY PRAYERS"

"Wherefore I also, after I heard of your faith in the Lord Jesus, and love unto all the saints, Cease not to give thanks for you, making mention of you in my prayers; That the God of our Lord Jesus Christ, the Father of glory, may give unto you the spirit of wisdom and revelation in the knowledge of him:"
-Ephesians 1:15-17.

Prayer has been described as the highest activity of the soul. It is worship in and of itself. Prayer tells on us because when we empty our hearts unto God we find what was really in there! If we are full of ourselves, that is what God hears about.

We sometimes think of prayer as the simple task of talking to God, yet, it seems to be much more complicated than this when we read the prayers of the Bible. No wonder the disciples asked our Lord, "Teach us to pray". As they followed our Lord in His earthly ministry, they witnessed the frequent and fervent prayers of Jesus. It was by seeing and hearing Jesus pray that they realized something was lacking in their prayer life. These men began to consider what they should be praying about, how much time should be spent in prayer, what language they should adopt as they approached the God of glory and who they were to address their prayers to.

Thus, we come to our scripture today, which is the beginning of an intercessory prayer by the apostle for the church at Corinth. Paul was certainly a praying man and his writings are pregnant with his petitions for the church. As we read his words, suddenly and unexpectedly, his pen bursts forth in prayer, and from his pen, we get a glimpse of the most important things we should be praying for today.

First, let us notice who the apostle is praying to: "the Father of glory." That is who Jesus taught the apostles to pray to: "Our Father, which art in heaven". There are some who think it is more spiritual to pray to Jesus. Yet, we are instructed to approach God the Father with our prayers. It is Christ who knows our hearts and makes *intercession* for us and the Spirit makes groaning for us which we can not utter(Romans 8:26,27). It is an amazing thought to realize that the Holy Trinity is present at every petition!

In this prayer, we find a triad of *praise*, *thanks* and a *petition* for others. Prayer should be divided with praise, thanks, intercession for others, repentance and then personal requests. This is a good order, place self last. Paul addresses the "Father of Glory". What better way could one begin a petition? By his thanks he acknowledges former blessings received and prayers answered!

The heart of Paul's petition is noteworthy. He was in prison and he was not asking for the members of Corinth to get together and form a committee to get him out. He was more worried for the Corinthians outside the prison in the world than he was for himself being in prison! His request was for God, the Father of glory, to give these church members wisdom and revelation in the *knowledge* of Him. In other words, he wanted them to KNOW GOD more and more. Though they were baptized members of

Corinth, he was not satisfied with their condition. This is our supreme need: to know God. Sometimes, we get caught up in our problems and the problems of churches and we forget that all would be cured if we had what this man has requested in his prayer. May his prayer become our own and may God, the Father of glory grant us our request, that we may know Him.

Helpful Hints:
1. Consider Paul's other prayers in this epistle.
2. Break his prayers down and consider the importance of each part of his prayers.
3. Look at Paul's prayers in the other epistles.
4. Let us make a solemn promise to pray the same things.

"THOU HAST ENLARGED ME"

"Hear me when I call, O God of my righteousness: thou hast enlarged me when I was in distress; have mercy upon me, and hear my prayer."-Psalm 4:1

Many were the distresses of the sweet psalmist of Israel. Though David was greatly loved of God, his life was full of trials. Saul, the king of his people, his brother in the faith, sought his life, hunting him like a wild animal. Satan was always at his heels, tempting him with the lust of the flesh and the pride of life as we read of his mistake with Bathsheba and numbering Israel. Absalom, his own son, rose up against him. So it is with the righteous. Our constant enemy is like a baying hound, either attempting to bite us himself or turning other dogs upon us. Though the weary pilgrim may be discouraged, in the midst of it all, something amazing happens. When he holds on to his faith, discouragement turns in to strength, sorrow into joy and Satan is revealed. The world is seen for what it is as affections are shifted from trusting and loving the world into trusting and loving the Lord: he is *enlarged*.

Let us note: David's enlargement was not the result of *victories*. It was not the result of personal *success*. It was not even the result of his *popularity* or *power*. It was the result of *distress*. The most beautiful flowers do not grow upon the mountain top, they grow in the valleys. Mountain top experiences are wonderful but God does not grow his crop there. Though one may be enlarged in the eyes of the world by all of the above, spiritual enlargement, which in the eyes of the Lord is what really matters, only comes by *distress*. This is the only way. We constantly hear people talk about our need for revival. But do we know what we are asking for? Revival is not this mountain top experience. True revival begins in the valley. It is when we feel rotten. Revival comes when we see ourselves as we are: bankrupt, guilty sinners. Revival comes when we see our mistakes in the church, in our misgivings, in our shallowness, in our personal sins which include our temper, our tongue and our worldliness. It is when we see our lack of commitment to God and His house. Distress is the beginning of revival, both personally and congregationally.

This word *distress* is full of meaning. It means a narrow, tight place where there are many enemies. Soul trouble, depression, personal problems, financial struggles, are among the distresses of mankind. "Man that is born of a woman is of few days, and full of trouble" writes the learned patriarch. Modern man has forgotten this and is perplexed when he is not happy at all times. Yet, God has ordained that it is here, and here alone, that the Christian grows!

There are many scriptural illustrations of distress: Daniel in the den of lions; the three Hebrew children in the fiery furnace; Paul in prison; and David's struggles are widely known by Christians everywhere. Even in conversion, the Christian experiences distress. Consider the events which fueled Pentecost or the Philippian jailer's repentance. When Christ is revealed, the heart is pricked as sins are revived before our eyes and we are in great distress. The way up is down! Figurative language like: "Take away the dross from the silver, and there shall come forth a vessel for the finer"(Proverbs 25:4) and "I counsel thee to buy of me gold tried in the fire, that thou mayest be rich"(Rev. 3:18a) indicate distress and how it enlarges those who are exercised thereby.

Yet, let us take courage. The same God that brings our distress also has promised: "When thou passest through the waters, I *will be* with thee; and through the rivers, they shall not overflow thee: when thou walkest through the fire, thou shalt not be burned; neither shall the flame kindle upon thee." (Isaiah 43:2). Our Lord is faithful in times of distress and He brings us through it all. Christians today are not exempt from distress nor should they think themselves to ever be so. Divers temptations must be viewed as a time to grow, to be enlarged, to seek the Lord's face. Lord, lead us not into temptation. Help us in our distress to be faithful and submissive. Enlarge us in all of our distresses that we may give thee glory!

Helpful Hints:
1. A good time to share your distress and enlargement with others.
2. Why is this necessary in our pilgrimage here?
3. Consider the distresses of Christ compared to our own.
4. Talk about the many distresses of the faithful in the Bible such as Joseph, David, the apostles and etc.

ABOUT THE AUTHOR

The author has pastored churches for over 15 years. This second book is the result of his labors. He has published his own periodical, *The Pastoral Letter,* as well as writing for other church papers and editorials during this time. He writes a religious column for the local newspaper in the town where he lives and continues to pastor and preach. This second book is similar to the first, *The Daily Record,* which is full of short devotions taken from his sermon notes. He graduated from Northeast Louisiana University School of Pharmacy and became a pastor and preacher 15 years later. He has four children, Kelli, Ryan, Neil and Bryant. He and his wife, Marilyn, have been happily married for 25 years.

Printed in the United States
32768LVS00008B/217-240

9 781420 857375